EX-NEOCON

Ex-Neocon

Dispatches from the Post 9/11 Ideological Wars

Scott McConnell

foreword by
Philip Weiss

Algora Publishing
New York

Library of Congress Cataloging-in-Publication Data —

Names: McConnell, Scott (Journalist), author.
Title: Ex-neocon. Dispatches from the Post 9/11 Ideological Wars / Scott McConnell.
Description: New York: Algora Publishing, [2016] | Includes bibliographical
    references.
Identifiers: LCCN 2016004347| ISBN 9781628941951 (soft cover: alk. paper) |
    ISBN 9781628941968 (hard cover: alk. paper)
Subjects: LCSH: Conservatism—United States. | United States—Politics and
    government—1989- | United States—Foreign relations—Middle East. |
    Middle East—Foreign relations—United States.
Classification: LCC JC573.2.U6 M367 2016 | DDC 320.520973—dc23 LC record
available at http://lccn.loc.gov/2016004347

Printed in the United States

To Margaret, and to Neil, Kristen, and Anna

Table of Contents

FOREWORD

By Philip Weiss

Though we are contemporaries, it was fitting that Scott McConnell and I knew very little of one another until 2004. Our social and political communities were almost entirely distinct. Scott's was uptown conservative, mine was downtown and left. He was from the aristocracy—a Columbia WASP who knew his way around clubs—while I am from the meritocracy—which is to say, I got work from Jews I had known at Harvard. My wife had known McConnell in the eighties; and she told me he was proper, shy, conservative, and extremely intelligent.

What brought us together was a project that transcended our backgrounds and temperaments, and that animates the essays in this book: the fight for the country we love against the influence of the neoconservatives. That is a bold claim, but McConnell has done the intellectual labor to earn it in the pages that follow. "Ex-Neocon" tells an important story about the power of ideas. The neoconservatives succeeded in effecting policy beyond their own dreams, and both vision and policy were narrow and dangerous. And undying. McConnell saw early on that despite the patent failure of their crowning project, the Iraq War, the neocons weren't going away. They had too much going for them, in terms of financial backing and cultural cohesion inside the new Jewish establishment.

It was those sociological observations that drew me to McConnell. I first read "Among the Neocons" in 2004, a year after it came out, and was moved by the author's willingness to take risks so as to be honest about his own experience. At a time when others were pointedly ignoring the elephant in the room, McConnell spoke about the neocons' devotion to Israel and the money behind their network. He explained that neoconservatism came out of the Jewish community, but it gained many non-Jewish adherents. McConnell had joined up because of the vitality of their conservative revisions; and he found their brilliance and mobility to be glamorous. He had treasured the company of the late Eric Breindel, his former colleague at the *New York Post*.

McConnell was a philo-Semite. He had witnessed the crumbling of the old WASP order that had sustained some of his own ancestors, but saw a fairness in it; he was eager to see what Jews would do with their entrance into the elites. For years when he was young, he had aspired to be published by *Commentary*, then a publication of the American Jewish Committee—the same magazine that piled up in my parents' breakfast room, and was so confident about its intellectual attractions that it had only headlines and bylines on the cover.

The neocons' concerns were, of course, broader than Israel, and McConnell did little Israel duty himself. He writes:

> I remember thinking generally that Israel was a burden, or perhaps a cross, which my Jewish neoconservative friends had to bear. While I often admired their ingenuity and tenacity in defending the Jewish state—rather the way one might admire a mother who gives effective care to a child with special needs—I was glad their burden was not mine. Beyond that, I didn't pay much attention; there were then many other subjects in *Commentary* and in the neoconservative universe to attend to.

Though in 1992, McConnell was induced to bash Gore Vidal over his satire of Norman Podhoretz and Midge Decter as dual-loyalty cases, he would come to regret the attack. He reflects with typical wryness:

> I had the lesson reinforced that it is seldom a bad career move for someone with an 'Mc' in their surname to accuse someone of anti-Semitism, especially if there's any basis for the charge.

These essays are often charming, but it's their directness that makes them memorable. McConnell broke with the neocons over immigration issues, when they turned on people McConnell knew who were for restrictions, but it was Palestine that ended the relationship. At a time when his wife and church were guiding him toward the (sadly remarkable) understanding that Palestinians were as deserving of dignity as other human beings, his neoconservative friends were deriding them in terms that would make a Jim Crow southerner blush.

McConnell was too much of a realist to be an ideologue. As the plans for the invasion of Iraq ramped up, he predicted the damage. The neocons were leading the country on perhaps the most perilous course in its history, and had done so using children's slogans and deception. Weeks before Shock and Awe, he wrote:

> America has fewer real friends and more ill-wishers than ever in its history. This is in considerable part the 'accomplishment' of America's neocons, the fruit of the power they have achieved in the conservative movement, and the influence they wield with an inexperienced and simple president. It will take years to undo the damage they have done, but there is no choice but to begin.

McConnell's disturbance over the war led him to Israel at last, and to plain descriptions of the Palestinian experience. The elegance and passion of the following passage—objecting to *Washington Post* columnists David Ignatius and Charles Krauthammer's repetition of the claim that Israel withdrew from Gaza and just got rockets in return—is worthy of any collection of American moral writings, from independence to abolitionism to the antiwar movement:

> Does not publishing this kind of narrative, again and again, constitute a kind of journalistic malpractice, an abrogation of a major newspaper's responsibility to inform? To imply that the Palestinians have no cause to resist, when rather plainly they exist in circumstances no people on earth would tolerate, is not really different from an actual lie.

As a conservative who had volunteered for Obama, McConnell had no desire to overturn the Washington consensus: he supported the two-state solution and the liberal Zionist group J Street. Myself, I have too much faith in human progress to accept those disappointments; but McConnell's seriousness and wit were rewards of our friendship, and the same manners elevate these essays.

Of course, there have been several books now documenting the neoconservative rise. The news in these articles is the documentation of intellectual crimes of staggering size: the neocons were able to sell an aggressive foreign policy as an appropriate nationalist response to the 9/11 attacks, and in doing so cloak their core concern, Israel's security.

I say it is news, because I have never seen this argument made with such force and lightness. I have read almost all these pieces before, and this constitutes one of the book's achievements: by collecting and shaping these pieces, McConnell has formed an indictment of intellectual transgressions that we have never heard before, and that is still necessary. Yes: Walt and Mearsheimer blew the bridge back in 2006 when they published the Israel lobby paper (which McConnell emailed to me that day in excitement). But as McConnell writes of the scholars' subsequent book, understanding what befell Washington required a more literary, precise, and discursive treatment; and there are elements of that quest here.

When contemplating the effect of Oslo's endless promise on the Palestinian people's experience of occupation, McConnell cites De Tocqueville: evils endured when they seem inevitable become intolerable once escape from them appears on the horizon.

Lenin is apostrophized when McConnell explains that neoconservatism doesn't just overlap with the Israel lobby, it "is the highest stage of the Israel lobby."

There is this observation of McConnell's own social class, in dispatching George Bush: "a man who unlike anyone else you've ever known suffered no adverse professional consequences for being an alcoholic with no real accomplishments at age 40."

And in laying out the historical significance of Bill Kristol's *Weekly Standard*, he writes:

> If Rupert Murdoch's purpose was to make things happen in Washington and in the world, he could not have leveraged it better. One could spend 10 times that much on political-action committees without achieving anything comparable.

Many of these essays have a meditative personal quality. There is also a deep feeling of betrayal, a feeling I shared, over the fact that the neoconservatives were not being upfront with Americans about their values. McConnell quotes the late essayist Sam Francis: "What neoconservatives have done is to design an ideology ... that offers ostensible and plausible rationalizations for the perpetual war in which Israel and its agents of influence in the U.S. government and media seek to embroil the United States (and which all too many American conservatives, out of a foolishly misplaced patriotism, are eager to support) without explicitly invoking the needs and interests of Israel itself."

McConnell's reserve saves these articles from crankiness. Some readers will surely bridle at his general and conservative opposition to immigration, as being a source of disruption to a society he cherishes. I have a very different view from his of the issue, one in keeping with my own camp; the society he would conserve is one in which whites have long been at the top of the scale. But I would point out that McConnell has demonstrated some fluidity on the question, and recognized that the browning of America may make the country's politicians less likely to go in for dangerous adventures like Iraq. He is well aware that the Democratic Party, or its base anyway, has been less disappointing in foreign policy than American conservatives; and so he has been willing to bend a bit on a core issue out of the very realistic aim of building a coalition. (Which is more than you can say about some left-wingers.)

McConnell's concern with Jews is neither cranky or prejudicial. An interest in Jewish intellectual culture, its rise and its power, runs through this book. As I share this interest, I don't think it requires any defense: the role of Zionist Jews in foreign policymaking is an important area of inquiry. And McConnell addresses the matter straightforwardly, without hints or exaggeration or code.

It is his genuineness that made McConnell such an important guide to me, the sense that he is telling you what he thinks without inhibition. This quality makes his charges against the neocons even more persuasive, for it is on that ground that they failed most of all; they were insincere.

Philip Weiss
Writer and creator of the Israel–Palestine blog Mondoweiss

INTRODUCTION

By Scott McConnell

If someone had told me at age 40 that I would devote many future years of my career to helping found and edit a magazine dedicated to opposing the main tenets and policies of neoconservatism, it would have struck me as daft or ridiculous. To the extent that any gentile could be a neoconservative (and many were), I was one. I worked at the editorial page of the *New York Post*, the culmination of a career path that had begun in earnest ten years earlier when I first published in *Commentary*. The vast majority of my friends were New York neocons—if my wife and I had a party, which we did a few times, three fourths of the guests would be writers and editors for *The Wall Street Journal*, or *City Journal*, or *Commentary*, or whatever. I knew Midge Decter and Norman Podhoretz pretty well, liked them enormously, and they liked me. Eric Breindel, the flawed and once fallen prince of the second generation neocons, a star at Harvard who had become a heroin addict and then righted himself to become editorial page editor of the *New York Post*, was not only a colleague but probably my closest friend—the person with whom I shared more thoughts in the course of the day than anyone else.

But things began to shift. The Cold War ended. Immigration emerged as an issue, and I was sympathetic (as a conservative logically would be) to changing the demography of the United States slowly, rather than rapidly: demographic transformation through mass immigration seemed an unnecessary and radical experiment. Neoconservatives disagreed, and mounted vicious and often effective internecine campaigns against the immigration restrictionists in conservative ranks. On foreign policy, like Jeane Kirkpatrick (another goy neocon), I felt the United States could become "a normal country again" after the Soviet Union collapsed. The main neoconservatives had other plans, which became evident in the 1990s with their publication of bold schemes to get the United States to enforce unipolar dominance over the planet.

The natural result of such falling out of step was a turn toward Pat Buchanan, whom I had mildly supported in 1996 (as a *Post* columnist) and worked for in 2000 in his ill-fated Reform Party presidential candidacy. What I had learned in those intervening years formed the seeds of the views I held when the 9/11 hijackers struck: it was almost instantly obvious to Buchanan, to myself, and to quite a few others who paid attention to such things that the neoconservatives would seek to use the attacks to set a country resistant to their bellicose entreaties on the warpath. Opposition to them should not be left to the Left alone. That essentially was the ideological platform of *The American Conservative*, which became financially and logistically possible because I was friendly with both Pat and Taki Theodoracopulos, a dauntless and flamboyant Greek millionaire interested in right-wing politics and magazines. I thought that bringing them together would create a bit of a media stir, and provide a necessary boost to a new publishing venture.

These essays are a representative sample of pieces I wrote for TAC and other publications in the dozen years after 9/11. At least half of them, it will be clear, are the arguments of a former neoconservative against a set of attitudes he knows intimately, and now finds reckless and dangerous. To acknowledge that could seem dismissive or a kind of pigeonholing, though less so when one considers how much political writing is inevitably done in reaction against a dominant paradigm, and how influential neoconservatism remains in Washington and elsewhere, despite its record of egregious and costly policy failures.

Prelude to War

Though this short piece is no longer timely, it is memorable for obvious and less obvious reasons. It was written on 9/11, begun a few hours after my wife phoned from her downtown Manhattan law office to say that she was okay, but that I should turn on the TV. It resurfaced 18 months later when David Frum tried to use it as evidence against me in his notorious National Review piece, "Unpatriotic Conservatives." Frum was attempting to impugn the loyalty of Pat Buchanan, Robert Novak, Justin Raimondo, myself, and several others—conservatives and libertarians who warned that invading Iraq would turn out very badly for the United States and Iraq. Frum noted that Novak and I had cited America's obsessively close relationship with Israel as one reason the United States was so hated in the Arab world. American intelligence analysis of the 9/11 attack subsequently confirmed our observations. I responded to Frum in "Among the Neocons."

Why Many Arabs Hate America

After the assassination of John F. Kennedy—before today, the most traumatic event for Americans in my lifetime—Malcolm X said that, "the chickens have come home to roost." Malcolm was reportedly gleeful and rancorous, and his audience laughed at his words: he meant to convey that Kennedy's death meant very little compared to what whites had done to his people. But the phrase would not be inappropriate today—if said in sorrow—after thousands of innocents were killed in the worst terrorist assault in American history.

Whether the World Trade Center perpetrator is Osama Bin Laden, or one of countless Arab or Muslim subgroups, we should not have any doubt: this attack was welcomed in much of the Arab and Muslim world. Palestinian leaders may have given it pro forma condemnation, but the people on the Arab "street" were smiling and flashing "V" signs when they heard the news.

Before Americans set their sights on revenge (and revenge is expected, and necessary), they should at least understand why this attack delighted many, why United States foreign policy makes it hated in much of the world.

The reasons were spelled out in part last month by Egyptian President Hosni Mubarak's foreign policy advisor Osama Baz. He came to Washington carrying the urgent message from the Arab world's most populous state: the United States would face mounting rage in the Middle East unless it did something to diffuse the escalating Israeli–Palestinian conflict.

He was received politely by Colin Powell and Condoleezza Rice, and otherwise more or less ignored. A month before, Senator George Mitchell's carefully modulated plan for a Middle East cease-fire, which incorporated a freeze on new Israeli settlements in the Palestinian territories, had been allowed to die on the vine after Israel said no dice to a settlement freeze. America's unanimously pro-Israel pundit class paid no heed to Baz's visit, instead using their columns to shill for an Israeli military reoccupation of the West Bank, supposedly to solve Israel's terror problem once and for all.

But the United States, supplier of the tanks and helicopters and rockets that Israel uses to control the West Bank and to assassinate the odd Palestinian leader, cannot opt out of the Middle East peace process. By its large scale arms shipments and financial subsidies to Israel, it is already engaged. It is a key partner. The Oslo peace process has aroused Palestinian hopes for a viable state, and one can't imagine that they would relinquish them now. In his attempted mediations, Bill Clinton eloquently gave voice to the reasonable core of Palestinian aspirations. Now George W. Bush, whose knowledge of the Middle East seems little deeper than what he picked up from a ride with Ariel Sharon on a helicopter, has decided to snub the Arab world.

Israel and Palestine are not the only issues that arouse Arab rancor. The embargo on Saddam Hussein's Iraq, organized and led by the United States, and now 10 years old, is responsible, United Nation officials estimate, for the death of more than half a million Iraqi children. Saddam Hussein—one of the world's cruelest tyrants—bears no small measure of responsibility for the current horror in Iraq. But while American policies have left him in power, they have done grievous harm Iraq's weakest, the old, the sick, the very young. Americans don't read or hear much of this—it is not on their front pages or TV screens. But there now must be at least tens of thousands of Iraqi parents who know that their children are dead because of the American embargo. It creates a sentiment—now widespread throughout the Middle East—that allows for the perpetrators of today's horrific deeds to be recruited.

America's airwaves are alive now with ordinary people calling for vengeance against this most vile of attacks. I don't feel differently, and if I had lost a loved one, would volunteer for a revenge mission myself. But we shouldn't delude ourselves about why there is so much hatred for the United States. It does not come out of the clear blue. It is not because we represent freedom and virtue and light while the Arabs stand for darkness and repression. American culture may represent something corrosive and immoral to certain Islamic sensibilities—that can't be helped. But that isn't what provokes suicide bombers. American policies often kill, directly and indirectly—and this is why people are willing to sacrifice themselves to kill us in return.

Antiwar.com
September 14, 2001

In the late 1980s, I got to know David Horowitz, the former leftist and Ramparts editor who was making a second or third career as scourge of the cultural remnants of '60s radicalism. I had been young and somewhat sympathetic to the New Left in 1970, and generally approved of David's campaign for "second thoughts." David was smart, energetic, fearless—and a decade or so younger than the older generation of neoconservatives I knew. He differed from them in part by being less viscerally hostile to the immigration worries that began to grow on the Right in the early 1990s, worries that I shared. He lived in California, and surely recognized that importing a large poor and less educated immigrant population was very much a mixed blessing, that concerns over the consequences were quite legitimate and not simply to be shouted down with accusations of racism and nativism. In any case, I liked David, and he published in his journal Heterodoxy my account of being fired as editorial page editor of the New York Post in 1997 (in part for publishing too many "let's slow down immigration" pieces, in part for publishing an editorial skeptical about statehood for Puerto Rico). I remember particularly a long lunch I had with him at a beachfront restaurant in Los Angeles. I had just turned in the Heterodoxy piece, had a photo taken, and was walking out to the car when he suddenly appeared in the parking lot and coaxed me to lunch. We drove to a beachfront restaurant and downed two bottles of white wine in the middle of the day. Over dessert he told me that he was not a Zionist, had never been to Israel, had no interest in it—an attitude I found refreshing after long association with the New York neoconservatives.

A few years later, in his sixties, Horowitz discovered Zionism, and the political uses of Islamophobia, and has since become an American publicist for the most toxic of right-wing Israeli attitudes. With his campaigns against antiwar and pro-

Palestinian activism on campus, David seems somehow driven to recreate the kind of McCarthyism that was used against his communist parents, and this time to be on the McCarthyite side. I would disagree violently with David if we met now, and he would surely find my views reprehensible. So I prefer to remember him by our lunch on the beach in the fall of 1997. I wrote this piece several months after 9/11, after realizing from something he had written that David no longer felt the indifference to Zionism he had expressed to me four years earlier.

An Open Letter to David Horowitz on the Israeli–Palestinian Conflict

Dear David,

I read with great interest your 5,000-word polemic on the Israeli–Palestinian issue both because I have long been an admirer of your rhetorical abilities and analytical fearlessness, and because it is quite effective for drawing readers toward your point of view. I don't agree with a good deal of it, but hope something positive can come from a candid exchange of opinions.

I admit to some worries that such an exchange might not be possible. I've found in the past several months that when one disagrees with one's Jewish friends about Israel, one risks losing those friends. I would add that few things in my political and journalistic experience have been more personally dispiriting.

Not long ago, I had, in the course of a long and wine-filled dinner, a spirited argument about Israel and the Mid East with a Jewish colleague from the *New York Press*. I commented afterward that this "Jewish–Christian debate," so rare in New York, had been quite refreshing. He agreed, saying the problem was that there were generally "not enough Christians" to carry their end.

Odd as it might seem, he was right: most American Christians who have given some thought to the issues involved have views similar to mine, but given the rank hostility their expression can provoke from Jewish friends and colleagues, they have learned to simply keep their opinions to themselves. In so doing, they do a disservice both to their friends and to their own interests as citizens. I am not inclined to follow their example.

At the outset of your piece, you write (correctly) that Zionism is the national liberation movement of the Jews, and then remark how curious it is that Zionism is opposed both by some leftists who typically back all national liberation movements and by some conservatives who are habitually hostile to left-wing guerrilla organizations like the Palestinian Liberation Organization. Your point is to account for such opposition to

Israel by linking it to the long history of European anti-Semitism, whose consequences made the quest for a Jewish national state seem necessary.

I don't disagree with this general point, but in making it you cite Patrick Buchanan as an example of a conservative supporter of a left-wing Palestinian national liberation movement "aimed at the Jews" and thus expressing "unique opposition to a Jewish homeland."

This is an error, and forgive me if I sound for a moment like the Buchanan campaign staffer I once was in correcting it. While Patrick Buchanan has made hundreds and possibly thousands of on-the-record statements about Israel, has published countless columns and discussed Israel and the Palestinians in several books and speeches, he has never been in "opposition to a Jewish homeland."

By contrast, he has opposed certain policies carried out by the Jewish homeland, including those that involve the suppression of the prospect for a Palestinian homeland. But to conflate, as your sentences do, opposition to Israel's maintaining control over the lands and peoples it conquered in 1967 (in a war for whose outbreak the Arab leaders bear most of the blame) with "opposition to a Jewish homeland" is not a fair accounting of Buchanan's position—which is quite explicit in its support for Israel in its pre-1967 boundaries. Nor does it fairly summarize the views of millions of others, in America and around the globe, who see no better solution to the Palestine problem than two states, side by side, one for the Palestinians and one for the Israelis—with the latter's boundaries conforming to the spirit if not the precise lines of pre-1967 Israel.

There is another, more conceptually ambitious, thread to your piece: the argument that the Palestinians, unlike the Jews, have no solid national claim to land their fathers and forefathers lived on before the Zionist enterprise began.

To this end, you argue that the Palestinians never had an independent national existence for the arriving Zionist Jews to suppress, and therefore are not entitled to one now. They were, you write, "largely nomads who had no distinctive language or culture to separate them from other Arabs ... the idea of a Palestinian nation did not even exist ... [in 1950] they did not attempt to create a state of their own ..." and so on. You probably overstate the case—there clearly was agriculture and commercial life in Arab Palestine before the Zionists arrived.

But you are right to say there was no Palestinian nationalism at the time of the Balfour Declaration. Furthermore, that Palestinian "nationalism," which had come into existence a generation later by the time of the U.N. partition plan, was not nearly so politically developed as Zionism. Another way to say this is that Jewish nationalism was derived from (and a response to) the European nationalism of the nineteenth century; Arab nationalism (including Palestinian nationalism) arrived one or two or even three generations later, as part of the wave of Afro-Asian nationalism born after World War I.

At every stage in the confrontation between the original Zionist settlers and the Palestinian Arabs, the consequences of this Zionist head start were manifest. The Zionists had leaders (of every ideological stripe) with a clear sense of the Jewish national mission; the Palestinians were represented by local "notables" who reigned over a semi-feudal system. A typical Palestinian Arab in the years before 1948 might have had a sense of his own village and those in the next valley. He did not think of "the Palestinian people."

The Zionist settlers, by contrast, were among the most sophisticated and nationally conscious people the world had ever seen. The Jews were all literate, many Palestinians, not; the Jews could understand the necessity of training and arming all their available men (and many women); the Palestinians' armed resistance was, by comparison, haphazard and formless. The Zionists could tax their entire community (in Israel and, in a way, in the Diaspora) to subsidize the building of an army and of a new state; the Palestinians were unable to do so. The Jews had leaders who could move effectively in corridors of world power; the Palestinians were geographically remote from key decision-makers and feeble in their ability to estimate accurately the political situation they faced.

It is not too much to say that it took establishment of Israel and the experience of Israeli rule on the land occupied in 1967 to give birth to a genuine Palestinian nationalism, and spur the Palestinians to embark on the long course of trying to catch up. Of course, if the Palestinians had been as nationally self-conscious as the Jews from the outset, Zionism would never have fulfilled its ambitions, at least not in Palestine.

But it has never been customary for the United States to recognize as legitimate only those national movements that arrived first. Nor does the important fact of earlier political development grant the more advanced people a moral right to perpetual domination. The fact of Irish ancestry may have rendered me (actually of mixed Anglo-Irish descent) somewhat more conscious of how this can work. For hundreds of years, the British who ruled Ireland were better organized, more literate, more technologically advanced, more adept at the mobilization of men and resources, in short more powerful. The phrases they used to describe the Irish were seldom more generous than those you use to describe the Palestinians. Many intelligent Englishmen could not imagine decent Irish self-government . . . ever, nor conceive of the development of a political entity that might allow the Irish to look the English in the eye as equals.

Yet history has almost finished making that turn in the Irish Republic and Northern Ireland, and (however the remaining embers of that conflict are ultimately disposed of) has provided a striking example of how comparative latecomers to modernity and nationalism can narrow gaps in national development that once seemed completely unbridgeable.

You make an important point about the U.N. partition plan that created the legal basis for Israel's establishment: had the Arabs accepted it, there would be no Middle East conflict. I certainly concur that the Arabs would have been better off if they had agreed to partition, instead of initiating wars they were not prepared to fight. But I'm not sure that their acceptance would have put an end to the conflict.

As you know, from the time of the state's very founding, there have been important Israelis (and not only in the Likud Party) who aspired to expand Israel to what they called its "natural borders," who wished to ethnically cleanse the Palestinians whose lands they coveted. ("Transfer" was the preferred euphemism.) Diplomatic necessity prevented the Israelis who thought this (including Ben-Gurion, for instance) to restrain themselves, but I am not sure that Arab acquiescence to the original partition agreement would have satisfied the Zionists who had long dreamed of the lands of Biblical Judea and Samaria.

You yourself seem relieved that the Palestinians did not accept their half a loaf in a timely manner, devoting several paragraphs in support of the notion that Jordan is the logical place for a Palestinian state anyway. Ariel Sharon is known to share this notion of "resolving" the Palestinian problem, which would be acceptable neither to the Palestinians nor Jordanians.

You state that the Palestinians who didn't flee in 1948 and remained in what is now Israel have more political rights than any Arabs in the Arab world. This too is not an insignificant point—just as it was not insignificant when Senators from the segregationist South argued that American blacks had far more rights, and were far more prosperous, than blacks in Africa. But the yearning for political self-determination (or equal civil rights) has become a nearly universal political drive whose claims any political realist has to acknowledge. I can think of no instance in which it has been trumped by the allure of exercising circumscribed minority rights in an alien and hostile polity.

When your essay reaches the Oslo period, I sense some uncertainty creep into your argument, as if you yourself are not sure whether you are disappointed, relieved, or ecstatic at the apparent breakdown of the peace process. If, like Ariel Sharon, you believe the "Palestinian homeland" is "Jordan"—then, of course, you would be delighted at the failure of Oslo, and can look forward to further Israeli measures to demolish homes and drive the Palestinians from Gaza and the West Bank.

But something tells me you aren't completely comfortable there. You are, of course, on strong grounds when you decry the Palestinian Authority's failure to more effectively prepare the Palestinian people under its jurisdiction for peace. But your treatment is one-dimensional: there were years during Oslo when the PA's behavior was quite responsible, when its suppression of those Palestinian elements that rejected Oslo and any peace arrangement were sincere and forceful. The PA's behavior seemed to correlate with the actual state of the peace process—the Palestinians acted responsibly prior to Yitzhak Rabin's assassination, far less so after Netanyahu succeeded him and began to stall and delay full implementation of the agreement.

Remarkably, in such a long essay, you fail to mention even once the word "settlements"—though, of course, you must know that the settlements are the main locus of tension between the occupying forces and the Palestinians on the West Bank and Gaza. In political terms, the settlements are "facts" by which the Israelis say to the Palestinians: We have power here in your home and you do not. We control your water supply and your movements; we build roads that are for our use only while choking yours with military checkpoints. You will never establish full sovereignty over this, your ancestral land.

I'm sure, David, that there is much in Arab political culture that is irrational, inured to the spirit of generous compromise, and even hateful, but I can think of few peoples in the world who would accept such treatment without resisting. And as you know, during the Oslo peace process, which was supposed to lead to the creation of a Palestinian state, the Israelis increased the number of settlements, and all the access roads and checkpoints that go with them by roughly one-third. This did much to sour the peace process, and stands in my mind in a sort of rough moral equivalence to the anti-Zionist propaganda taught in Palestinian schools that you quite rightly despise.

Your largest point is that the Palestinian national grievance is "a self-inflicted wound." Perhaps you mean that the Palestinians did not have leaders with the intelligence and foresight to recognize that Zionism was the greater force—there to stay—and make a timely accommodation with it. This is undeniable—the Palestinians waited far too long to recognize Israel and give up the idea that other Arab armies, or even they themselves, would destroy the Jewish state.

But that doesn't mean the grievances of the present Palestinian people are not legitimate. When Palestinian children are shot for sport by Israeli marksmen (*New York Times* correspondent Christopher Hedges describes this ugly enterprise in the September *Harper's*) or Israeli special forces leave booby trapped bombs on the pathways outside Palestinian elementary schools (as happened last month), these actions create grievances as compelling and legitimate as those felt by the Jewish victims of suicide bombers in Haifa or Jerusalem.

When Palestinian women are forced to give birth in ditches, because Israeli checkpoints make it impossible to reach the hospital, that is not a manufactured grievance but a real one.

I of course agree with you that the Palestinians erred grievously in failing to make a realistic counterproposal to Ehud Barak's offer at Camp David; and that the Palestinian bid for "right of return" for their refugees to pre-1967 Israel is a complete nonstarter. I have heard sophisticated and politically active Palestinians make these same points. I was glad to see that Arafat's latest appointment as the PLO's political representative to Jerusalem, Sari Nusseibeh, has said much the same thing. His appointment I think belies your contention that no Palestinian leaders acknowledge Israel's ties to the Holy Land.

There were several spots in your essay in which I thought your summaries or brief quotations didn't convey the full sense of the facts—your depiction of the Mitchell Commission report as exonerating Sharon's behavior when he marched with 1,000 troops up the Temple Mount/Holy Sanctuary is one such instance. But since you cover so much ground so artfully, I will spare you arguments that might seem like nitpicking.

But I don't want to leave you without asking one major question: how you think American interests would be served by adoption of the policies implicit in your argument? You paint the Palestinian national movement as a fraud and the effort to build a state in the occupied territories as a nonstarter, and suggest the Palestinians "try Jordan" if they want a state of their own. Though this is not an uncommon view on the Israeli Right, it is generally kept under wraps, because sophisticated Israelis understand how poorly it plays with international audiences.

So, again, what are the American interests in this situation? Of course, you recognize that Israel's day-to-day suppression of the Palestinians is now covered by television throughout much of the Muslim world, and for numerous reasons (in part surely to deflect popular attention from the shortcomings of Arab governments) the Arab–Israeli conflict has become the emotional center of Arab politics. Though Israel might well be able to dominate the Palestinians without American weaponry, financial assistance, and diplomatic support in the U.N. and elsewhere, the fact that it is generously supplied with all three makes that domination easier.

The Arabs know this. Arab leaders who are friendly to the U.S. had been warning Washington with increasing urgency of the explosive feelings the unresolved Palestinian problem was generating among their own people. Last September 11, Americans got a bitter taste of the consequences. Not because the bin Laden crew was directly linked to the Palestine problem, but because the widespread anti-Americanism in the Arab world that provides, as it were, the sea in which Al Qaeda's fish can spawn and swim is inexorably linked to Israel's unrelenting domination of the Palestinians.

In short, Israel's efforts to deny the Palestinians a homeland on the territory that the United Nations allocated for that purpose poses a problem for the United States, for the way Americans are perceived and treated in the world. Washington is rightly committed to Israel's security, and if a peace settlement gave Israel recognized borders, I would support guarantees to protect those borders—not that Israel, with its extremely competent military and advanced weaponry would have any trouble defeating any conventional assault. (The potential long-term security threat to Israel from ballistic missiles containing non-conventional weapons is hardly attenuated by Israel's domination of the West Bank and Gaza.)

But as Israel's sole and generous patron, the United States risks the unleashing against its own citizenry of the anger felt by the Palestinians (and spilling into the rest of the Arab world) over their continued national dispossession. Indeed, that anger has already been unleashed. Even if—as you argue—it were the Palestinians' own fault that they lost their homeland, or that they have no legitimate claim to any of the territory allocated them by the United Nations partition of the Palestinian mandate, why would it be in America's diplomatic and strategic interests to endorse such arguments, considered completely ridiculous in most of the world?

A relevant analogy here might be the civil rights movement and the Cold War: many American southerners argued that American blacks were better off than those in African countries, and there were sound reasons why they should attend separate schools or be denied the same rights as white people. But even if such arguments had been right (they were not), there were far more compelling global reasons during the Cold War 1950s and 1960s that made it imperative for the United States to end segregation.

Similarly, at a moment when the United States, facing a long and treacherous struggle against a ruthless terrorist enemy, must wage a focused and successful campaign for the hearts and minds of a billion people in the Arab and Muslim world, why should it continue to subsidize an Israeli occupation that undermines everything else it is seeking to accomplish?

David, I hope you know this letter is written in a spirit of friendly, even comradely, disagreement, and that it comes from someone who has plenty of appreciation for everything you have done since you came out as a "Lefty for Reagan" 17 years ago, and who was an avid *Ramparts* reader a dozen years before that.

Best wishes,
Scott McConnell

Antiwar.com
January 15, 2002

President Obama

"Untested Savior" was the first time I wrote about Barack Obama, and it showed me to be 100 percent wrong, more decisively, I believe, than I had been on any other political question as an adult. I corrected myself, endorsed Obama, and I find seven years later that I still agree with all the points I wrote in that endorsement.

To my surprise, Obama has turned out to be my favorite president in the past 30 years, though I am no "progressive." He strikes me as more or less a liberal Republican, which no doubt frustrates his progressive base, but doesn't displease me at all. His opening to Iran has been historic and took great political skill to achieve, given the influence of the Israel lobby on both sides of Congress. His appointment of Chuck Hagel took nerve; it showed early in his second term that Obama was ready to take risks in combating the neoconservatives.

Despite initially underestimating Obama's viability as a national politician, I ended up canvassing for him in both elections, first in Roanoke and then in the very poor towns of southeast Virginia. I hadn't done that kind of volunteer election work since 1968. It was fun and memorable, but I certainly can't see a candidate in this election cycle who would tempt me to do it again.

Untested Savior

The nation's Barack Obama swoon has eased, arrested by Hillary's swell of tears. But the force behind it gathers for resurgence. Its intensity is driven by yearnings as old as society itself, for a politics of the transcendent. Some intellectuals who fled Europe in the 1930s described a continent-wide "wholeness hunger"—a longing for release from corrupt, narrow, divisive parliamentary factions, a search for a more poetic, more binding politics.

There is some of that in the Obama fervor. In the wake of his Iowa triumph, one young light of the progressive blogosphere wrote, "Obama's finest speeches do not excite. They do not inform. They don't even really inspire. They elevate. They enmesh you in a grander moment, as if history has stopped flowing passively by, and, just for an instant, contracted around you, made you aware of its presence, and your role in it. He is not the Word made flesh, but the triumph of the word over flesh, over color, over despair." One Chicago newspaper reporter's book on Obama is proceeding with the working title *The Savior.*

Obamaism responds to a specifically American need. In his lucid study of the candidate, *A Bound Man,* Shelby Steele notes that America has "has undergone a moral evolution away from racism so transformative that there is now something like a desire in the body politic to see a truly qualified black person in the White House." But no previous black candidate has been plausible. Obama is, passing without ambiguity the ability threshold for holding the highest office.

In the age of affirmative action, attending Harvard as a black man would not suffice. Winning the editorship of the Harvard Law Review—a position, Steele notes tersely, "gained through competition rather than through the suspension of competition"—most emphatically does. And Obama's political talent mitigates his experience deficit. He bests his rivals at responding to tedious political questions with a nuanced or memorable phrase. He was correct about the Iraq War from day one. He can write. The autobiographical *Dreams from My Father,* with its vivid portraits and sardonic self-awareness, is a literary accomplishment no contemporary senator could match. Again, Steele: "The point is that Obama has separated himself from the deadly stigmas of black inferiority and white paternalism. This does not mean that people won't consider his race in some way as they ponder his candidacy. It only means they can consider his candidacy without feeling guilted, intimidated, or otherwise manipulated by his race." Not only is he plausible, his candidacy implicitly promises the healing of America's oldest wound.

National polls show Obama running as well or better than Clinton in match-ups against Republicans. The conventional wisdom is that while a dissolving GOP coalition could be re-united against Hillary, Obama would have greater appeal to independents and restless Republicans. Such prognoses come not only from progressives, happy to tell you that leading Republicans have no idea how to run against a black candidate, but from conservatives, too. David Brooks has touted Obama's moderate, consensus-seeking character in language so glowing some liberals interpreted it as a prelude to endorsement.

There is another opinion about this, however. It is held by some traditional conservatives who oppose Bush's Iraq and Iran policies, those most open to supporting a Democrat if the Republicans, as seems likely, promise a foreign policy of more of the same. In a nutshell, this view is that Hillary would face a difficult race, but would probably prevail, as could have Edwards or Joe Biden or a fairly generic Democrat in a year when the Dems have a major tailwind. Obama would be their weakest candidate, who could lead his party into an electoral disaster.

This is not because of Obama's race, which—other factors held equal—probably attracts more voters than it puts off. The weakness is the other major quality that progressive intellectuals find appealing in him: his cosmopolitanism, his relative unrootedness, the sense that he is harbinger not only of a new America in which race doesn't matter but of a globalized world in which national sentiment is on the way out. He would not only be the United States' first black president, but, to borrow immigration activist Mark Krikorian's useful term, its first post-American one as well.

In his foreign policy address before the Chicago Council on Global Affairs last April, Obama asserted that America's security is "inextricably linked to the security of all people," a recipe for global interventionism so promiscuous as to make neoconservatives almost prudent by comparison. He is a proponent of global free trade and high levels of immigration. Much of his memoir is devoted to his quest to connect with an extended family in Africa. This world-man aura is not without appeal, especially after eight years of a president deaf to what foreigners think and feel. But taken as far as Obama does, it would be an electoral liability.

One must also consider that the Republicans—perhaps especially those now overflowing with praise for Obama—might actually want to win the presidential election. In Obama, they would have an opponent who has never faced a well-funded foe in a tough one-on-one race, never encountered a barrage of negative TV advertising. He might be able to take a political punch well, he may not have a glass jaw. But there is no evidence for it. Obama's one statewide campaign was a romp over Alan Keyes, prompting one wag to remark that Obama's general-election prospects would indeed be excellent if the Republicans nominated Alan Keyes.

Obama has never faced a white opponent who hit hard or low or who struck at the very quality that makes him most appealing to the Left blogosphere, his exoticism. He won't face that test in the primaries: the nearest the Hillary camp might come is former Nebraska senator Bob Kerrey's probably disingenuous claim that he "liked" Obama's name and background and presumed ability to connect with the world's 1 billion Muslims. Liberal bloggers slammed Kerrey for propagating a vicious "smear," reminding one and all that multicultural good manners and political correctness are still the single factor that unites Democrats.

Republicans would not necessarily share such qualms. What might their campaign look like? You needn't be a political consultant to imagine a pretty effective one. The natural point of approach, of course, would be the name. Can we acknowledge that no contemporary Trollope or Allen Drury seeking to dramatize the emergence of a talented half-African presidential contender would consider burdening his hero with a name that evokes both of America's best-known enemies in the War on Terror? It would be far too over the top for social realism.

As the Democratic presidential nominee, Obama could quickly become known as Barack Hussein Obama. Republican commercials and talk radio would guarantee it. Negative TV spots could be relatively banal, pointing to some liberal highlights from Obama's state legislature record—one very strong pro-abortion vote and another against people who used unregistered guns to protect their homes against intruders would do the trick. And then, a voiceover, intoning something like "Barack Hussein Obama—Right for America?"

A colleague asserts that this would be seen as no more than a childish playground taunt, that by autumn Americans will be so acclimated to Obama's name that no repetition of it could weaken him. I doubt this. The political class, far more cosmopolitan than the rest of the country, has been intrigued with Obama for years. But by this summer, both parties will be playing to a broad electorate, in most cases more than twice the percentage of voters who turn out for a contested early state primary. Compared to primary voters, November voters are lower on the political awareness scale, less educated, less prosperous, less tuned in. Many will be forming an opinion about Barack Obama for the first time during and after the conventions, and branding him could be done comparatively quickly. Democrats in 1988 were astonished at how rapidly Michael Dukakis was "defined" by Willie Horton and how fast the Duke's double-digit lead in national polls evaporated. They of course knew that Dukakis was a competent and tested governor, a proven debater, no slouch on law and order. How could blue-collar voters not see this? Similarly, John Kerry's team found the Swiftboat charges so ludicrous they didn't deign to answer them. But, to the campaign's remorse, many voters found them believable enough. On what basis should we assume that white working-class voters (precisely those most resistant to Obama's electoral appeal thus far) would be completely unmoved by a campaign geared to question Obama's "American-ness"?

There is another vulnerability to Obama that his Democratic opponents would never exploit. Shelby Steele is right that America is more than ready for a black president and that Obama, in his present persona, does indeed embody "something that no other presidential candidate possibly can: the idealism that race is but a negligible human difference." Like Tiger Woods, the nation's most popular sports figure, he is a child of two races, embodying racial reconciliation in his very person. Hybridity, to use the fashionable academic term, is a growing phenomenon in America, driven by a burgeoning number of interracial marriages, visible in every large American city and even more so on elite college campuses. Obama is a natural beneficiary of this trend.

But there is another Obama, a young man abandoned at age 2 by his African father, who spent decades trying to fill the resulting void, in great part by trying very hard to become African American. In his "60 Minutes" interview, Obama describes himself as "rooted in the African-American community" and also "more than that." But this claim to "rootedness" in black America is nonsense. *Dreams from My Father* is a sometimes fascinating story of a sensitive young man trying to graft for himself an African-American identity, with very limited opportunities to do so. Obama was raised by his white mother, by an Indonesian stepfather, and then by his maternal grandparents in multiracial but not very black Hawaii. His efforts to become "black" without the context of any serious African-American community are labored. One of the book's charms is that Obama the writer sometimes seems to recognize this, describing his self-absorbed quest, then stepping outside to ever so faintly mock the character trying so earnestly to be black.

But while the quest for black identity is interesting on a human level, it is not necessarily the fodder of a mainstream presidential campaign. One of Obama's major stepping stones toward blackness was his membership in Jeremiah Wright's Trinity United Church of Christ, a sprawling Afrocentric enterprise on Chicago's South Side. Obama first became involved with Wright as a poverty organizer and later joined the church, with its "black value system," "black freedom," black this and black that. Trinity United is an atavism of the 1960s, with all the ties anyone would care to find to Louis Farrakhan and Muammar Gaddafi.

Identity politics is always understandable and often forgivable. I know of no evidence that Trinity United Church harmed anyone, and it probably did many attendees a lot of good. Nevertheless, Obama's long-time membership gives rise to Steele's impassioned and eloquent question:

> That he would join a church so steeped in blackness, with so many other churches available, only underscores his determination to be transparently black. How else to reconcile this church membership (and for over a decade) with the fact of his own family—his white mother, grandmother, and grandfather. It was not a "Black Value

System" that prepared Obama so well for the world. Nor was it "black community" or "black family." It was not black anything. One could more easily argue that his good luck was to be born into a white "family," "community," and "value system." ... So how can Barack Obama sit every week in a church preaching blackness and not object—not stand and proclaim that he was raised quite well, thank you, by three white Middle Westerners?

If that might be difficult to answer, the politics of it are not. Presumably they explain why, at the last moment, Obama cancelled plans to have Reverend Wright give the convocation at his campaign kickoff. A great part of Obama's appeal is his blend, his hybridity—a brand in danger of being undermined by his very biography. If Republicans want to link Obama to the kind of black nationalism that would make many of his would-be supporters (and not only them) uneasy, they have only to make Jeremiah Wright and his preaching well known in the months leading up to November. This would be denounced as race-baiting, and may indeed be unfair. My guess is that the present-day Obama has moved beyond the young man searching for ways to be authentically black and is now more in sync with the Ivy League intellectuals who have flocked to his banner than with Afrocentrists of the South Side. But politics is often unfair.

Perhaps the Republicans have so internalized political correctness that it would be unthinkable for them to chip away at Obama's character. But political parties, by their nature, want to win. John McCain has already opined, "Obama wouldn't know the difference between an RPG and a bong," foreshadowing a campaign that emphasizes personality more than issues, terrain hardly favorable to Obama.

Obama's backers seem strangely overprotective of their man, as if they can't conceive how any fair-minded person would not adore him. The few times questions like those raised above have been posted in the comments section of the highbrow progressive blogs, the reaction has been visceral, immediate, strident: it is racist even to mention this stuff, a point pounded home in vitriolic terms. The intense repudiation of Bob Kerrey's rather innocuous observation about Obama's name and background was astonishing, suggesting not confidence but fear that a very tender area was being exposed. It would seem that they too worry that their poetic and exciting candidate may actually be far weaker than the polls show.

The American Conservative
January 28, 2008

OBAMA OVER McCAIN

Remember the neoconservatives? Three years ago they were a hot topic, as people all over the world tried to understand why the United States had invaded a country that had nothing to do with 9/11. Then interest waned. First Paul Wolfowitz, then Doug Feith, then Don Rumsfeld left the administration. George W. Bush, who asked his dad "What's a neocon?" in the summer of 2004, took their counsel less. Core neocon concepts—a blend of forceful rhetoric about expanding democracy, contempt for most existing democratic countries, and enthusiasm for starting wars—began to seem unhinged from reality. They had dreamed up the Iraq War to transform the Middle East, argued it was pointless for Israel to make peace with the Palestinians, agitated for attacks on Iran. Without repudiating them directly, Robert Gates and Condi Rice eased them from the stage.

John McCain wants to bring them back, in triumph, on horseback. Unlike Bush, McCain is a neocon true believer; Wilsonian bellicosity has visceral appeal for him. A McCain victory would mean, in short order, an attack on Iran's nuclear facilities. Joshua Muravchik, a candid and well-connected neoconservative whom I've known for 25 years, affirmed this unequivocally at a Nixon Center debate last month. Iran is now the principal neoconservative obsession—as it is for Israel's hawks, who ludicrously paint Tehran as Nazi Berlin. McCain jokes about bombing Iran, but the consequences would not be amusing. Admiral Mike Mullen, chairman of the joint chiefs, has warned that an Israeli strike would put American forces in Iraq at grave risk. If America bombs, the consequences would be worse. As Secretary of Defense Gates warned a group of senators recently, "We'll create generations of jihadists, and our grandchildren will be battling our enemies here in America."

That's not all. Top McCain advisers like Robert Kagan seek to reignite a Cold War with Russia: Kagan recently told a Washington audience he wouldn't want to live in a world in which Russia had a preponderance of influence over Georgia. Elliott Abrams, son-in-law of Norman "World War IV" Podhoretz, is reportedly in line to head McCain's National Security Council. As a Bush appointee, he's worked at stymieing the peace process between Israel and the Palestinians. Expect a McCain administration to back the Netanyahu policy of turning the West Bank into isolated bantustans instead of a Palestinian state.

For these reasons, I'm voting for Obama. While he doesn't inspire me, he does impress. His two-year campaign has been disciplined and intelligent. He has surrounded himself with the mainstream liberal types who staffed the Clinton administration. Like countless social democratic leaders before him, he probably was more left-wing when he was younger. Circumstance and ambition have pushed him to the center. If elected, he will inherit an office burdened with massive financial and foreign-policy problems. Unlike John McCain, he won't try to bomb his way out of the mess.

The American Conservative
November 3, 2008

GOLFER IN CHIEF

"Ike's not a communist, he's a golfer." The quip comes from paleoconservative sage Russell Kirk when asked about John Birch Society chief Robert Welch's charge that President Eisenhower was a Communist agent. Ike wasn't the only Red in Welch's sights. "I personally believe [Secretary of State] Dulles to be a communist agent," he wrote, and CIA chief Allen Dulles "is the most protected and untouchable supporter of communism, next to Eisenhower himself, in Washington." Further, "The chances are very strong that Milton Eisenhower is actually Dwight Eisenhower's superior and boss within the Communist Party."

What chance has Barack Hussein Obama to be judged by more sober standards? Granted, Welch in his heyday was considered a kook while Obama is viewed as secretly disloyal by meatier segments of the Right. Rush Limbaugh, probably the most influential voice of the conservative movement, recently told listeners that Obama is governing with "the express purpose of overthrowing this country." Rush believes (or at least says) that Obama is not driven by communist doctrine but a Third World desire for payback for America's historical crimes. The president has been on this mission, Rush asserts, "far longer than you think."

Most modern-day conservatives do not disassociate themselves from Limbaugh the way Bill Buckley and Kirk distanced themselves from Welch and the Birchers. The comment boards on big conservative websites are full of Obama-the-totalitarian, Obama-the-closet-Islamist rhetoric. A few conservatives find this rhetoric distasteful and self-defeating, not to mention remote from observable facts. But the best retort to the reckless charges may be the same as Kirk's: No, Obama's not carrying out a long-term plan to overthrow the United States. He's a golfer.

Unpacking Kirk's remark requires some sense of the game and its impact on the personality. Obama has clearly become hooked. It was reported that he had played 32 times prior to the funeral of the Polish prime minister, when, seizing the opportunity provided by the volcano air-travel shutdown, he teed it up. This is a pace of about 24 rounds a year, well short of Eisenhower's hundred. Unlike Ike, Obama doesn't walk around the residence with a pitching wedge in hand or practice eight irons on the White House grounds. But he plays golf with the frequency of a man committed to the game.

By most accounts, Obama is still a mediocre player. Reports have him shooting in the nineties and low hundreds. He has poor technique in greenside bunkers, a sure recipe for fattening a score, but he plays seriously, recording real scores without mulligans.

Obama was a varsity basketball player in high school who still looks athletic on the court, and he has a fluid-looking golf swing. I'm sure he hits plenty of fine shots, the kind that tell him, "If I could only play and practice a bit more, I could get pretty good." Most people who were strong high school athletes can. One of golf's wonders is that a reasonably fit adult can continue to improve throughout his fifties. Last year Tom Watson nearly won the British Open at age 59, beating a field of men half his age. That was exceptional, but in any other sport, it would be out of the question.

Let's dispense with platitudes about golf being a great way to relax, to put aside the cares of the office, to bond with friends, to commune with nature. All are true, but the same could be said of fishing or hiking. Those pastimes don't become obsessive. Golf does.

For the avid golfer, few pleasures rival hitting a good shot. Sex, sometimes. Exquisite food, maybe. Doing something very well in your profession, certainly. But striking a good golf shot pushes a lot of psychic satisfaction buttons. It requires both physical grace and mental control. The margin between hitting well and hitting poorly is small. A good shot rewards, however fleetingly, with a sense of mastery.

Some writers describe this in mystical terms. Here's John Updike in *Rabbit, Run*. His protagonist, 20-something former high school basketball star Harry "Rabbit" Angstrom, is playing golf with Eccles, an Episcopal priest. Rabbit has a busted marriage and is having trouble with adulthood. There is something, some "it," that was missing from his marriage and remains absent from his life. Perhaps it's God or the sense of wholeness and peace that some people seek in church. Eccles isn't convinced and indeed questions whether there is any "it" at all. He asks Rabbit to describe what he's looking for:

> In avoiding looking at Eccles, he looks at the ball, which sits high on a tee and already seems free of the ground. Very simply he brings the clubhead around his shoulder into it. The sound has a hollowness, a singleness he hasn't heard before. His arms force his head up and his ball is hung way out, lunarly pale against the beautiful black blue of storm clouds, his grandfather's color stretched dense across the north. It recedes along a line straight as a ruler-edge. Stricken; sphere, star, speck. It hesitates, and Rabbit thinks it will die, but he's fooled, for the ball makes its hesitation the ground of a final leap: with a kind of visible sob it takes a last bite of space, before vanishing in falling.

"That's it," he cries, turning to Eccles with a grin of aggrandizement. "That's it."

The satisfaction doesn't last, and even avid players lose interest in the game. But those who are getting better tend to stay committed. Obama, who started playing in his late thirties, is still on the upward stage of his golf trajectory, the most rewarding stage, and the one most likely to border on compulsion.

Some on the Left have already complained that golf is damaging his presidency. *The New Republic's* Michelle Cottle laments that the spirit of "change you can believe in" is being dissipated on the golf course. She is on to something. A disciplined person can compartmentalize, shove the golf thoughts into a corner, and let them out only for their allotted ten or 15 hours of the week. But their presence makes a difference. Golf crowds out other, potentially competing, obsessions. A golfing president can put in the focused hours his job requires, but grandiose dreams about what his office can accomplish are likely to be restrained. Golf teaches the recognition of limits. Don't swing too hard. Power is found in balance, in tempo, in not overreaching. No golfer is a revolutionary.

Does the president's mind wander to the pure six iron he hit in his last round while he is working on talking points that recommend Elena Kagan to the Supreme Court? I would bet it does. Does Obama think more about his next round and how to play better infinitely more than he does about overthrowing the American system? Without a shadow of a doubt. Does golf limit his motivation even to transform the country, with the bitter, all-consuming fights this would require? Quite possibly that, too.

The American Conservative
July 1, 2010

On the Trail in Virginia

I spent the weekend canvassing for Obama in the Virginia Beach area. The task for the hundreds of volunteers who descended from Washington, D.C., and New York was to make sure the maximum number of Virginia's "sporadic Democratic voters"—a designation which seemed to mean, pretty much, poor minorities—get to the polls on Tuesday. People needed to know where their polling place was, what ID they needed, be reminded that it's important, and make a foolproof plan to vote.

And, of course shooting down the various disinformational memes that "someone" has been circulating in the area: that "because of the hurricane" you can vote by calling this number, or that you can't vote a straight Democratic ticket—if you do, your Senate or Congress vote won't count.

It is a core axiom among Democratic activists that the essence of the Republican "ground game" is to suppress the Democratic votes with lies, intimidation, and whatever might work.

It was a curiously moving experience. Much of the sentiment comes from simple exposure. I have led most of my life not caring very much whether the poor voted, and indeed have sometimes been aware my interests aligned with them not voting at all. But that has changed. And so one knocks on one door after another in tiny houses and apartments in Chesapeake and Newport News, some of them nicely kept and clearly striving to make the best of a modest lot, others as close to the developing world as one gets in America. And at moments one feels a kind of calling—and then laughs at the Alinskian presumption of it all. Yes, we are all connected.

At times when I might have been afraid—knocking on a door of what might well have been a sort of crack house —I felt no fear. I was protected by age and my Obama campaign informational doorhangers.

And occasionally, one strikes canvassing gold. In one decrepit garden apartment complex, where families lived in dwellings the size of maybe two large cars, a young man (registered) came around behind me while I was talking to his mother. "Yeah" he said, "Romney wins, I'm moving back to the islands. He's gonna start a war, to get the economy going." Really. He stopped to show me a video on his smart phone of one of his best friends, a white guy in the Marines. I couldn't make out what the video was saying, but I took it as a *Monthly Review* moment. In a good way.

And Tomiko. Plump, pretty, dressed in a New York Jets jersey and sweatpants. "If the campaign can get me a van, I can get dozens of people around here to the polls on Tuesday." Yes, Tomiko, the campaign might be able to do that, and someone will be calling you.

A very small sample size, but of the white female Obama volunteers with whom I had long conversations, 100 percent had close relatives who had failed marriages with Mormon men. I think Mormonism is the great undiscussed subject of the campaign, and I don't quite know what to make of it myself. But contrary to Kennedy's Catholicism (much agonized over) and Obama's Jeremiah Wright ties (ditto), Mormonism is obviously the central driving factor of Romney's life. This may be a good thing or a bad thing—but it is rather odd that it is not discussed, at all. I think it's safe to say that if Romney wins, the Church of Latter Day Saints will come under very intense scrutiny, and those of us who have thought of the church as simply a Mountain West variation of Protestantism will be very much surprised.

I spent a good deal of time driving and sharing meals with three fellow volunteers, professional women maybe in their early forties, two black, one white, all gentile, all connected in some way, as staffers or lobbyists, to the

Democratic Party. All had held staff positions at the Democratic convention. They had scoped out my biography, knew the rough outlines from neocon, to Buchananite, to whatever I am now. They knew my principal reason for supporting Obama was foreign policy, especially Iran. They spent many hours interrogating me about my reactionary attitudes on women, race, immigration, all in good comradely fun of course. At supper last night before we drove back to D.C., I asked them (all former convention staffers) what they thought about the contested platform amendment on Jerusalem. Silence. Finally one of them said, with uncharacteristic tentativeness, "Well, I'm not sure I really know enough about that issue." More silence.

Then I told them I thought it was a historic moment (though I refrained from the Rosa Parks analogy I have deployed before), which portended a sea change in Democratic Party attitudes on the question. I cited various neocon enforcers who feared the same thing.

And now, with permission to speak freely, they spoke up. It came pouring out. Yes, obviously Israel has to give up something. There has to be a two-state solution. We can't just one-sidedly support Israel, and so on. But really striking was their reluctance, perhaps even fear, to voice their own opinions before hearing mine.

LobeLog.com
November 5, 2012

The Neocons in Action

Among the Neocons

In what may be the twentieth example of the genre in the past decade, a neoconservative has written a magazine article excommunicating from the conservative movement Patrick Buchanan and others who fail to embrace warmongering neoconservatism. A comedy skit could be made about these repeated efforts, as the excommunicated faction somehow fails simply to shut up and disappear as it is supposed to. David Frum's *National Review* article (April 7) is longer than most of its kind but predictable in its wielding of the standard neocon rhetorical weapons: those who disagree with his faction are racist, nativist, anti-Semitic, and of course "unpatriotic."

However tendentiously, Frum is addressing an important subject. There is a full- scale ideological war in the ranks of those who think of themselves as conservative and, if they were of age, supported Ronald Reagan a generation ago. As Frum notes, the split became apparent in the mid-1980s, spiked briefly in the early 1990s, and smoldered on through to the present. The neocons have always been the dominant side in the contest; they are more internally cohesive and far wealthier. Nonetheless they often, and rightly, feel unappreciated by those they believe should admire them, and they are constantly on the lookout for ideological deviancy. Their opponents include the disparate right-wing sorts mentioned by Frum and—just as significantly—a far larger number of moderate, centrist, or establishment-oriented Republicans who are not by temperament given to ideological battling but who tend to perceive the neocons as dangerous zealots. This magazine was founded in great part to engage in the battle that Frum depicts.

The neocons would prefer to ignore their challengers. On paper, they should be able to: they hold key jobs in the Bush administration; control virtually all the major "conservative" media outlets—from the magazines, to the major television and radio shows, to the significant editorial pages—and play the dominant role in the better-funded think tanks and foundations. And yet they don't breathe easily. Frum's piece is a sequel to attacks on antiwar conservatives by Max Boot in the *The Wall Street Journal* and Lawrence Kaplan and Robert Kagan in *The Washington Post*. All betray the same anxiety: that despite their wealth and position, the neoconservatives sense that they are no longer gaining adherents and now are losing them.

For me, these battles are intensely personal. Not because I harbor any rancor toward individuals on the other side, or because I have come under personal attack myself, but because my own bit of foot-soldiering in the ideological wars is virtually defined by the split between the neocons and traditional conservatives. As I write this, in my New York apartment there sits (sorted and labeled in plastic organizers) virtually every issue of *Commentary* from 1976 to the present. The contents include some fifteen pieces I wrote for the magazine, long essays and short reviews, between 1982 and 1995. I still take pride in virtually all I wrote there. I remember vividly the joyous moment when I learned I could actually get published in my favorite magazine, and, some years later, my giddiness at being invited to a small dinner at the Podhoretzes'. I remember with a wistful affection my close friendship with the late Eric Breindel, my admiration for the incisive mind of *Commentary* editor Neal Kozodoy. They all make up a big part of the person I am today.

I remember too my puzzlement upon hearing the first rumbles of the "paleo" insurrection in the late 1980s: "What is their problem?" I might have said in the solicitous tone one uses about those who are not necessarily rational. My reaction to reading *The New York Times* account of Richard John Neuhaus's eviction from the Rockford Institute's New York offices was, I would guess, very much the same as David Frum's. My views on Lincoln and Churchill were and remain boringly conventional. So what happened during the 1990s that could have transformed me from a neoconservative into the co-founder of a magazine that is anything but that?

Two new issues broke apart the 1980s Reaganite conservative consensus. The first was immigration. By the late 1980s, the impact of the 1965 immigration law had begun greatly to accelerate the pace of immigration. Younger readers may not recall the vital role *National Review* began to play in analyzing that law and the social, environmental, and political consequences it brought about. The battle was joined when John O'Sullivan (*NR*'s editor since 1988) published in 1992 Peter Brimelow's explosive "Time to Rethink Immigration," which quickly became the most debated conservative magazine article of the year. The piece forced the immigration debate into the open within the conservative movement, where it fused with the populist revolt breaking out in California over Proposition 187, an anti-illegal alien measure. For the next five years, the magazine put what it called "The National Question" in the spotlight, publishing cover stories by Brimelow, Fred Iklé, O'Sullivan, and eventually (as I was won over to the magazine's position) one by me.

The neoconservatives, to my complete surprise, were not pleased.

In the summer of 1995, Neal Kozodoy gave me a copy of a letter. Written by Irwin Stelzer to the *The Weekly Standard*'s Bill Kristol, it was making its way around the upper echelons of the neocon magazines and think tanks. Stelzer is a Bronx-born economist and *Weekly Standard* editor who lives part-time in London. While a gifted economic essayist, his most important function is surely as the ideological *gendarme* for Rupert Murdoch's American media properties.

Stelzer wrote to Kristol (and the wider world) that he was canceling his subscription to *National Review* because of its "increasingly offensive positions on such topics as immigration." He went on then to complain about a piece by Richard Neuhaus on anti-Semitism, which, Stelzer charged, was itself anti-Semitic. He added, apropos of a quote of Kristol's that appeared in Neuhaus's article, that he was "always suspicious" of Father Neuhaus's excerpting, "particularly in an article which contains cunningly placed little adjectives and descriptions." He concluded with a more general comment about John O'Sullivan's *National Review*: "Add to this *NR*'s applause for the immigration statutes of the 1920s, designed to keep eastern European Jews out, and you have a not-very-subtle form of anti-Semitism, dressed up as an attack on liberalism."

Bill Buckley stood by his editor initially, but not for long. Within two years, O'Sullivan was eased out, replaced by the youthful Rich Lowry, who immediately upon assuming his new post fired Peter Brimelow.

In the very early years of the neocon-paleocon skirmish, Russell Kirk, the somewhat fogeyish father of postwar American intellectual conservatism, gave a speech about the neocons at the Heritage Foundation. He generally praised them but added some words of caution. Quoting from a friend's letter, Kirk said, "It is significant that when the Neo-Cons wish to damn any conservative who has appealed for a grant from a conservative foundation, they tell the officers of the foundation the conservative is a fascist." I, of course, had heard of neocon campaigns against other conservatives, but the targets were not men I knew or agreed with. But I did know O'Sullivan and Neuhaus, and the Russell Kirk remark that had once seemed overheated became a good deal less so.

If *National Review* did not entirely drop the issue of immigration, in the post-O'Sullivan era it addressed it with markedly diminished zest. Mark Krikorian contributed some solid but uncontroversial pieces. John Miller, who had written a book that attacked several immigration reformers while calling for a renewed effort to "assimilate" an ever-growing number of new immigrants, replaced Brimelow on the masthead. The flame of "nativism" in the nation's leading conservative publication was safely extinguished, and the neocons breathed more easily as 1.5 million new immigrants entered the country every year.

Soon gone too was the magazine's intellectual flair and unpredictability, as it abandoned its role of pre-eminent arbiter of different voices within the conservative movement (and occasional critic of Republican politicians) for that of simple cheerleader for the GOP establishment. Readers would no longer find articles like Fred Iklé's on the perils of worshiping the measures of economic growth for their own sake, or Dan Seligman on "IQ and National Prosperity." Seldom was anything published that might complicate the thoughts of the average Rush Limbaugh listener.

At roughly the same time that O'Sullivan was pushed from the helm of *National Review*, I was fired as editorial page editor of the *New York Post*, ostensibly for publishing an editorial opposing statehood for Puerto Rico and standing by it after the pressure started. The morning I was sacked, the *Post*'s editor pointed out to me an op-ed in that day's paper by Mark Krikorian (the most measured of immigration-reform writers). He said accusingly, "You keep putting things in the paper like that."

In the mid-1990s, the post-Cold War debates on American foreign policy began to assume a definitive new shape. When not focused on the Clinton sex life, *The Weekly Standard* agitated for a more belligerent U.S. stance in several areas of the world: first (and always) Iraq, then the former Yugoslavia, China, and Iran. The *Standard* was aware of the visceral resistance to this more aggressive Kristol-Kagan-Perle-Wolfowitz line within the traditional Republican Party, both from politicians with some residual isolationist tendencies and from the realist-internationalists who predominated during the Cold War period. Writers of the latter persuasion had found a home in *The National Interest*, a quarterly founded in 1986, a time when neoconservatives and realists were more often allies, and edited from its inception until 2001 by the Australian, by way of Wales, Owen Harries.

Harries's journal was perhaps even more eclectic than *NR* under O'Sullivan, and like *NR* it gave a voice to all the major conservative tendencies.

Harries had been a Cold Warrior, but became worried that America would overreach after having established itself as the "sole-surviving superpower." He frequently quoted Edmund Burke's admonition against nationalistic hubris: "I dread our being too much dreaded."

By the end of the 1990s, neoconservative tolerance for such perspectives was wearing rather thin. Lawrence Kaplan in *The Weekly Standard* lambasted *National Interest* writers who "blame America first," singling out James Schlesinger, Jack Kemp, James Kurth, Samuel Huntington, and Walter McDougall. All were faulted for advocating a foreign policy too solicitous of the sensibilities and cultures of other nations. Two years later, Kaplan published a similar article in *The New Republic*, attacking conservative foreign policy intellectuals who were skeptical about the good that would come from hegemonic America as "yearning to see U.S. power erode." Huntington (who worried about the impact of high immigration on national unity) and Schlesinger (who had the temerity to call attention to the prominent role of the Israel lobby in formulating American Mideast policy) were singled out as particular offenders. "Guess Who Hates America," *The New Republic* titled Kaplan's piece. David Frum's attack on "unpatriotic conservatives" has a well-established pedigree.

While the attacks on Harries's journal and its contributors were more polite than Stelzer's smear of Neuhaus and O'Sullivan, they revealed something important about the state of neoconservatism: many of the Christian intellectuals of the first rank who identified quite wholeheartedly with the tendency during the 1980s did not anymore, and the neocons knew it. It was one thing to go after a Mel Bradford or a Samuel Francis (who identified too closely with the Old South to be widely accepted as mainstream). But Harries, Neuhaus, and O'Sullivan were public intellectuals of the highest caliber, the sort of people who really made the neoconservative ascendance of the 1980s far broader and more important than a simple "New York intellectual" (i.e., Jewish) phenomenon. Add to them Samuel Huntington, the Harvard political scientist who—if he wasn't a neocon by virtue of institutional ties, as a moderately hawkish and conservative Democrat seemed to be an almost pure representative of the ideological tendency—and you had a situation in which the neocon bastion was riven by defections of major figures.

Of course, this was muted: to most, the neocon world seemed to be growing more dominant. And on many levels it was. The mid-'90s infusion of Murdoch cash (through *The Weekly Standard*, the Fox News Channel, and, of course, the *New York Post*) helped secure neocon ascendancy. Even *National Review* was safely in neocon hands. But unlike the 1980s, the hegemony was based increasingly on fear rather than respect. Conservatives who still had jobs in the seemingly ever-growing network of neoconservative magazines and think tanks learned that the place for many of their real political views was private life. As Owen Harries explained to me, "That is what an establishment is."

There are three main elements to Frum's indictment: racism ("racial passions run strong among the paleos"); antipathy toward Jews (he quotes something from Joe Sobran); and lack of enthusiasm for America's hand-in-glove alliance with Israel's current right-wing government (he quotes several writers who have appeared in this magazine). I obviously cannot speak for all those he mentions, many with views that don't resemble mine. But I can discuss Frum's charges through the prism of my own experience, as a neocon and after.

I was far more conscious of "racial passions" during my neocon years climbing the greasy pole at the *New York Post* than subsequently. No doubt this is partially due to the period (framed by the Tawana Brawley case and the O.J. trial, with the LA riots in between) and the job (writing mostly about urban politics). But I suspect some part of the difference is due to the surrounding culture of neoconservatism. It may not prove much of anything, but a dinner with Sam Francis (or virtually any other "paleocon") is less tinged with snickers and winks about the behavior of people of color than a dinner in the New York neocon world.

Another difference: church. Sometime in 1995, I began attending services for the first time since prep school, showing up sporadically at a mainline Presbyterian church in Manhattan. No big epiphanies to relate, and unlike George W. Bush, I cannot claim Christ as my favorite philosopher. But something rubs off from the Christian liturgy—its all-embracing quality, its summons to universal brotherhood—that makes "racial passions" of any sort seem a bit shameful. That's my experience anyway, but I suspect it is why the country's hard-core racialists are so vehemently anti-Christian.

From church may have come the spark of another realization: that the Palestinians, many of whom are Christian, are people deserving of dignity and rights. In one of the first Christmas services I attended, the minister alluded to Jesus' mother Mary as "a poor Palestinian woman." For a new congregant who had spent the previous decade in circles where the word "Palestinian" was rarely uttered without a sneer implying a congenital predilection for murder and mayhem, the phrase about Mary rattled around the mind for a while. During the Cold War, Israel-Palestine was a very secondary issue for me, and at the Cold War's end there came Oslo, which seemed certain to set matters to right. During the 1990s, the neoconservative I knew best (Eric Breindel) invariably spoke and wrote of Oslo as "a fact." Though Breindel had significant ties to the Israeli Right (Bibi Netanyahu spoke at his wedding party), he was friendly as well with Shimon Peres and Yitzhak Rabin's widow, Leah. It would shock me if he could have made common cause with such current Bush administration figures as Douglas Feith and Richard Perle, who worked with Netanyahu to undermine the Oslo Accords in the mid-1990s.

It is by now beyond serious dispute that the vast and uncritical American support for Israel looms large among the factors making the United States disliked and feared in the world. The push for an even great number of wars in the Middle East—Norman Podhoretz now demands the U.S. overthrow the regimes of six or seven Muslim countries—is quite clearly driven by a concern for Israel's needs, not America's. Washington's commitment to Israel's existence is a given—a logical and moral goal. But support for Israel's suppression of the Palestinians, whose lands the Israeli Right covets, does nothing but generate hatred for the United States. In the aftermath of 9/11, some neoconservatives (and others who are simply gullible) have touted the line that the United States is hated "because of its freedom." This slogan fit for small children contradicts what virtually any American with business, diplomatic, or military experience in the Middle East will say. Sadly, it wouldn't be the first time that a great nation came under the spell of a tragic delusion.

Frum's other indictment against the antiwar conservatives is anti-Semitism, the nuclear weapon accusation in American public life. The simple point to be made is that neoconservatism is not synonymous with Jewish opinion. (And indeed, several of the movement's prominent figures are gentiles.) In their effort to marry American policies to the goals of the Israeli far Right, the neocons have embraced Norman Podhoretz's definition of anti-Semitism: if you are supportive of Israel, everything is fine. The neocons have no problem with those parts of the Christian Right that view the gathering of Jews in the Holy Land as a prelude to the final Armageddon, in which all Jews will convert to Christianity or perish. Such believers stand meekly in the Amen Corner for the Sharons, Netanyahus, and Meir Kahanes of the world, and the neocons are well pleased. But conservatives who evince any public doubts about where the Israel tie is leading us are seen as dangerous anti-Semites, ripe for smearing.

The good news—because the Jewish contribution to nuanced and sophisticated political discussion in America is quite substantial—is that many (and perhaps most) politically engaged Jews consider the neocon view of the world to be rabid nonsense. To turn one's back on the Richard Perles and Paul Wolfowitzs and David Frums, who have worked to trash America's good name with their incessant warmongering, does not mean that one is turning one's back on Thomas Friedman, or Joe Klein, or Leonard Fein, or

Michael Kinsley or anyone else in what would obviously be a very long list of non-extremist Jews, some who are conservative, many more who are not.

No matter how quickly Baghdad is conquered, it is clear that the neocons have led the United States into an extremely perilous situation, perhaps the most dangerous in its history. As strident advocates of open borders and the sworn enemies of immigration reform—they have helped bring about a situation where it was easy for terrorist cells to hide themselves within the nooks and crannies of the "first universal nation" they espouse.

Their unceasing agitation against a compromise peace in the Middle East, coupled with their lobbying for America to endorse to Sharon's ongoing humiliation of the Palestinians, has managed to make America hated in parts of the world where it used to be admired, even loved. Some of that hatred has been turned—should we be surprised?—into anti-American terror. Now, as it prepares to occupy Iraq against the will of much of the Middle East while facing a rejuvenated al-Qaeda, America has fewer real friends and more ill-wishers than ever in its history. This is in considerable part the "accomplishment" of America's neocons, the fruit of the power they have achieved in the conservative movement and the influence they wield with an inexperienced and simple president. It will take years to undo the damage they have done, but there is no choice but to begin.

The American Conservative
April 21, 2003

THE WEEKLY STANDARD'S WAR

As *The Weekly Standard* celebrates its 10th birthday, it may be time to ask whether America has ever seen a more successful political magazine. Many have been more widely read, profitable, amusing, or brilliant. But in terms of actually changing the world and shaping the course of history, what contemporary magazine rivals the *Standard*? Even if you believe that the change has been much for the worse, the *Standard*'s record of success in its own terms is formidable.

At the time of the *Standard*'s founding, in 1995, there was considerable speculation among neoconservatives over whether the movement had run its course. In "Neoconservatism: A Eulogy," Norman Podhoretz argued that neoconservatism had effectively put itself out of business by winning on its two major battle fronts: over communism and the residue of the 1960s counterculture. In the process, it had injected itself into the main body of American conservatism to such a degree that it was no longer particularly distinct from it. The eulogy was not a lamentation, more an appreciation of a job well done.

But while there was something to the Podhoretz argument, the American Right in 1995 did not have a neocon-ish feel. Newt Gingrich and the new Congress were the center of gravity; Rush Limbaugh was a far more important figure than Bill Kristol; the issues that most agitated the Right, gays in the military and Whitewater, were either the province of religious and social conservatives or committed Republican partisans.

On other national issues, neocons were either uncertain or not on the cutting edge. Charles Murray's 1994 bestseller *The Bell Curve*, which argued that IQ was hereditarily based and was increasingly and ineluctably correlated with career success and life outcomes, was the most discussed and controversial book on the Right, but neocons were split over whether to distance themselves from it or quietly embrace at least some of its analyses. Immigration, already an issue of intense popular concern in California, was a key cause for *National Review*, the oldest and most popular magazine on the Right. But most neoconservatives deplored the immigration-reform impulse, with many claiming to see in it an echo of the restrictionists of the 1920s, whose legislation had the (obviously unintended) result of closing America's door to Jewish refugees a decade later.

Foreign policy, which had been a prime unifier of the Right during the Cold War, was on the back burner. Norman Podhoretz's *Commentary* had been waging a lonely battle against the Oslo peace process (a track leading to a Palestinian state in Gaza and the West Bank), but its position was very much in the minority among both foreign affairs experts and American Jews. In the quarterlies, foreign-policy specialists debated America's role in the post-Cold War world, but it was hard for most newspaper readers to keep up with obscure struggles on the Balkans or complicated debate about NATO expansion. America, it seemed, had no real enemies. Thus in 1995, it could be rightly claimed that the original neoconservative movement had spawned a successor generation, even two. But it was not clear what that generation's role would be, if any.

Enter *The Weekly Standard*—edited principally by William Kristol, a genial and sharp son of an eminent neoconservative family—which arrived on the scene thanks to a $3 million annual subsidy from Rupert Murdoch. It is not always understood beyond the world of journalism that political opinion magazines almost invariably lose money—sometimes a lot of it. The deficits are usually made up by their owners and subscribers' contributions, some quite substantial. *Commentary* was supported for most of its life by the American Jewish Committee and now has a publication committee of formidably wealthy people. William F. Buckley's *National Review* always had angels; Buckley once answered a query about when his magazine would be profitable by saying, "You don't expect the Church to make a profit, do you?" The venerable *Nation*, at the time of the *Standard*'s founding, had an annual deficit of roughly $500,000, made up by owner Arthur Carter. The prestigious *Atlantic Monthly* reportedly loses between $4 and $8 million a year.

That said, while the *Standard*'s reported subsidy was gigantic for a small ideological niche magazine. If Rupert Murdoch's purpose was to make things happen in Washington and in the world, he could not have leveraged it better. One could spend 10 times that much on political-action committees without achieving anything comparable.

It has never been obvious, however, what Murdoch's ideological and political ambitions were. A brilliant businessman, he was generally right-wing—though his newspapers and networks hardly humored socially conservative sensibilities. His papers tended to endorse conservative candidates who had a good chance of winning. More than anything else, he seemed to relish his triumph over the British press unions. He was not an immigration restrictionist, but didn't share the neocon antipathy to them. In 1993, it took considerable effort by *New York Post* editorial page editor Eric Breindel to persuade Murdoch that Rudy Giuliani was vastly superior to the incumbent David Dinkins as a candidate for mayor of New York. In one conversation I had with him (during my own brief tenure as *Post* editorial page editor) about the paper's foreign policy positions, he told me, when the discussion had veered to Israel and the Middle East, "Well, it might not have been a good idea to create it [Israel], but now that it's there, it has to be supported." A splendidly ambiguous statement—perfectly consistent with a strong pro-Israel position, but not the sort of thing an American neoconservative would ever say.

The subsidy Murdoch accorded the *Standard* assured the new venture would be highly visible by the standards of start-up political magazines. It could afford a wide newsstand presence: it is costly for any new magazine to print issues that will in most cases not be sold. The *Standard* not only passed out thousands of complimentary issues around Washington, it had them personally delivered to Beltway influentials as soon as they were printed. Above all, the new journal provided employment for a small coterie of neoconservative essayists and a ready place to publish for dozens of apparatchiks who held posts at the American Enterprise Institute and other neocon-friendly think tanks.

With the fledgling Fox News Channel, the *Standard* soon emerged as the key leg in a synergistic triangle of neoconservative argumentation: you could write a piece for the magazine, talk about your ideas on Fox, pick up a paycheck from Kristol or from AEI. It was not a way to get rich, but it sustained a network of careers that might otherwise have shriveled or been diverted elsewhere. Indeed, it did more than sustain them, it gave neocons an aura of being "happening" inside the Beltway that no other conservative (or liberal) faction could match. Murdoch had refuted the otherwise plausible arguments in Norman Podhoretz's eulogy.

But what was the *Standard*'s type of neoconservatism? To some degree the new magazine echoed the most popular GOP obsessions, exhibiting for example a limitless enthusiasm for Kenneth Starr's inquisition into Bill Clinton's sex life. It warned Republican lawmakers against supporting a 1996 immigration reform that would have reduced the numbers of legal and illegal immigrants. (Asians and Hispanics had "increasingly Republican partisan inclinations" the magazine claimed, without evidence.) It had a moment—one issue, precisely—of Great Fear when it seemed possible that Pat Buchanan would capture the 1996 Republican presidential nomination and devoted a three-article cover spread to bemoaning the possibility. (One piece was a smear, one a reasoned look at Buchanan's protectionist economic views, and one contained the interesting assertion that Buchanan's views on issues were not particularly extreme—and in fact shared by tens of millions of Americans—but his way of presenting them was, and therein lay the problem.) It published Robert Kagan's attack on Samuel Huntington's "Clash of Civilizations" under the charming neo-McCarthyesque title "Harvard Hates America." But except for its foreign policy stances, the *Standard* seemed a bit theme-less throughout its early life.

Nor does the recently released *The Weekly Standard: A Reader 1995-2005* pinpoint the editorial heart of the publication. The volume (as does the magazine itself) contains several excellent pieces, exuding an urbane and sophisticated moderate conservatism. Worthy of note is what may be the finest appreciation in print of the Columbia literary critic and neoconservative precursor Lionel Trilling, written by Gertrude Himmelfarb (Bill Kristol's mother). The collection also contains essays by Christopher Caldwell, Joseph Epstein, and Andrew Ferguson that any editor would be proud to publish. The magazine's hawkishness is not exactly swept under the bed; Kristol and Robert Kagan's "Saddam Must Go" editorial of November 1997 is reprinted: "We know it seems unthinkable to propose another ground attack to take Baghdad. But it's time to start thinking the unthinkable." Charles Krauthammer's "At Last, Zion" (May 1998) is a powerful and moving explanation of why Israel is at the center of his (and much neoconservative) consciousness. In "The Holocaust Shrug" (April 2004), David Gelernter wheels out the tried and tested appeasement analogy in support of the Iraq War. Saddam is no Hitler, Gelernter acknowledges, but "the world's indifference to Saddam resembles its indifference to Hitler."

But these foreign policy essays, making up perhaps a fifth of the volume, don't do justice to the central role the Iraq War played in establishing the

Standard's identity. For despite the publication's subsidy and visibility, before 9/11 it seemed to be floundering. It was unable to push George W. Bush in a direction it wanted. Most of the editors had supported John McCain in the Republican primaries; no neoconservatives received cabinet-level posts in the administration. The varied balloons Kristol and company hoisted to give a focus to their politics ("national greatness conservatism" was one, with an emphasis on an assertive foreign policy and constructing patriotic monuments) never gained much altitude. In 2001, Kristol mentioned to some that he was considering closing down the magazine. The *Standard*'s last cover story before 9/11 was a long meditation by David Brooks on the TV show "Gilligan's Island" and what the evolution of pop culture said about globalization.

One day a novel must be written that conveys the sense of purpose and energy that surged through the *Standard*'s offices—and that of the whole Washington neoconservative network—in the days after September 11, 2001. No more esoteric musings about Gilligan and the Skipper. The Project for a New American Century (PNAC)—a Bill Kristol-founded pressure group that specialized in gathering the signatures of the obscure and moderately famous in support of a more militarized foreign policy—would be ignored no longer. At long last, there would be an audience.

Inside the administration were Dick Cheney, Donald Rumsfeld, and their staffs, heavy with signatories of the original 1998 PNAC Saddam-must-be-removed letter. They set out to neutralize the skeptical CIA and Colin Powell's more cautious State Department and rush the White House into a war in Iraq. Their story has been told in several book-length accounts and administration memoirs. Outside, with the vital task of shaping public opinion, the *Standard* emerged as the nerve center, a focal point to concentrate and diffuse the message of the Beltway neocons. For these bookish men, it was a Churchillian moment, an occasion to use words to rally a nation and shape history.

Their job was to divert America's wrath away from those who perpetrated the attack and turn it against those who did not. It was, on the face of it, quite a stretch. The day before 9/11, the idea of a ground invasion to overthrow Saddam Hussein's Iraq was as "unthinkable," as it had been when Kristol and Kagan had first broached it four years earlier. But the country was confused—in shock and primed for vengeance. Suddenly, there was a large national audience for foreign policy discussion on the TV networks and talk-radio programs. The whole conservative movement was looking for guidance. If repetition could somehow insert into the national consciousness and thereby render plausible an idea that would otherwise have occurred to very few, the *Standard* would be up to the task. Again and again the refrain would be pounded out, "Saddam Must Go!," and would be picked up by commentators further down the ideological food chain.

In the first issue the magazine published after 9/11, Gary Schmitt and Tom Donnelly, two employees of Kristol's PNAC, clarified what ought to be the country's war aims. Their rhetoric—which laid down a line from which the magazine would not waver over the next 18 months—was to link Saddam Hussein and Osama bin Laden in virtually every paragraph, to join them at the hip in the minds of readers, and then to lay out a strategy that actually gave attacking Saddam priority over eliminating al-Qaeda. The first piece was illustrated with a caricature of Saddam, not bin Laden, and the proposed operational plan against bin Laden was astonishingly soft. "While it is probably not necessary to go to war with Afghanistan, a broad approach will be required, " they wrote. Taliban failure to help root out bin Laden ought to be "rewarded by aid to its Afghan opposition." Presumably Ramsey Clark was tendering advice more dovish than this, but it could not have been by much.

Against Saddam, by contrast, no such caution was contemplated. "To be sure," the PNAC duo intoned, "Usama bin Laden and his organization should be a prime target in this campaign. ... But the larger campaign must also go after Saddam Hussein. He might well be implicated in this week's attacks ... or he might not. But as with bin Laden, we have long known that Saddam is our enemy, and that he would strike us as hard as he could. ... The only reasonable course when faced with such foes is to preempt and to strike first." "Eliminating Saddam," they concluded, "is the key to restoring our regional dominance."

If by week two the *Standard* had laid out a grand strategy (focus on the Saddam end of the fanciful "Saddam-bin Laden axis"), by week three, it had found an iconic cover photo to reinforce the message. Max Boot's "The Case for an American Empire" was illustrated with two Navy enlisted men in bright white uniforms, one black, one white, raising (or perhaps lowering) the stars and stripes, the sea stretching before them. This imperialism, the photo said, would be based on racial harmony. It evoked the "France of 100 million" posters that recruited soldiers from the empire to fight the Huns in World War I. "Afghanistan and other troubled lands today cry out for the sort of enlightened foreign administration once provided by self-confident Englishmen," Boot wrote.

Once Afghanistan has been dealt with, America should "turn its attention to Iraq." "Who cares if Saddam was involved" in the 9/11 attacks? Boot did not. Saddam "has already earned himself a death sentence a thousand times over. ... He is currently working to acquire weapons of mass destruction that he or his confederates will unleash against America. ... Once we have deposed Saddam, we can impose an American-led, international regency in Baghdad to go along with the one in Kabul. With American seriousness and credibility thus restored, we will enjoy fruitful cooperation from the region's many opportunists."

Standard writers would repeat these arguments for the next 17 months. "If two or three years from now Saddam is still in power, the war on terrorism will have failed," wrote Gary Schmitt some weeks later. Several weeks after that, it was Reuel Marc Gerecht's turn: "Unless Saddam Hussein is removed, the war on terror will fail." The line derived from the letter of menace Kristol and PNAC had addressed to George W. Bush on September 20, 2001. Failure to attack Iraq, they told the president, would "constitute an early and perhaps decisive surrender" in the War on Terror.

A magazine communicates through its covers as well. Most telling was one of George W. Bush, gesticulating before an audience of troops, arm extended in a Caesarian pose. "The Liberator," the *Standard* headline proclaimed. Flatter the leader who will do your bidding. It was February 2003, and the editors knew by then that war was almost certain.

Bush and his team have since fallen out of favor in *Standard* land. The magazine has begun blaming the bungled prosecution of the war on Secretary of Defense Rumsfeld and has called for his resignation. As Bush sinks in the polls, the journal will surely look to other politicians to carry out its aspirations. If David Brooks, now a *New York Times* columnist, is an indicator, that figure is likely to be a centrist or a "progressive" in the Joe Lieberman mode—conservatism as a vehicle for neoconservative foreign policy goals having been pretty much run into the ground.

During the second week of the Iraq invasion, the Israeli newspaper *Haaretz* interviewed several intellectual supporters of the war. *The New York Times*'s Thomas Friedman (who backed the war despite being haunted by its similarities to Israel's 1982 invasion of Lebanon, which he saw firsthand) suggested that this was very much an intellectuals' war.

> "It's the war the neoconservatives marketed. Those people had an idea to sell when September 11 came, and they sold it. Oh boy, did they sell it. So this is not a war that the masses demanded. This is a war of an elite. ... I could give you the names of 25 people (all of whom are at this moment within a five block radius of this office) who, if you had exiled them to a desert island a year and a half ago, the Iraq War would not have happened."

Then Friedman paused, clarifying:

> "It's not some fantasy the neoconservatives invented. It's not that 25 people hijacked America. You don't take such a great nation into such a great adventure with Bill Kristol and *The Weekly Standard* and another

five or six influential columnists. In the final analysis what fomented the war is America's over-reaction to September 11. ... It is not only the neoconservatives that led us to the outskirts of Baghdad. What led us to the outskirts of Baghdad is a very American combination of anxiety and hubris."

That kind of ambiguous conclusion about the *Standard*'s and the neocons' role in starting the war is what the undisputed and public evidence will sustain. The *Standard* was important. It amplified the views of "the 25" the way luncheon seminars at the American Enterprise Institute and other neocon think tanks never could have.

Its role can be likened to the yellow press, the Hearst papers and Pulitzer's *New York World*, which did everything they could to instigate a war against Spain over Cuba in the 1890s, and boosted their circulation mightily in the process. In the wake of 9/11, the *Standard* didn't have to create the martial atmosphere artificially, just divert it from Osama to Saddam.

Without *The Weekly Standard*, would the invasion of Iraq taken place? It's impossible to know. Without the *Standard*, other voices—including those of the realist foreign-policy establishment, which had been dominant in the first Bush administration and which opposed a precipitous campaign against Saddam—would have been on a more level playing field with the neocons. That would have made a difference.

So in a sense the Iraq War is Bill Kristol's war as much as it is George W. Bush's and Dick Cheney's, and the *Standard* is the vehicle that made it possible. It should go down in history as Rupert Murdoch's War as well, and thus becomes by far the most significant historical event ever to be shaped by the Murdoch media.

How ironic it would be if it were not, in the end, a war Rupert Murdoch particularly wanted.

The American Conservative
November 21, 2005

Let Me Shine Your Shoes, Sir

The biggest question raised by Fred Barnes's *Rebel-in-Chief* is whether the author's embarrassment is a closely held secret among family and close friends, or more widely admitted. Embarrassment there must be, for Barnes is a capable writer, even a good one. To those who read him in *The New Republic* or saw him on "The McLaughlin Group" in the 1980s and 1990s, he was a refreshing type in a throwback sort of way: a not terribly ideological, intellectually unpretentious conservative, Republican in his instincts; a suburban Virginia family man; a reporter with good sources and a crisp, fact-filled prose style. Perfect for the slot of token Republican at *The New Republic* in its 1980s heyday.

But for readers who might wonder what it is like to be North Korean and required to read formulaic biographies of great helmsman Kim Il Sung and his son, an afternoon spent with *Rebel-in-Chief* should provide a proximate answer.

In Barnes's defense, the book is a representative product of a large neo-Republican publishing industry that has sprung up in the past five years to tap the market for conservative books aimed just below the middle of the brow—gifts to give the friend or parent who is an avid Hannity and O'Reilly watcher, to be thumbed through perhaps more than read. This is a large market, previously underserved.

In his acknowledgments, Barnes tells of writing an opinion piece for *The Wall Street Journal* on George W. Bush as an "insurgent" president. Many would find this an unlikely designation for a man who was essentially anointed as heir apparent by Republican elites, a very fortunate son who floated from business partnerships where he did no real work into the Texas governor's mansion, a man who unlike anyone else you've ever known suffered no adverse professional consequences for being an alcoholic with no real accomplishments at age 40. But for Barnes, this experience was the perfect training for the president "as rebel," enabling him to disregard conventional Beltway knowledge, the tiresome stuff of diplomats, science advisors, and other "experts."

It is as if the Bush presidency were the Chinese Cultural Revolution (Better Red Than Expert!) reformulated GOP-style, a place where experience and specialized knowledge are always the subject of suspicion. (Why was it not surprising when news leaked out that a 24-year-old campaign worker without a college degree, promoted to a NASA press aide position by the Bush administration, tried to block the director of NASA's Goddard Institute for Space Studies from speaking to the public about global warming?) Bush, of course, doesn't send the pointy heads to re-education camps, but, as Barnes reports cheerfully, he ignores them.

Barnes's *Journal* piece led inevitably to a book contract with, one imagines, a wink and a nod that the book wouldn't actually require, as a real book would, concentrated work that would distract Barnes from his day job at *The Weekly Standard* or TV show "The Beltway Boys"—neither negligible in their demands of time and energy. If the advance is good enough, why not take the bait?

The core of *Rebel-in-Chief* is that George W. Bush, by virtue of his rebellion against conventional liberal/centrist Beltway counsel and the prudent, cautious conservative establishment wisdom, has been an astonishingly successful president, well-deserving of Natan Sharansky's flattery—"Mr. President, I see you are a dissident. Dissidents believe in an idea. They suffer a lot. But history proves them right." The main evidence for this success has been Iraq and the war on terror, so naturally Barnes attests that the Bush foreign policy is working out swimmingly. For example:

> During the Iraq War and its aftermath, non-Bush Washington hollered repeatedly for an announced exit strategy. Bush demurred, arguing that a declared plan for getting out could only prolong a conflict and encourage the enemy to hang tight. With the success of the Iraqi election, Bush was vindicated.

And:

> For Bush, the tight partnership [with Tony Blair] is an essential ingredient of his new foreign policy in the aftermath of the terrorist attacks of September 11, 2001 on the World Trade Center and the Pentagon. It is a world-changing policy crafted mostly by Bush himself, not his advisers. And it is a policy that has significantly strengthened America's strategic position in the world.

And:

> The 9/11 assault by al Qaeda terrorists changed Bush's approach to foreign policy in important ways. Within hours of the attacks, Bush was already fashioning a new policy. It was a Bush policy, not the work of his advisers. He was no longer the attentive student. Now he was the policy maker. And the president was soon finding new allies and shedding old ones. National Security Adviser Rice, Vice President Cheney, Defense Secretary Donald Rumsfeld, Secretary of State Colin Powell—they followed their leader.

There are dozens of paragraphs like this, emphasizing Bush's "bold vision" vindicated by "dazzling" democratic elections, portraying Bush "taking charge" and "deftly" moving Israelis and Palestinians closer to peace "than at any time in decades" and thereby turning the whole volatile Middle East into "Bush Country." Iraq, Barnes tells us again and again and yet again, is now, thanks to George W. Bush, a "pro-American democracy" because Bush, "adamant about democracy," with his "hands-on style," has never been afraid to override the crabbed views of experts. And, lest we forget, it is Bush alone who has done this, not his advisors. The cynical might suspect that this last is a form of neoconservative special pleading, designed to spirit the war party intellectuals away from the scene when the Bush policy goes down in flames. It might even be charitable to Barnes to think so, for the alternative is to believe that the courtier style that saturates *Rebel-in-Chief* is without guise.

As I write, the American ambassador to Baghdad, a veteran neoconservative hardly given to public pessimism, is warning reporters that Iraq remains on the brink of a civil war, requiring an overstretched U.S. Army to remain there at full strength for several more years. "Right now there's a vacuum of authority, and a lot of distrust," says Zalmay Khalilzad, though the poor country has gone through not just one but three of Barnes's "dazzling" elections. The risk if American troops don't remain is a regional conflict that would be a more encompassing version of the Iran-Iraq War. Religious extremists could take over sections of Iraq and expand outward, making, in Khalilzad's words, "Afghanistan look like child's play."

The audience for books like *Rebel-in-Chief* doesn't hear such news as Zalmay Khalilzad is commenting on. It blocks it out, as it would news emanating from some foreign and ignoble land. That may not matter much— not every citizen needs to be well-informed about everything. But Fred Barnes, despite his protestations, is himself a member of the Beltway elite, a top editor at a leading conservative magazine, a veteran TV performer, from a distance at least a likeable and sane individual. What does it say about contemporary American politics if he believes basically in the bulk of what he has written here? What does it say if he doesn't believe it? Neither alternative is especially reassuring.

The American Conservative
April 10, 2006

They Only Look Dead

Republicans may have gotten "a thumpin'," but the neocons appear to be suffering a full-fledged rout. The intellectual faction that had its origins in City College's storied Alcove No. 1 during the 1930s (home of the "anti-Stalinist" socialists) has become a household word, and not in a good way. Apolitical grandmothers write their children e-mails deriding "the neocons and their war." Intellectuals who have logged years on the payroll of well-funded neoconservative institutions forward little ditties through cyberspace (to the tune of "Thanks for the Memories"):

But thanks to the neocons,
For every war a shill,
We're driven from the Hill
But their mission was accomplished
Since our troops are dying still.
A cakewalk it was.
Thanks for the neocons
Those late-night shows on Fox
We watched while drinking shots

> Sure Cheney lied and soldiers died
> But ain't Ann Coulter hot?
> A kegger, it was.

If disrespecting the neoconservatives is emerging as a minor national sport, it should be enjoyed, and tempered, with realism. The last few years have been difficult for the faction, the years to come perhaps more challenging still. But they are as aware of their own vulnerabilities as anyone—much more so than the Bush-Rove Republicans with whom they have been allied. Neoconservatives have faced the political wilderness before, and survived. They have other political options.

Moreover, whatever one might feel about "the neocons and their war," it is difficult not to experience some twinges of remorse over the movement's decline. For decades, *The Public Interest* was a penetrating and groundbreaking journal. *Commentary* in the 1970s—when it turned hard against the countercultural '60s—was brave and forceful. Nathan Glazer may never have written anything void of wisdom. To see the movement that spawned this grow into something bloated, stupid, and ultimately dangerous to America is to see the terminus of a vital part of our intellectual history.

The neoconservative lines were first broken two years ago when Iraq War architects Douglas Feith and Paul Wolfowitz were ushered out of the Pentagon—a virtual decapitation of the cadre that planned the war. Scooter Libby's indictment and subsequent departure from Dick Cheney's side was a further blow. By last summer, George Will, the dean of establishment conservative journalism in Washington, had turned openly against the group. Noting *Weekly Standard* editor Bill Kristol's call for the U.S. to use the Lebanon war as a pretext to bomb Iran, Will remarked, "The most magnificently misnamed neoconservatives are the most radical people in this town." Kristol received more of the same medicine when he appeared on National Public Radio with Gen. William Odom, director of the National Security Agency under Ronald Reagan: "Mr. Kristol certainly wants to make [Lebanon] our war. He's the man with remarkable moral clarity. He tends to forget the clarity he had on getting us into the mess in Mesopotamia. I think if you look at his record, you'd wonder why anybody would allow him to speak publicly anymore." Thus moral clarity—that robust quality the neoconservatives had long ascribed to themselves—is returned as mockery.

A main dilemma for the neoconservatives is their relationship to Bush's lame-duck presidency. Neocon doubts that Bush will stay true to the course they have helped set for him are widespread. Addressing these fears, this summer Norman Podhoretz argued that the president was still their man. Quoting Bush speeches at length, Podhoretz insisted the evidence showed Bush still believed in the "Bush Doctrine." But it is not clear that neoconservatives will be rallied by such hallucinatory observations as:

> I must confess to being puzzled by the amazing spread of the idea that the Bush Doctrine has indeed failed the test of Iraq. After all, Iraq has been liberated from one of the worst tyrants in the Middle East; three elections have been held; a decent constitution has been written; a government is in place; and previously unimaginable liberties are being enjoyed.

Veteran pamphleteer Joshua Muravchik recognized the larger problem, that the current neocon brand—now defined by Bush, the Iraq War, and American global hegemony—has become broadly unpopular. Writing in Foreign Policy, Muravchik observed, "some among us, wearying of these attacks, are sidling away from the neocon label." He raised a bugle to stem the retreat. Neoconservative ideas are "as valid today as when we first began." George Bush "has embraced so much of what we believe that it would be silly to begrudge his deviations." Neoconservatives, he mused, should acknowledge mistakes, if necessary—"We were glib about how Iraqis would greet liberation." And they should concentrate on their greatest strength—"political ideas." While Muravchik unsurprisingly called for renewed agitation to bomb Iran, his most amusing recommendation may have been that neocons should "volunteer" to train U.S. Foreign Service officers in the "war of ideas"—and make sure their trainees were assigned to every overseas post.

Podhoretz (writing this past August) and Muravchik (published in late October) may have been anticipating the remarkable neocon self-immolation that would appear in early November on Vanity Fair's website in the form of David Rose's interview notes for a forthcoming article. Rose quotes neoconservatives who had played major roles in the formulation and selling of the Bush administration's foreign policy all lamenting that Bush has proved himself unworthy of the sound advice they gave him. Eliot Cohen, whose pre-Iraq War book stiffened the Bush team to ignore the reservations of America's top generals, fears America will need "another big hit" to spur it to the warpath again. Michael Ledeen, a confidant of Vice President Cheney, laments that the most powerful people in the White House are the women who are in love with George W. Bush—Condi, Karen, Harriet, and Laura. In the neocons' heyday, he formulated what Jonah Goldberg admiringly called the "Ledeen Doctrine": "Every ten years or so, the United States needs to pick up some small crappy little country and throw it against the wall, just to show the world we mean business."

Unlike Norman Podhoretz, these neoconservatives were realistic about what a charnel house Iraq has become, but this was Bush's fault, not theirs.

Richard Perle, who left his chairmanship of Bush's Defense Policy Board in 2004, acknowledged that had he "seen where we are today," he would not have advocated the invasion of Iraq. But he attributes the current failure to Bush's bumbling: "[Decisions] did not get made in a timely fashion ... you have to hold the president responsible. ... Huge mistakes were made, and I want to be very clear on this: they were not made by neoconservatives who had almost no voice in what happened ... and certainly no voice in what happened after [Saddam's] downfall. ... I'm getting damn tired of being described as an architect of the war."

Perle chose not to dwell on his associate of more than 20 years, Douglas Feith—the man he recommended to Donald Rumsfeld for the number three slot at the Pentagon, the same Douglas Feith that Rumsfeld entrusted with planning for post-Saddam Iraq.

David Frum's complaint is more interesting. Frum was a principal author of Bush's "axis of evil" designation, which placed Iran on Washington's enemies list, put a damper on Iranian co-operation in rolling up al-Qaeda, and helped cut the legs from under moderate reformist elements in Iranian politics. Says Frum, "I always believed as a speechwriter that if you could persuade the president to commit himself to certain words, he would feel himself committed to the ideas that underlay those words. And the big shock to me has been that although the president said the words, he just did not absorb the ideas."

But Bush's lack of ideological aptitude was predictable, a bone neocons had chewed over for a long time. As Bush advisers, both Frum and Perle had a difficulty: they felt themselves to be far more intelligent than Bush (as surely they were) and yet needed Bush to sell their global political ideas to the American people. Perle never proved able to mask his condescension. Years before, he had commented, "The first time I met Bush, two things became clear. One, he didn't know very much. The other was that he had the confidence to ask questions that revealed he didn't know very much."

Frum made a real effort to finesse the matter. After leaving his White House speechwriter job, Frum wrote a memoir depicting Bush as "The Right Man"—one who was "nothing short of superb as a wartime leader." Bush, he said, combined moderation, persistence, and boldness in just the right measure. Temperament, it appeared, could trump the ability to "absorb the ideas." Frum's book would set the standard for hagiography of the one-time master of Baghdad. The genre was later supplemented by John Podhoretz's *Bush Country: How Dubya Became a Great President While Driving Liberals Insane* and Fred Barnes's amazingly sycophantic *Rebel-in-Chief*. The neocons may not have believed all they wrote in these courtier volumes, but they certainly believed it should be published. Extricating themselves from the Bush embrace will be awkward and risks burning the faction's bridges to more conventional Republicans.

But I predict that they will manage it. Despite the obituaries now being written, neoconservatism will not soon be over with and certainly won't disappear in the way that American communism or segregation have. The group has always been resilient and tactically flexible.

Recall the state of neoconservatism in the early 1990s. The neocons could point with pride to their role in the Reagan presidency—though America's Cold War success owes as much to the times when Reagan ignored their advice as when he took it. George H.W. Bush granted a presidential pardon to Iran-Contra figure Elliott Abrams, allowing him to continue his career. But that was all Bush 41 did for the group. When the elder Bush, after evicting Saddam from Kuwait in 1991, tried to put America's weight behind settlement of the Israel-Palestinian conflict, many neoconservatives suddenly remembered their Democratic Party roots and bolted. In 1992, a significant group of neocons signed on as advisers to Bill Clinton, and the Democratic standard-bearer, eager to shed the McGovernite label neoconservative publicists typically draped around his party, entertained their counsel during the campaign.

But appointing them to strategic foreign policy posts in his administration was another matter. Soon enough, press coverage of the Clinton transition was filled with neoconservative grumbles of being shut out. In one noteworthy example, Beltway neocons strongly backed Joshua Muravchik's aspiration to be assistant secretary of state for human rights. But like many neoconservatives, Muravchik had a long paper trail, and his job search did not survive *Washington Post* columnist Mary McGrory's illumination of it. "Plainly if the president-elect is looking for a human rights director who thinks Mrs. Clinton is a post-Cold War Communist dupe, the search is over," wrote McGrory.

What is basically a group of intellectuals interested in foreign policy has not always found it easy to acquire powerful political sponsors. Senator Henry "Scoop" Jackson was the archetype, a "labor" Cold War Democrat and the man who originally brought Richard Perle and Paul Wolfowitz to Capitol Hill. A force in the Senate, Jackson could delay or even thwart policies he opposed, and he (and aide Richard Perle) did a brilliant job of tying Henry Kissinger's détente policy in knots in the mid-1970s. But that was the power to negate, not create. Jackson induced sleep on the stump, as his two presidential bids revealed. Replacing him as the great hope for the neocons was Daniel Patrick Moynihan, the New York-born Harvard professor who was, in the 1960s and '70s, a flamboyant and often brilliant intellectual. But once elected to the Senate in 1976, Moynihan proved a disappointment, turning out to be not remotely as hawkish as neoconservatives expected.

For the older neocons, with backgrounds as Democrats and even socialists, embracing the Republican Party always seemed a date on the wild side. But not so for those now under 60, who came of political age under Reagan. Republican ties were natural. And as the experience with the Clinton transition demonstrated, crossing the floor to the Democrats will not be easy.

But if Bush has failed them, what options remain? Joe Lieberman has less national appeal than Henry Jackson did, and once you have been embedded in the Pentagon and the vice president's office, forays from the Senate will seem a weak brew. John McCain is another matter, and if Americans can be persuaded that the solution to their Middle East, terrorism, and other diplomatic dilemmas lies in more troops and invasions, neoconservatism will have springtime all over again.

In the short run at least, neoconservatism is wounded and is likely to present a different public face. The soaring language about how it is America's destiny to spread democracy throughout the globe, the efforts to define an American global empire as something greatly to be desired—this will dropped, a casualty of the Iraq fiasco. But it's not clear that the neocons will miss the democracy baggage. Jeane Kirkpatrick's famous essay "Dictatorships and Double Standards"—the one that landed her the post of Ronald Reagan's ambassador to the United Nations, was published in *Commentary* and considered a primary example of "neo" conservative thinking of the period. But recall that her argument was that "authoritarian" regimes could be reliable American allies in the Cold War, and Washington was destabilizing them by hectoring about human rights and democracy. Kirkpatrick was wrong in the end about how durable communist "totalitarian" regimes turned out to be (compared to the authoritarian dictatorships she favored), but the dominant perspective of the essay was undeniably realist—an attempt to take the world with its myriad political cultures as it was rather than imposing upon it a pre-fabricated American model.

What won't be dropped is the neoconservatives' attachment to Israel and the tendency to conflate the Jewish state's interests (as defined in right-wing Israeli terms) with America's. So one can look forward to neoconservative agitation on two fronts: a powerful campaign to draw the United States into a war to eliminate Iran's nuclear potential and an equally loud effort in support of maintaining Israeli dominance over the West Bank and denying the Palestinians meaningful statehood. Those who argue effectively for a more even-handed American policy toward Israel and Palestine will risk the full measure of smears linking them to historical anti-Semitism. The archetypical neoconservative argument will no longer be Bob Kagan and Bill Kristol's call for American "benevolent global hegemony," but Gabriel Schoenfeld's attack on John Mearsheimer and Stephen Walt in *Commentary*, an essay that sought to connect the pair's work to "The Protocols of the Elders of Zion."

This election season ends with neoconservatism widely mocked and openly contemptuous of the president who took its counsels. The key policy it has lobbied for since the mid-1990s—the invasion of Iraq—is an almost universally acknowledged disaster. So one can see why the movement's obituaries are being written. But the group was powerful and influential well before its alliance with George W. Bush. In its wake it leaves behind crises—Iraq first among them—that will not be easy to resolve, and neocons will not be shy about criticizing whatever imperfect solutions are found to the mess they have created. Perhaps most importantly, neoconservatism still commands more salaries—able people who can pursue ideological politics as fulltime work in think tanks and periodicals—than any of its rivals. The millionaires who fund AEI and *The New York Sun* will not abandon neoconservatism because Iraq didn't work out. The reports of the movement's demise are thus very much exaggerated.

The American Conservative
December 18, 2006

In Search of Forever War

The publication of Norman Podhoretz's *World War IV: The Long Struggle Against Islamofascism* provides one answer to the question of whether neoconservatives are experiencing second thoughts about the militarized foreign policies they have advocated. The answer given by the venerable former editor of *Commentary* and now foreign policy adviser to Republican frontrunner Rudy Giuliani, in a word, is "no."

The book is a polemic made up largely of essays that have appeared over the past five years in *Commentary* and circulated on the internet. Podhoretz readers are likely to find little with which they are not familiar.

That need not be fatal. Podhoretz has published some vignettes from his long life among New York intellectuals again and again. Many readers will take pleasure, as I did, encountering for the umpteenth time Marion Magid's quip about the few dozen down-at-the-heels leftists attending a 1960 union-hall debate about American foreign policy. Every one of these young people was "a tragedy to some family or other." Yet the point was how quickly things could turn around. Within a handful of years, their oppositional attitudes would infuse a resurgent New Left and nearly upend the American establishment.

But *World War IV* provides few such moments. Those hoping for Podhoretz near his best, a writer capable of wonderfully subtle distinctions and penetrating dissections of other thinkers, will be disappointed. Those content with a somewhat more sophisticated version of Sean Hannity-style tub-thumping about "Islamofascism" will be well satisfied.

World War IV is written to shore up what Podhoretz calls the "Bush Doctrine," to revive waning enthusiasm for the war in Iraq and for new wars Podhoretz wants Washington to initiate—especially a campaign against Iran. He seeks to infuse Bush's foreign policy with a spirit of world historical mission while regretting that the White House and its backers have not done the job themselves. He wants Bush to adopt the name *World War IV* to encourage Americans to see Iraq as an episode in a grander struggle, as epochal as the battle against the Axis powers in World War II and the Communists in the Cold War (which Podhoretz dubs World War III). The enemy in this case is not Iraqi insurgents, or even al-Qaeda, but Islamofascism.

It is worth noting that this term, unlike "Communist" or "Nazi" or "Fascist," is not one the adversary has chosen for himself. It is instead of fairly recent invention and is now deployed as a propaganda tool to persuade Americans that all of their various Muslim foes—be they real, latent, violent, non-violent, or even fanciful—are pretty much alike. Thus Palestinian nationalists, Sunni Islamist terrorists, Shiite radicals, Baathist insurgents, and, most especially, the government of Iran are to be considered part of the same "two-headed monster." Defining the adversary is a way to guarantee, in Michael Vlahos's apt phrase, a "Forever War" that will continue as long as there are regimes to be labeled "fascist," Muslims who resist American military presence in their lands, and, of course, people who oppose Israel for any reason. Islamofascists, claims Podhoretz, "like the Nazis and the Communists before them ... are dedicated to the destruction of the freedoms we cherish and for which America stands." Perhaps aware that this claim would come as news to anyone with professional or passing firsthand knowledge of the Arab world, Podhoretz brandishes a torrent of quotations from people with Muslim names. See, he says, citing a sentence from some Palestinian cleric who rails against America, Israel has nothing to do with their hatred!

With a keen marketer's insight, Podhoretz supposes the battle for American public opinion is more than half won if things can be named correctly. So after "World War IV" and "Islamofascism," Podhoretz constitutes (with more fanfare than the White House ever assembled) a "Bush Doctrine" from the speeches the president has made and is so enamored of a passage delivered nine days after 9/11—"I have seen their kind before ... heirs of the murderous ideologies of the 20th century"—that he quotes it twice. This oblique reference to fascism, reportedly added at the last minute at State Department insistence to avoid giving offense to Vladimir Putin, proves a godsend to those who want to convince us we are at war with the successors to Nazi Germany.

By defining a Bush Doctrine to his liking, Podhoretz seeks to put Bush in a bottle, to make sure that the most hawkish phrases in his speeches can never be forgotten, to guarantee there is no change of course. But he is also skating around a subject of some debate in neoconservative circles: whether George W. Bush can be relied upon to pursue the wars to the extent the faction desires. Podhoretz, citing the limits on any politician, and recalling his own dismay at Ronald Reagan's seeming shrinking from confrontation with Moscow, remains a Bush stalwart. So he mocks the now commonplace perception of the Bush Doctrine as "the voice of the neoconservative ventriloquists who were using [Bush] as their dummy," saying it was unreasonable to suppose that underlings could convince "strong-minded" people like Bush and Cheney and Rumsfeld to do their bidding. But this argument can't help but bring to mind a comment of David Frum, who actually worked as a White House speechwriter during the post-9/11 period. After his tenure, Frum said, "I always believed, as a speechwriter, that if you could persuade the president to commit himself to certain words, he would feel committed to the ideas that underlay those words. And the big shock to me has been that although the president said the words, he just did not absorb the ideas."

If Frum does not go so far as to endorse the "Bush as dummy of the neocon ventriloquists" argument, he does call into question, in a way Podhoretz does not, whether Bush fully understood the implications of what he was saying in those speeches. All the more reason then for Podhoretz to elevate hurriedly pulled-together strands of presidential rhetoric into an immutable "doctrine."

Podhoretz's depictions of the Iraq War have a Hail-to-the-Great-Five-Year-Plan-Harvest quality to them, as if writing this book required that he refrain from reading any newspapers: "Iraq had been liberated from one of the worst tyrants of the Middle East; a decent constitution had been written; three elections have been held; a government was in place; and previously unimaginable liberties were being enjoyed." One wonders, can he really be that ignorant of the accounts of the Iraqi middle class in exile in Jordan and Syria, reduced to penury, making the invasion of Iraq the cause of one of the most dramatic migrations of educated people in our lifetime, one as vast and tragic as the boat people exodus from Vietnam?

Much of *World War IV* is a survey of American elite debate, which Podhoretz places in the context of his own biography. As the editor of *Commentary*, he witnessed the shift from the Cold War liberal consensus of the 1950s and early 1960s to the radicalism of the late 1960s, which in turn gave rise to neoconservatism in the 1970s. He welcomed the prodromal stirrings of this radicalism in the early 1960s, then recoiled against it as it expanded through the polity and has since been on constant guard against its recurrence. Now he fears it may be happening all over again, professing shock at the speed with which intellectual opposition to the Iraq War gathered steam, noting it is broader now than the Vietnam-era antiwar coalition ever was.

He spends some time parsing the intellectual factions that have turned against the war: realists, paleoconservatives, liberal internationalists, and finally long-established mandarins of the Right like George Will and William F. Buckley. But his efforts to explain and pick apart their arguments are weak and pro forma, as if he hardly had patience to understand or even read them. Podhoretz in the 1960s and '70s had known personally many of those whose ideas he would combat; it was generally a strength of the neoconservatives that they knew, in an intimate and sometimes even familial sense, whom and what they were against. That world of clashing opinions, so vibrantly conveyed in earlier Podhoretz works like *Breaking Ranks* and *Ex-Friends*, is absent from World War IV. Podhoretz writes as if he hadn't had an actual conversation with a foreign policy realist in years, much less with a paleoconservative. His depictions of them—sprinkled with sneer words about "hating America"—never rise above the one-dimensional, and are often mere caricatures. By the book's end, he hasn't answered why Americans have turned against the war in Iraq more quickly than the one in Vietnam, probably because the most simple explanation, that it is alien to the American experience to invade a country in order to turn a region democratic, is too difficult to refute.

An anecdote of my own suggests the source of Podhoretz's problem. I had known him since the mid-1980s and admired him for a decade before that. We had been friendly, if not close, for a dozen years. Five or six years ago, a hostess sat us near one another at a dinner. As I approached to shake hands, he appeared uncomfortable, saying, finally, "I always liked you, Scott, but you wrote something that was anti-Israel, and on that subject I'm very ideological." There was to be, he made clear, no talk between us at the dinner.

World War IV reads as if there have been many such cut-offs, often inspired by disagreements about Israel—I had written critically of the West Bank settlements and roadblocks—but perhaps other matters as well. The Norman Podhoretz who once engaged forcefully and even joyously a wide spectrum of political-intellectual opinions exists no more. Those who have read his earlier books will recognize the loss.

The American Conservative
September 24, 2007

CHOSEN PEOPLE

Measured in terms of military dominance, Israel has never been stronger. But Israel's campaigns against its Arab neighbors no longer receive the international applause they once did. Many Europeans consider Israel a regional bully. Even in the United States, a recent essay in *The New York Review of Books* argued that a state grounded in ethnicity is an anachronism, a throwback to the ethnonationalism that the West sought to transcend after World War II.

In the realm of soft power, Israel finds itself somewhat beleaguered, with its cultural and economic exports facing incipient boycotts and its military actions scrutinized and rigorously condemned by prestigious international jurists. Among gentiles, Israel's strongest support comes from Christian Zionists, but the country's more sophisticated enthusiasts recognize that Armageddonite eschatology is not a solid foundation from which to ensure Washington's unconditional backing.

To Zion's rescue comes George Gilder, veteran luminary of the American Right, author of a successful polemic against feminism and a Reagan-admired ode to the free market, and publisher of a newsletter touting technology stocks. *The Israel Test* is in many respects a crackpot work, but it is more original than most contemporary political bestsellers, and it is bold.

Some mainstream conservative magazines have dutifully reprinted excerpts, and a few right-wing bloggers have praised the book. Still, one senses hesitation: is this an argument conventional Republicans really want to embrace?

Stripped to its basics, Gilder's book attempts to view the Arab–Israeli conflict through the prism of the scientific and racialist thought influential in Europe and America in the first decades of the last century. By the 1920s, scientific racism was already facing intellectual resistance, perhaps most insistently from Catholics such as Hilaire Belloc, and its later association with Nazism eventually brought about its near complete demise. A generation before Hitler, Madison Grant, then scientific racism's most prominent American exponent, had been a friend of presidents and a stalwart of the Eastern establishment. He published *The Passing of the Great Race* in 1916 to wide readership and considerable acclaim. The "Nordics," claimed Grant, had given the world most of its explorers and leaders, the organizers of great endeavors. Indeed, it is not hard to imagine how an Anglo-Saxon might survey the world early in the last century, observe where its most fertile centers of economic, scientific, and technological innovation were located, and construct a plangent theory about endangered Nordic superiority.

George Gilder takes this template and recasts it, deploying group IQ data that didn't exist in Grant's time. For Gilder, the superior men are not

Teutonic explorers or generals but Jewish scientists and financiers. He takes a brief tour through the birth of quantum physics, the Manhattan Project, and the computer revolution and finds Jews central at every stage. It is indisputably the case that in proportions much greater than their share of the population, the leading scientists and mathematicians of the twentieth century have been Jewish. Half of them? Probably not. Over a quarter? Almost certainly. No surprise then that America won the race to build the first atom bomb with a boost from Jewish refugee scientists from Central Europe or that the computer revolution took off in a region congenial to Jewish talent and innovation—that is, California.

Gilder takes these facts, which are neither novel nor very carefully explored, and grafts them to an argument about Israel, the Middle East, and America's broader conflict with the Muslim world. At the core of this struggle, he sets his "Israel test." Is one able to admire and embrace Jewish superiority and creativity, or does one, out of envy, oppose it? This is the examination we all must face. The Nazis failed, of course, and so, he says, have the Arabs. Gilder does not concede that the anti-Semites of the past century were more likely to dwell on the prevalence of Jews in the upper echelons of Bolshevism than in the physics lab. Yet the envy that he describes has often been an unacknowledged part of their complaint.

In transporting his "Israel test" to the contemporary Middle East, Gilder runs awry. To pass the test, one must accept propositions held almost solely on the far Right of the Israeli political spectrum. He argues that no accommodation with Palestinians is desirable or possible. Those who suggest otherwise, even such robust friends of Israel as Thomas L. Friedman and The Atlantic's Jeffrey Goldberg, Gilder labels weak-kneed appeasers.

Though this book is leavened by cheerleading for Israeli high-tech entrepreneurs and digressions into the theory of computers and the history of the Manhattan Project, the bulk consists of Gilder repeating the same argument: all opposition to Israel is rooted in anti-Semitism, a resentment among the masses for the brilliant and creative. Support for Israel is the only way to honor the Jews. Capitalism is the only social system that honors creativity and innovation. Hitler was an anti-capitalist, thus anything less than wholehearted support for the Likud and the Israeli parties to its right is rooted in envy, anti-Semitism, and Nazism.

When addressing conditions in the Middle East, Gilder sinks to cartoonish agitprop. Palestinian leaders are "mostly Nazis." "[W]ithout the presence of the Jews, there is no evidence the Palestinians would want these territories for a nation," he writes. During Israel's war of independence, "Palestinian Arabs fled, chiefly evicted or urged to flee by Arab leaders." This catchphrase of Israeli propaganda, repeated a million times in the past 50 years, is designed to absolve Israel of any responsibility for Palestinian refugees—they did it to themselves. But it is contradicted by a powerful and growing historical literature, much of it based on Israeli military and government archives, which records Israel's ethnic cleansing of Arabs from Palestine in 1948, including drawing up lists of Arab men who were to be seized and assassinated before the villagers were driven out. One can—and many Israelis do—debate the morality of these acts, central both to Israel's founding and the sense among Palestinians of their own tragic history. Pretending they did not happen cannot be the basis for a serious book.

Similarly fanciful is Gilder's assertion, oft repeated, that Arab leaders claim "the right to banish or kill 5.5 million Jews." He names no Arab leaders making this claim and would be hard put to do so. Is Gilder simply being mendacious? It's hard to know.

By the book's end, one senses the author's exasperation. Gilder seems to know that most readers welcome Jewish excellence in the sciences. But what does that have to do with the Arab–Israeli conflict? It pains him that many brilliant Israeli innovators seem to want nothing more than to lead their lives and build their companies in Europe and the United States. A frantic tone creeps in: "We need Israel today as much as Israel needs us, as much as we needed Jewish physicists and chemists [for the Manhattan Project]."

Gilder never explains why, beyond misty paeans to the spirit of enterprise and capitalism and Jewish genius. ("Jews have known before the fatherhood of Abraham that it was the word that made the world—the ultimate assertion of algorithmic power.")

But what kind of Israel does America "need"? The 9/11 Commission Report, stating the obvious, noted that American support for Israel's treatment of the Palestinians is a prime theme of anti-American terrorist propaganda. Why should Americans support roads designated for Jews only and a web of checkpoints that strangles Palestinian life? The United States has strived with difficulty to overcome its own history of racial discrimination. Why should it embrace a stronger version in Israel? And the Israel of scientific advancement—not to mention the growing contingent of Israelis abroad— hardly needs the violent West Bank settlers to make a positive contribution to the world.

While there are other examples of authors writing books about the superiority of ethnic groups to which they do not belong, they make up a small subset in the literature of ethnonationalism.

After thumbing through *The Israel Test*, blogger Matthew Yglesias speculated that Gilder may be a kind of WASP who "likes Israel in part because he wishes American Jews would leave him alone and go live there instead." This interpretation strikes me as insufficient. Perhaps a better one can be derived from Gilder's final chapter, in which he paints a portrait of his artistically and financially successful ancestors and the upper-class WASP world in which he was raised. The focal point is an incident that occurred when he was about 17. While trying to impress an older girl, his summer tutor in Greek, he blurted out something mildly anti-Semitic. The young woman dryly replied that she was in fact "a New York Jew." Gilder was mortified. He relates that he has never quite gotten over the episode. It is the kind of thing a sensitive person might long remember. Variations on this pattern are not uncommon in affluent WASP circles to this day: guilt or embarrassment at some stupid but essentially trivial episode of social anti-Semitism serve as a spur for fervent embrace of Likud-style Zionism. Atonement. It would not be surprising if a similar process helped to shape George W. Bush's mentality.

This sequence might be amusing if the real-life consequences were less sinister. It is now often acknowledged—if not widely regretted—that Palestinians have had to pay the price for Nazism and the Holocaust. It is they, after all, not the Germans, who are now stateless. But Gilder's confession, and the book it animates, establishes a corollary to this truism: Palestinians are now required to pay not only for the crimes of the Nazis but for the genteel anti-Semitism of America's fallen WASP elite.

The American Conservative
December 1, 2009

Thought Leader

Already the world's most studied group of writers since Bloomsbury, the neoconservatives aren't even close to passing into history. If one counts *Ex-Friends*, Norman Podhoretz has produced three memoirs. Add to that a score of sympathetic studies and an equal number of critical ones, and one wonders what more can be learned from a new history of *Commentary* magazine.

As Benjamin Balint's very readable book shows, quite a lot. A young former assistant editor at the magazine, Balint is a fellow at the neocon-friendly Hudson Institute and now lives in Jerusalem. Yet *Running Commentary: The Contentious Magazine That Transformed the Jewish Left Into the Neoconservative Right* is neither apologia nor hagiography. It explores its subject with both real familiarity and a critical distance all the more refreshing for being unexpected.

There has been some recent controversy over whether to describe neoconservatism as, in the main, a Jewish phenomenon. It was fueled by some neoconservatives who charged that critics of the Iraq War were using the term as a coded anti-Semitic slur. Eschewing such silliness, Balint situates the movement firmly in the stream of Jewish-American history.

That history was inseparable from *Commentary*, founded, housed, and supported by the American Jewish Committee for the purpose of providing "informed discussion on the basic issues of our time, especially as they bear on the position and future of Jews in our country and in the world scene."

From its first issue in 1945, *Commentary* seemed ideally fitted to its time. It could tap a surge of new Jewish literary talent as the first college-educated generation had burst forth from the confines of the immigrant neighborhood, the Yiddish press, and Marxist sectarianism. Add to this a wave of refugee intellectuals from Hitler's Europe—probably the most concentrated stream of brainpower to settle on these shores—and there existed a can't-miss recipe for a vital magazine.

Commentary's first editor, Eliot Cohen, held one guiding restriction: the magazine would be staunchly anti-communist. It gives a sense of the talent available to Cohen to note that during one early period, the magazine had Nathan Glazer and Irving Kristol as assistant editors, soon joined by Norman Podhoretz. Balint's account gives much evidence of how freewheeling and irreverent American Jewish intellectual life was during the '40s and the allegedly conformist '50s. For instance, in 1949, *Commentary* ran a satirical piece, "Adam and Eve on Delancey Street," by the young novelist Isaac Rosenfeld. He speculated that kosher food taboos against the mixture of meat and dairy symbolically functioned as sex taboos, keeping Jews away from the unrestrained sexuality of the goyim. The piece provoked several "not since Julius Streicher"-type denunciations from prominent rabbis, and some tried to kill the magazine. But after an apology, Cohen and *Commentary* survived.

Zionism, too, was subjected to probing criticism. Even the limits of what the magazine would publish revealed a breadth of debate. When Norman Podhoretz assigned Hannah Arendt to explore Little Rock and school desegregation, she made the kind of argument that Rand Paul would find ill-tolerated 50 years later: the use of federal troops to enforce integration imperiled the Constitution. Podhoretz's superiors stepped in to spike the piece, prompting Podhoretz to claim that "it was dereliction of intellectual duty" not to run it and to resign in a huff. Remarkably enough, Arendt was able to publish her piece in the further Left quarterly *Dissent*.

Commentary's trajectory after Podhoretz reappeared as the top editor in 1960 is better known: after a measured flirtation with writers of the prodromal New Left, *Commentary* shifted rightward in the late 1960s. By the 1970s, the magazine was engaged in full-scale war against "the movement" and the counterculture. By the late '70s, it was benefiting from the New Left's collapse: the Cambodian genocide, the Vietnamese boat people, and the Soviet invasion of Afghanistan brought in new refugees from '60s liberalism. Israel's 1973 war, in which the country desperately needed an American military airlift, had been a turning point for many Jewish New Leftists. Podhoretz's magazine was there to welcome them.

And, of course, not only Jews. Daniel Patrick Moynihan, who seemed in the mid-1970s the most serious intellectual in American politics, wrote there, to his and the magazine's mutual benefit, as did James Q. Wilson, Robert W. Tucker, and Owen Harries.

Balint's illumination of some of the magazine's internal gears, especially the role of Neal Kozodoy, who worked as Podhoretz's right hand from the 1960s to 1995, when he took over as editor, is especially valuable.

Seemingly blocked as a writer, Kozodoy has often been described as self-effacing for his long career in Podhoretz's shadow. Few of those who knew him would attest to the description. For *Commentary*'s younger contributors (those born after 1940 or so), Kozodoy's was the self-confident voice of the magazine, the man who read their pitches, judged their submissions, and did the lion's share of their editing. Handsome in an understated 1950s sort of way, Kozodoy was almost certainly the only middle-aged neoconservative to attract beautiful young women.

His considerable erudition, grounded as an scholar of accomplishment in Jewish studies, was clothed in gruffness, making him an unusual mixture of earthy and intellectual. Balint captures this nicely in a vignette. At an editorial meeting, a title was being sought for a piece about interfaith dialogue. Senior Editor Gabe Schoenfeld protested that the proposed "How Not to Conduct Interfaith Dialogue" didn't work. It implied that *Commentary* knew the proper way to conduct such dialogue. "We do," Kozodoy replied. "F-k you! No, f-k you! F-k me? F-k you."

To the author of one piece he had solicited, he eventually said, "Yes, we're going to run it." When the writer asked if he had liked it, Kozodoy replied, "What are you, needy?" But he had more than one tone: for many younger writers, he was tremendously encouraging. When you did well, and heard back quickly on the phone, "Great! Just great!" it was worth far more than the modest sum you might eventually be paid. For a gentile, publishing in *Commentary* was a badge of intellectual and moral seriousness, one that could open as many doors in New York City as a Harvard degree might have done for a young Jew in Walter Lippmann's day.

By the end of the Cold War, many believed neoconservatism had run its course. Midge Decter's Committee for the Free World declared victory and disbanded. In *Commentary*'s own pages, Norman Podhoretz proclaimed that neoconservatism was no longer distinct from the American mainstream variety—such had been its triumph. The one distinctive passion the magazine had was Israel, a topic it worked hammer and tong from a Likudist perspective, opposing the Oslo Accords and any effort to bring about a Palestinian state.

As mentioned above, Commentary had not always been dogmatically Zionist: in its early days, it had run such leading dovish intellectuals from Palestine as Uri Avnery. In 1946, Hannah Arendt assessed Theodor Herzl's legacy 50 years after the publication of The Jewish State. She found the Zionist idea flawed: there was no country to be had without displacing the original inhabitants, and such a state would not end anti-Semitism in the world. Four years later, Clement Greenberg wrote that if Jews could survive only by becoming aggressive nationalists, they would have lost justification for persisting as a group.

Anti-Zionism receded after Israel's founding, in the magazine and beyond. Commentary devoted little space to Israel before 1967. By the 1980s, however, Podhoretz could be counted on to slam critics of Israel as anti-Semitic. By the 1990s, advocacy for Israel and alarmist pieces about Iraq's supposed weapons of mass destruction were Commentary staples.

To his credit, Balint treats the debates swirling about the magazine in the age of 9/11 with considerable dispassion. He claims it is a "canard" that neocons cared more for Israel than the U.S., but quotes without sneering many of those who make the charge. In his epilogue, he adds this assessment from the late paleoconservative essayist Sam Francis: "What neoconservatives have done is to design an ideology ... that offers ostensible and plausible rationalizations for the perpetual war in which Israel and its agents of influence in the U.S. government and media seek to embroil the United States (and which all too many American conservatives, out of a foolishly misplaced patriotism, are eager to support) without explicitly invoking the needs and interests of Israel itself."

It is a damning indictment, on the mark in my estimation. And how rare is the Commentary editor who would present it for contemplation, not, of course, with an endorsement, but without insinuations about Father Coughlin reincarnated! Perhaps it is due to Balint's living in Israel, where debate has traditionally been much freer than in New York.

As for the rest, from Balint one receives a full and vivid sense of Commentary's achievement. Eliot Cohen and Neal Kozodoy were enormously successful editors. Norman Podhoretz—a talented and pugnacious ideologue with control of a nicely subsidized magazine—could well be counted the most influential American intellectual of the postwar era. Commentary has since been passed to Norman's son John, whom no one believes is on the same rank as his predecessors. But this may not really matter. Neoconservatism has made solid and probably irreversible inroads among most politically active and influential American Jews, for whom hawkishness and resolute

Zionism (regardless of party affiliation) have become the default majority positions. That is an historical development with major global consequences, and for which *Commentary*'s editors deserve a great share of credit or blame.

The American Conservative
August 1, 2011

THE NEOCONS OVERREACH ON HAGEL

The neoconservative decision to charge that Chuck Hagel is an anti-Semite strikes me as a tactical blunder—a decision grounded in the idea that since they can't defeat the nominee on the issues, their better option was to try to assassinate Hagel's character, presumed to be one of his greatest strengths. Such accusations raise the temperature around the nomination, with consequences difficult to foresee. But just as anti-Semitism is a blight, so are false accusations of it. Peter Beinart has perceptively noted that no one in America ever pays a penalty for falsely maligning someone as an anti-Semite. This may be true today, but like all social rules, it is subject to renegotiation.

Ali Gharib at *The Daily Beast*'s *Open Zion* has done a superb job deconstructing the evidence, or, I should say, "evidence," on which the charge is based: leaders of the Nebraska Jewish community who are alleged to think that Hagel has a Jewish problem deny there is anything of the sort. Hagel may not always have acted like Alfonse D'Amato in his attending to them, but really, why should he?

Since we know that genuine anti-Semitism has deep social and psychic roots in Western societies, it shouldn't be surprising that the leveling of false anti-Semitism charges for political ends also has contours worth exploring. Quite unexpectedly, the Hagel nomination is opening a rich vein for their study. One thing one finds is that those who are quick to deploy false charges of anti-Semitism have begun to take on traits historically associated with bigoted paranoia.

Take for example *The Wall Street Journal*'s Bret Stephens, the first to play the anti-Semitism card against Hagel. Last month, he notoriously wrote, "Prejudice—like cooking, winetasting, and other consummations has an olfactory element. [With] Chuck Hagel ... the odor is especially ripe." Beinart and others have deconstructed Stephens's charge, the centerpiece of which is that Hagel, in an interview, used the term "Jewish lobby" instead of "Israel lobby." But connoisseurs of literary criticism may notice an eerie parallel to Stephens' toxic paragraph.

If evidence of Hagel's anti-Semitism cannot be substantiated by facts or logic, it can nonetheless be smelled. It's as if Stephens is seeking to transport us back to the world of Marcel Proust and the Dreyfus Affair, where the anti-Dreyfusards (the anti-Semitic precursors of French fascism, and, via Theodore Herzl, a propellant fuel for the birth of Zionism) were confident they could smell the Jew, an outsider even when an habitué of the best salons of Paris.[1] Only, of course, Stephens has reversed the roles, as it is he who smells Hagel.

The charge has been raised not only by Stephens, but by Elliott Abrams, trumpeted repeatedly in Bill Kristol's *Weekly Standard*, and echoed by the American Enterprise Institute's Danielle Pletka.

But despite the axiom that false charges of anti-Semitism are cost-free for those who make them, there may be risks here. The neocons don't argue that Hagel suddenly became an anti-Semite at age 60 when his split with the Republican Party's foreign policy direction became too obvious to overlook. It was always there. According to them, it is deeply rooted in his Nebraska past, evident as long ago as the mid-1980s, if not before, when he supposedly was less than enthusiastic about securing funding for a USO facility at Haifa, Israel.

But what does this charge then say, not about Hagel, but about his best friend in the Senate, John McCain? On Saturday, the *Times* ran a lengthy piece reviewing that friendship and its eventual fading out over differences on the Iraq War. According to the account, Hagel, who was co-chair of McCain's 2000 presidential campaign, at one point more or less lived in McCain's Senate office, and vice versa. As veterans who both had tough wars, they shared much in temperament and spirit—an extraordinary "bromance"— almost to the point where they completed one another's sentences. If Hagel is, as Kristol, Abrams, Stephens, and Pletka now charge, an "especially ripe" anti-Semite, what do the neocons really think of John McCain (who is, not so coincidentally, one of the foremost advocates for neoconservative foreign policies in the Senate)?

Of course Hagel is not an anti-Semite and neither is McCain, but it is telling that Kristol, Abrams, and company are ready to slander (implicitly, to be sure) one of their best friends in the Senate to impugn Chuck Hagel's character. And who is to say there won't be some costs to this nest-fouling behavior down the road.

An early sign of the pushback against all this is the cold reaction to Elliott Abrams from the Council of Foreign Relations, where he is a senior fellow. Council President Richard Haas called Abrams's remarks charging Hagel as an anti-Semite "over the line"—probably the first time in history the Council has felt the need to rebuke publicly one its senior fellows. Abrams is an uber-hawk who has been convicted of perjury, so he seems an odd fit

---

[1] I am indebted to the discussion of the olfactory tropes of anti-Semitism in Jacqueline Rose's *Proust Among the Nations*.

for the once centrist and highly respected Council. But he is a darling of the neocons, married to one of Midge Decter's daughters. Rachel Abrams herself attracted considerable recent attention when *The Washington Post*'s Jennifer Rubin retweeted one of her posts calling for Israeli genocide against the Palestinians. No difficulty whatsoever imagining her braying for blood as part of a fascist mob. We might well wonder to what extent Abrams's reckless charges and the sensibility that produced them are influenced by his wife's genocidal sentiments. Indeed, it is something of a puzzlement why Abrams even seeks a role in American foreign policymaking, as he has written that unless they live in Israel, Jews are "to stand apart from the nation in which they live," though perhaps his views on this question have evolved.

In short, we are in for a wild ride. By raising charges against Hagel that those who know the man find bizarre and disgraceful, the neocons have succeeded in turning a spotlight on themselves—not only on their history of warmongering, but on their political tactics and on their character. They may regret it.

The American Conservative
January 15, 2013

ISRAEL

It would be difficult to overstate the importance of Israel to American political culture, and impossible to understand American foreign policy without reference to Israel and the Israel lobby. Such understanding came late to me. Some time after the assassination of Yitzhak Rabin, I began to fear the Mideast solution that many diplomats expected—a partition of the land, a Palestinian state on a small part of it—was not going to happen, however favorable this partition would be to Israel and however unfair to the Palestinians. Israel under successively elected Likud governments simply would not allow it: Netanyahu believed, as his party's founders did, that Palestinians should have no sovereign political rights on any part of Palestine.

This was of course dismaying, and equally dismaying was the discovery that one could not really state this without arousing the hostility not only of the neoconservatives but of parts of the mainstream right as well. National Review had become as one-sidedly dogmatic on the issue as Commentary.

With TAC as a platform, I began writing about Israel frequently. The connection between Israel and neoconservative campaigns to ignite wars against Iraq, and later Iran, seemed critical to understanding what was going on. I've visited the country twice, in 2006 and 2011, met many Israelis and Palestinians. Israel is a national success in many ways, of course, and there are many talented and admirable Israelis. But with its continued rule over the West Bank and its blockade, and de facto control of Gaza, it has also become, quite literally, an apartheid state. That the United States has begun to perceive, almost subconsciously, its overall Middle East policy through the lens of what is "good" for Israel's right-wing government has been an unmitigated disaster for the United States, and the results have fanned the flames of extremism in the Middle East as a whole.

Obama has been a partial exception to Washington's general obsequiousness toward Israel, and his views are shared by many of America's foreign affairs professionals and experts. But their freedom to maneuver is limited, given the realities of American campaign finance. The essays and reviews included here do not reach any conclusion; the problems of Israel, the Palestinians, and Washington may be more acute now than when I started writing about them 15 years ago. And yet the situation has evolved as well: there has been the important and quite widely read work of Stephen Walt and John Mearsheimer, discussed at length below, and the rise of the blogosphere, and the growth of campus activism that seeks to educate Americans about an occupation, abetted by their tax dollars and often enthusiastic governmental participation.

In a world where information flows fairly freely, it seems impossible that America's "special relationship" with a country run on unapologetically ethnonationalist foundations could endure unchanged over the long term. It simply contravenes too many American values and strategic interests. Right now, of course, major donors of both parties work effectively to ensure Washington does Israel's bidding, and Netanyahu still enjoys incredible support in the U.S. Congress. The battle over Israel's place in American foreign policy is likely to grow more intense in the years to come.

A Friend's Lament

In this snappily written book, Richard Ben Cramer argues that Israel has been corrupted by its thirty-seven-year-long occupation of the Palestinian territory on the West Bank and Gaza. The occupation has diverted the country from its historic mission—providing "a place where Jews could live the best life ... in accordance with their values"—to something less ambitious and admirable. Its energies and spirit sapped by measures to control an embittered foreign population, Israeli life has begun to coarsen.

Some of the consequences are internal: domestic assaults, road-rage killings, school violence are now part of the social texture. The once appealing smallness of the country, Israel as a modern village in which everyone felt mutually connected, is now gone. Gone too are such noble aspirations as the doctrine of "purity of arms," through which the army tried hard to avoid harming innocent Arab civilians; some of today's top commanders don't even pretend to care.

Cramer writes with great empathy about the life Israel has inflicted on the Palestinians, a captive people, shut off from all foreign contacts, locked into a hopelessly uneven contest against one of the best armies in the world. Though seldom voiced in the United States, such arguments are expressed often by Israelis unreconciled to Likud's policies. In Cramer's colloquial American idiom, they are sharp and refreshing. The "How Israel Lost" of the title sets down a challenge for admirers of Begin, Shamir, Netanyahu, and Sharon (including, it is now clear, George W. Bush) who would deny that Israel has suffered meaningful loss at all. But Cramer recalls how luminous Israel's reputation used to be in the United States and in much of the world, and that clearly has been lost. Was that reputation entirely deserved?

"A land without people for a people without land"—this was the most commonly heard shorthand for the Zionist project forty or fifty years ago. It was popularized in the movie *Exodus*, with Paul Newman as a Jewish underground fighter and "shiksa-goddess Eva Marie Saint as his home-from-the-holocaust honey" (a clause that could come with a "don't try this yourself" warning). But the "land without people" slogan was an element of what Cramer calls "hasbara"—Hebrew for "explaining" or spin—and one of the Jewish state's most successful exports. This bit of hasbara was a work of genius, as deeply burrowed into the American subconscious in the 1950s and '60s, as (Cramer puckishly notes), "Winston tastes good, like a cigarette should." Back then, most of America felt part of Israel's venture.

That sentiment is almost entirely gone. Relatively few believe the land of Palestine was "without people"—and while there is scant perception of moral equivalence between Israel and the Palestinians, no Israeli (or American) leader is now likely to say, as Golda Meir once did, "There are no Palestinians." Yes, Golda, there are, several million in the West Bank or dispersed throughout the world, many with the keys and title deeds to what were once their families' homes.

Cramer discovered this for himself in the late '70s, as *The Philadelphia Inquirer's* Mideast correspondent. He arrived buying into the whole hasbara package, but as he looked around him, it began to wear off. He began to write in his paper about the Arabs—who were, quite often, hospitable, dignified, rational, and oppressed. Above all, they were there. His pieces earned him a Pulitzer prize ... and several campaigns by committees of Jews trying to lose him his job. "Is it really Ibn Cramer?" they would ask.

The argument of this book is drawn mostly through the portraits and stories of individual Jews and Arabs. Cramer has a real gift for bringing to life the people caught up in the endless struggle—even, or indeed especially those whose politics are not his own. His portraits are usually sympathetic (Mariam Farhat, the "mother of martyrs," a Palestinian woman who has raised several suicide bombers, is an exception); some, like that of Menachem Furman, a charismatic leader a West Bank settlement, are exquisite. The portrait of Yehuda Meshi-Zahav, an ultra-orthodox Jew who has organized the ultra-orthodox haredim to gather body parts of the victims of terror bombings for ritually proper burial, seemed to me journalism as an act of love.

Nonetheless, the backdrop to all these conversations is an occupation that impinges on Palestinian life at every level—shutting off three million largely innocent people. When Sharon completes his fence, Palestinian encirclement will be complete. The most banal journey in the West Bank is determined by Israeli military checkpoints. Cramer describes the trip of one

Palestinian man who sets out to visit his elderly mother thirty miles away. He wants to avoid the checkpoints (which can take hours), so he tacks back and forth, up a riverbed, through a town, six separate taxis for the journey. Finally near the end, he climbs up a pile of stones to find an Israeli half-track and a soldier with a machine gun on the other side. Ordered to pull up his shirt to show he wasn't carrying a bomb, the Palestinian just froze. "Shy?" the soldier asked. "No, I am ashamed," was the reply. The soldier shrugged and let him pass—the man, whose journey had taken four hours, happened to be the newly appointed Palestinian minister of labor.

Arabs stopped at the checkpoints aren't always as fortunate as the minister. There is the elderly headmaster of a Palestinian school whom the Israelis regularly force to strip—in order to humiliate him in front of his students. As a Russian Israeli manning the checkpoints explains, "Because the bad attitude—you know? If they are acting like they are good, and we are the bad one. Then, you must show them control." Then there are other incidents, as when a Palestinian talks back in too fluent Hebrew, protesting against the soldiers who were throwing rocks at his rented car to amuse themselves. For his protest, he was shot in the head at close range.

Two poignant stories function as bookends, demonstrating how the conflict has worn down the morals of both sides. One is Kandil's, just a boy when the Israeli troops entered his village in June 1967. He noted to his surprise that the Jews didn't have tails, as he had been taught. Indeed, they seemed friendly enough, and within months Kandil and his friends used to cross the Green Line to play soccer with Israeli kids on a nicely leveled field. He later found employment at an Israeli nature reserve, learned to read and write Hebrew. When the second Intifada erupted, he ignored warnings to stop working for the "Zionist occupier." One day he was told to report to Palestinian Authority headquarters in Ramallah, where he was taken in and beaten daily for two weeks and hung from a hook during the evenings. Finally he signed a blank sheet paper, which was turned into a confession for informing on Palestinian militants. He was rescued only when Israeli tanks entered Arafat's compound in 2002.

The parallel tale, similar in spirit though mercifully lacking the sheer brutality, is that of Yossi, an Israeli art dealer from Tel Aviv. With his wife pregnant, Yossi was tempted by the prospect of subsidized housing in one of the new settlements near Jerusalem. But he didn't quite fit in, preferring not to go out in the evening with his fellow settlers and shoot holes in the hot-water tanks of his Arab neighbors for amusement. An artistic type, he also he didn't want a prefab house but one built of stone by craftsmen. He befriended the Arab artisans who lived nearby. As punishment for this fraternization, the settlement moved his trailer outside the fence. But Yossi found he could get along fine with the Palestinians—eventually proposing that the settlement create a joint kindergarten for Jews and Arabs. It was roughly at this point that the settler kids began saying "the house is unclean" and killed Yossi's ducks and geese—finally his new house was burned down. Harassment and arson quite clearly do not equal torture, but the two tales are driven by a quite parallel emotion.

During the 1980s, Cramer said he was optimistic about a peaceful solution. Israel could give up the territories, which would involve a fight with other Jews—the right-wing settlers—but they then were few in number. Or it could try to kill or expel millions of Arabs, which was "a tad Nazi-ish." Or it could hang on to the land and develop a policy of apartheid. The logic of the first choice was compelling—however, a conflict with other Jews was distasteful. But abrupt end of the Cold War and the arrival of a million "Jewish" immigrants from the Soviet Union suddenly made option three possible, at least for a while, and that is what the state has done.

Yet Cramer believes a peace is still possible. Palestinians are not especially religious and not committed to religious-based Jew-hatred; the conflict is entirely about land. Widespread anti-Israeli terrorism began only after Israel committed itself to a wholesale policy of expanding settlements, assassinations, and land appropriation—that is when expansion of Israeli settlement of the West Bank became the driving impulse of the Jewish state.

Cramer is one of the very few authors to deflate the myth of Ehud Barak's "perfect" peace offer at Camp David in 2000—97 percent of the land, an offer that Arafat rejected as "less than a Bantustan, for your information." Arafat and his cronies usually appear as self-serving thugs in Cramer's narrative, and yet on this question the PA chairman had a point. What Barak offered was to keep 6 percent of the West Bank, give the Palestinians 3 percent from some Israeli desert. The so-called nation of Palestine was to consist of three separate ghettos, each walled off by Israeli checkpoints and bases—so a citizen of "Palestine" couldn't go about his country without Israeli permission. In addition, Israel proposed to keep military bases on the far (Jordan) side of "Palestine" and control of the aquifers and the new nation's scarce water supply. Cramer acidly comments that the Barak proposal would have allowed Israel to continue the occupation policy under another name, "Palestine."

And yet, since the issue is territory (and honor), compromise remains possible. It would center on a slogan everyone knows would be a winner—Give Back the Land. Not the land "except for the settlements," or the land "except for the bases," but all of it. Of course, one can hear all the think-tank experts decrying the idea as simplistic or worse. But I am with Cramer here—

such a step would transform the Middle East (and America's now wretched image there)—and make Israel a better country as well.

This is a wonderful book, courageous and honest—though courage and honesty hardly suffice to make a book good. Cramer has brought Israelis and Arabs alive in his pages, effortlessly passing on to the reader his own deep affections. He writes as a Jew and lover of Israel, but is utterly persuasive in his argument that the occupation is gobbling up the soul of the state.

The American Conservative
May 24, 2004

DIVIDED & CONQUERED

Officially, we were a delegation from Churches for Middle East Peace (CMEP), a noble but desperately underfunded Washington group created to represent mainstream Christian churches on a vital issue. In more banal terms, we were 12 Americans following a tight schedule through Syria, Jordan, Israel, and "Palestine"—forever getting on and off a bus, shepherded from one meeting to another, following a daily rhythm not unlike children on a long elementary school fieldtrip.

The meetings devolved into a familiar pattern: CMEP's director Corinne Whitlatch described the group and its point of view—boiled down to support for a two-state solution in Israel and Palestine and a status for Jerusalem that reflects the city's importance to two peoples and the three Abrahamic faiths—our hosts made a presentation, we went through some questions, exchanged gifts, posed for a photograph. And then back on the bus, to the next place. Eventually one began to speculate how CMEP might appear to our hosts: why, they must have wondered, do America's most established churches have so little influence on America's actual policies? But they were never so tactless as to pose this question directly (though virtually every Arab intellectual we encountered brought up without prompting Stephen Walt and John Mearsheimer's now famous essay).

Our first stop was Damascus, the capital that has nearly achieved full "axis of evil" status in George W. Bush's Washington. Syria is under sanctions legislation rushed through Congress in 2003, the American ambassador has been withdrawn for "consultation," and the *chargé d'affaires* tells us that American policy is to "freeze" the country. An official Syria resistant to being frozen is delighted to welcome a group like ours and to demonstrate to its citizenry its ability to do so.

So on our first morning we had an audience with President Bashar al-Assad, a motorcade to whisk us up the mountain to a white marble presidential palace, our photograph on the front page of the next day's paper, our comings and goings chronicled on the TV news. Tall and gangly, educated in London as an ophthalmologist, Assad is articulate and well-informed. He is unassuming for a head of state (much less a dictator), a man who might pass for a wonkish professor of biology or computer science at an American university. Assad essentially inherited his post from his late father, Hafez al-Assad—posters of the two together are ubiquitous in Damascus—who had come to power in a 1970 coup. He is an Alawite, a minority Shiite sect, and his regime is vulnerable to ethnic pressures as well as political ones. Christians, who make up 10 percent of Syria's population and a much higher share of its professional classes, are in a similar minority position and are probably more at home in cosmopolitan Damascus than anywhere else in the Middle East.

Assad is worried about Islamic fundamentalism; he acknowledges that Islamists would do well if elections were held. Before democracy, he says, Syria needs an "upgrade"—more education, literacy, internet expansion—and then Islamic extremists would have less of an audience. No doubt this is a self-serving argument but not necessarily an incorrect one. There are genuine liberals in Syria's opposition, but the chances that they would emerge from the chaos if Assad were toppled are unlikely.

Half a million Palestinians dwell in slum-like refugee camps around Damascus, and they are a political wild card, a potentially volatile element in Syria's politics. Assad says they could return to a Palestinian state on the West Bank; he postures not at all about their possible return to ancestral homes in Haifa. Official Syria is altogether realistic about Israel's existence and eager to reap the practical benefits of a peace settlement.

Damascus is not wealthy but seems quite sane. We saw no troops in the city, virtually no beggars, and the streets felt safe. The traffic flow reminded my (veteran world traveler) wife of China in the 1970s, jammed with motorbikes and little trucks. Black-and-white TVs were visible in businesses open late but not selling very much. In the Christian neighborhood where we stayed, the sidewalks were full of young men and women milling about in same-sex groups, eyeing one another but seldom mingling.

The head scarf is making inroads—about half the women in the city now wear it, and as there are no religious police enforcing dress codes, it is a style freely chosen. While this surely reflects the growth of fundamentalist Islam, in Damascus at least it seems more a fashion statement and certainly not an effort to put a lid on female sensuality. Many "covered" Damascene women wear tightly fitted outfits and provocative eye makeup.

As CMEP is in part a religious group, several of our meetings were with archbishops of the Christian churches and prominent Muslim clerics. The interest of our Syrian hosts in putting on a real reception for a group that is hardly a powerhouse in American politics was remarkable. Sheikh Kuftaro's

Islamic Foundation, for instance, a huge institution with some 8,000 students, assembled, at 10 in the morning, a middle-school girls' choir and a group of about 20 clerics and professors to "dialogue" with us. Eight were women, tightly wrapped, unable to shake hands with the men in the reception line, smiling and touching their hearts as we passed. But, they avidly informed us, they are professors of comparative literature, doctors of medicine and pharmacy, and were eager to talk, especially to the women in our female-led delegation. Alas, we had only an hour, and once we got through the choir, the introductions, the now familiar presentation about Syria being a country of many faiths and how the Jewish and Christian prophets are honored in Islam, it was time to go. The women seemed visibly disappointed, anxious perhaps to dispel for their American guests preconceptions about women in Islam being powerless ciphers (or perhaps to illuminate them). But as always, the bus awaited.

We spent part of an afternoon at the American ambassador's residence, hearing our diplomats explain how they are keeping economic and political pressure on the Assad regime and about Syria's lack of progress toward real reform. Off the record, around a table of drinks and snacks, the tone softened. They all loved being stationed in Damascus and were delighted with their encounters with unofficial Syria. I told one diplomat that the evening before we had attended a concert at the city's largest Greek Orthodox church, hearing men's, women's, and children's choirs perform religious and folk songs. It was a large and formal event, a milestone in the Damascene Christian calendar. Watching the young choir boys fussing shyly with their uniforms or their mothers coddling younger brothers and sisters or gathering the kids together after the event, one could easily imagine this as a pre-Easter break convocation at Convent of the Sacred Heart in New York or any large parochial school in the Western world. I told the diplomat that there are many in the corridors of power in Bush's Washington who want nothing more than to smash the Syrian regime in the service of the "global democratic revolution" or whatever is the slogan of the moment at the American Enterprise Institute, and this smashing would have incalculably tragic consequences for the community whose celebration we had witnessed the night before. He nodded with a look of weary resignation.

We spent a day traveling through Jordan, stopping at the ancient Roman city of Jerash. Ruins don't move me, but none of us could ignore the shock of re-entering the "global marketplace." As soon as we stepped off the bus, we were accosted by ragged bands of little boys shouting "Mister, Mister" and trying to sell us postcards and umbrellas, followed immediately by grown men trying to do the same thing. In Damascus, one might receive a smile and polite expression of interest about where one came from, or occasionally, in the *souk*, an invitation to "please come in and take a look at my pottery." But Syria's isolation means the reflex of falling over oneself to accommodate the West's purchasing power has not taken hold.

It's a cliché, the short distances between Israel and its neighbors. Beirut and Damascus are only several hours' drive away. Once we cleared Israel's Allenby Bridge checkpoint—a six-hour ordeal—we were no more than an hour on mountain roads from Jerusalem, which along with its close suburbs of Bethlehem and Ramallah would fit comfortably into New York City's geographic limits.

Modern nationalism has inflicted a wound on a region once culturally diverse but geographically united, and it is not surprising to hear Christian clerics make wistful reference to "the Roman period" or "even the Ottoman" as better than the present. Nonetheless, it is hard to imagine any Mideast solution that does not follow the logic of the nation-state, or as CMEP puts it, "two viable states, Israel and Palestine ... side by side, with secure and recognized borders."

It is late afternoon by the time we arrive, pulling into the Lutheran World Federation on the Mount of Olives. The day is cool, the sun is bright, the hills are shimmering, the Dome of the Rock glistens below us. It is a scene of extraordinary beauty. But the human and political situation, as we would hear from virtually everyone we spoke to over the next week, is ugly and deteriorating rapidly. Two months prior to our arrival, Hamas had won the Palestinian election, and no Palestinian who met with us—none of whom were Hamas voters—failed to express pride in the vigorous and fair electoral process. "A successful delivery, but a sick baby" remarked an aide to Palestinian President Mahmoud Abbas. Sick and near death, too, is the peace process that had infused the region with hope in the early 1990s.

In retrospect, it may be that these hopes, which glowed so brightly among the Israeli Left and center and among virtually all Palestinians, were based on a misunderstanding: the Palestinians believed that in return for their recognition of Israel and renunciation of their claim to historic Palestine, they would achieve a viable and fully sovereign state on the West Bank and Gaza, the territories seized by Israel in the 1967 War; the Israelis believed they could give up nothing they really wanted for themselves and be rid of their Palestinian problem once and for all.

The geography in and around Jerusalem brings into sharp relief the difference between the two geographic visions. With many other Americans, I had my moments of impatience with the seemingly endless talks in the late 1990s when "final status" was at least nominally under discussion. The Israelis, one read repeatedly after the Camp David talks had broken down, were prepared to give Arafat 97 percent of the West Bank, or perhaps merely

94 percent. It seemed nearly the whole loaf, plus territorial compensation for the remainder, taken from "Israel proper." While the actual acreage offered to the Palestinians varied from account to account, it led to the same conclusion: why did the Palestinians need to haggle over a few hectares of land, a nominal percentage of the West Bank, when the prospect of a real independent state was within their grasp? I was, of course, aware of Israel's construction of a separation wall that stretched beyond Israel's internationally recognized borders and tried to read with necessary care the articles in *The New York Review of Books*, with their detailed maps and their many footnotes from Peace Now's Settlement Watch and B'Tselem, with their myriad references to new Israeli settlements whose names I couldn't pronounce. But this seemed more than one really needed to know if one was committed, as a matter of justice (and, not incidentally, of convenience to America) to a "two-state solution."

But this casual attitude toward a few percentage points of West Bank acreage here and there cannot survive a visit to Jerusalem, Bethlehem, and Ramallah. When we arrived, Israeli voters had just given Ehud Olmert's centrist Kadima party a narrow victory, while Hamas was trying to put together a cabinet. As several Palestinian intellectuals and American church officials mentioned to us, Hamas was the perfect foil for the Israeli Right. Because of the group's terrorist past and its caginess about recognizing Israel, the Olmert government has a credible excuse not to negotiate with the Palestinians and is under no American pressure to do so. As it happens, throughout the previous year, Israel had also refused to negotiate with Palestinian President Mahmoud Abbas for reasons that were less apparent, as Abbas clearly recognized Israel and sought a peaceful path to Palestinian statehood.

The essence of Olmert's convergence policy, a path initiated by Ariel Sharon, is for Israel to determine unilaterally its borders by withdrawing from isolated settlements in Gaza and some in the West Bank and building a wall—in places a 30-foot-high concrete structure—on the boundaries of its choosing to separate itself from the Palestinians. Halfway constructed, the wall has clearly been something of an impediment to suicide bombers, and no one could plausibly object if Israel decided to build a wall along the 1967 boundary line—Israel's internationally recognized border. But the wall's route expands Israel's territory considerably in key areas. It takes in the entire city of Jerusalem, including those sections that are historically Palestinian, and it thrusts eastward in various peninsulas and salients into the West Bank in order to gather in various newly constructed Israeli West Bank settlements. Routing the wall so that the settlements fall on the Israeli side, ensuring they have space for further expansion and access to all the water resources they might need, and satisfying the supposed requirement that the wall be constructed on "high ground" requires Israel to annex far more land than is taken by the settlements themselves.

The impact of the wall's construction on the major Palestinian towns of the West Bank is dramatic. For example, Bethlehem is now flanked on two sides by the wall and on the rest by a highway built for exclusive use by Israeli settlers. Cut off from its agricultural hinterland, lacking room for expansion or even parks, Bethlehem, in Olmert's vision, is to be surrounded by concrete, a walled-in urban ghetto.

To the east of Jerusalem, visible from the Mount of Olives, is the new settlement of Ma'ale Adumim, connected to Jerusalem through its own hinterland, called "E-1." This complex of vacant land and new suburb stretches eastward into the West Bank as far as the eye can see, dividing the future Palestinian state, in effect, in half. Meanwhile, in the interior of the so-called Palestinian area, Israeli military checkpoints are everywhere, fixed and floating. Even if one were to put aside the religious significance of Jerusalem for Muslims, the eastern parts of the city are the economic and cultural hub of the West Bank—as connected to the Palestinian towns of Ramallah and Bethlehem as McLean, Virginia, and Bethesda, Maryland, are to Washington, D.C. But the wall effectively severs Jerusalem to Palestinians from Bethlehem and Ramallah. If a man from Bethlehem were to marry an Arab Jerusalemite, the couple would face years of bureaucratic wrangling to get a Jerusalem residency permit, and until that time they could not live together.

The wall cuts off Palestinian farmers from their land and workers from their jobs, separates families, and prevents access to hospitals where they traditionally have gone for medical treatment and places where their children can pursue higher education. In *Haaretz*, the liberal Israeli paper that prints news that seldom appears in the American mass media, columnist Amira Hass writes, "Palestinians living under the Israeli occupation are imprisoned in a thicket of physical, corporeal barriers of all types and sizes (checkpoints, roadblocks, blockades, fences, walls, steel gates, roads prohibited to traffic, dirt embankments, concrete cubes) and by a frequently updated assortment of bans and limitations." The wall and checkpoints mean that Bethlehem University, the Catholic school founded 30 years ago with Vatican support, has increasing difficulty educating its students because travel to and from the school has become so arduous.

Among Palestinian activists and intellectuals, one often hears the word "bantustan" to describe the various cantons the West Bank has been divided into, cities where the Palestinians may practice "self-rule" while needing Israeli acquiescence for any movement of people and goods. It is clearly a polemical word, linking Israel to South African apartheid, and surely another term is needed. But it is clear that the boundaries Israel is now drawing for itself do not leave room for a viable Palestinian state. Dr. Mahdi Abdul Hadi of PASSIA, a Jerusalem-based think tank, says that Palestinians have taken up the term "Palestan" for their areas—the zone around the northern town of Nablus, one around Hebron, one around Ramallah, the Gaza Strip—four circles, surrounded by the Israeli security zone along the Jordan River, separated by the Ma'ale Adumin/E-1 complex and network of Israeli-controlled roads and checkpoints.

The Palestinian economy was in a free-fall even before the election of Hamas and the cutoff of Western economic aid. The out-migration of the Christian middle class is accelerating: students we spoke to at Bethlehem University talked of having no job prospects in Palestine. One young man exclaimed with mock defiance, "We will never leave our homeland!" and then smiled, explaining that is just "an emotional slogan." If he wants to work, he will have to leave.

The Israelis welcome such a result. If educated people are denied the possibility to travel, to pursue a profession, to raise a family in normal circumstances, they will seek other options. The policy that envelops the Palestinians in a maze of restrictions can't quite be called ethnic cleansing—it is milder, and always carried out under the sheen of legality. But the result is the same.

This anyway was the dire impression our group received during a week of meetings in Bethlehem and Jerusalem with Palestinian intellectuals and activists, Israeli human-rights organizations, the archbishops and officials of the main Christian churches, and international relief workers. Except for an Israeli brigadier general who was an eloquent advocate of his government's point of view and the American consul general, who was a caricature of smugness and nonchalance about the looming humanitarian collapse of the West Bank, everyone we spoke with was somber. "I wish I had better news for you" was a phrase we must have heard a dozen times. The core of the lament was that Israeli actions over the past 10 years are effectively foreclosing the possibility of a two-state solution, and Palestinian society is approaching a state of collapse with the intensification of every social ill—and all this before the American-organized cutoff of funds to the Palestinian Authority had its predictably disastrous impact.

It is a sociological truism noted by Tocqueville that there is no more dangerous period for a social system than when a time of gradual improvement suddenly ends: "Evils that have been patiently endured when they seem inevitable become intolerable once the idea of escape from them is suggested." The Israeli occupation that Palestinians endured through the 1970s and 1980s seemed, after Oslo, on its way out. And then, with the withering of the peace process, the idea of escape was suddenly foreclosed. The second intifada, inevitably crushed by Israel, followed, leaving nothing in its wake except deepening despair. As the Anglican Bishop Riah Abu El-Assal put it, "When you don't have money to buy bread, death becomes more worthy."

And so one can imagine that Palestine might yet become what it has never been, a recruiting ground for al-Qaeda, or, as B'Tselem's executive director, Jessica Montell, puts it, "a swamp for breeding terrorists around the world." The California-born Montell is young, dynamic, still seems American—and leads one to wonder how it happens that a liberal Jewish woman who made *aliyah* has a better sense of the strategic realities of the war on terror than 99 percent of those in the U.S. Congress. B'Tselem may be the foremost purveyor of research and documentation of the impact of Israeli policies on the Palestinian Arabs. Its point of view, of course, is not widely shared in Israel. Indeed, Montell explains, the dominant attitude is that the Palestinian problem is over as far as Israel is concerned. "They voted for Hamas" and Israel has "no partner" are the phrases one hears repeatedly.

So what are the options, beyond despair and waiting for the situation to deteriorate further? Mitri Raheb is a Palestinian Lutheran who has created the International Center of Bethlehem. He is a theologian, slight, balding, intense—an intellectual who can find new things to say about a situation that generates millions of words of commentary every week. His center, built with funds raised in Europe, is a testament to his vision: it is time for Palestinians to "stop whining" and begin to build their own institutions. It is hard, he acknowledges, to build a state under occupation—no society has ever been asked to do it before—but the Palestinians have no other choice. His center has an exhibition hall for student artwork, job-training programs for unskilled workers, conference centers, college-level classes—an effort to raise Palestinian political and social consciousness. "Our role as Christians is to give a foretaste of what Palestine will look like—to build facts on the ground that are as real as the wall." Go back to your churches, he exhorts us, and have them help us build a state. Israel, too, could never have been built without American help. His talk takes some surprising detours into self-criticism: Palestinian Christians put their eggs in the basket of Arab nationalism, which has proved a failure in a time when all the pre-twentieth century identities are asserting themselves. He quotes Tony Blair, who recently described his vision of "two states side-by-side, one Muslim, one Jewish"—perhaps Blair just made a slip of the tongue, he says wryly.

Raheb remains, just barely, an advocate of the two-state solution, but his mild demeanor softens what is an edgier analysis. "The state called Palestine has failed," he says, but "whenever Jewish leaders come, we tell them the whole project of Israel has also failed. The ghettoizing of Palestinians cannot be the fulfillment of the Jewish dream. ... If you read the Bible seriously, a project called Israel never succeeded. Its leaders sinned against God. A national state can never be the answer to people's aspirations. ... It is a time for repentance. Israel has been calling for churches to do repentance for years. Now it is time for Israel to do repentance. I know this is tough to say in the U.S., but most church people are cowardly and won't speak the truth."

Our group had some difficulty digesting this. "Uh, Mitri, are you suggesting that CMEP give up its advocacy of the two-state solution?" one of us asked. He replied, in the end, no, not yet, there is perhaps a tiny little window for a two-state solution still open. But he warned what was ahead: Israel would use its great marketing power to sell its unilaterally drawn boundaries as "a two-state solution," with boundaries giving Israel Ma'ale Adumim and the Palestinians the holes within the Swiss cheese, with tunnels connecting the various Palestinian areas so they can move between them underground like rats.

Other prominent Palestinians are also contemplating the end of two-state diplomacy. On our last day, we drove in our bus out to Ramallah, over rutted and dusty roads, so the 10-mile trip took nearly an hour, arriving finally at the Presidential Palace where Mahmoud Abbas exercises what power he has over the Palestinian Authority. This was mid-April, and the European and American financial freeze on the new Hamas government was just getting underway. We met there with several members of the PA's Negotiations Support Unit set up to give legal and strategic advice to Palestinians engaged in negotiation with the Israelis—except there are no negotiations to support, nor the prospect of any. So we sat in a room with able, Western-educated, secular Palestinian professionals, drinking tea in a newly constructed administrative office building—all with the sense that either humanitarian disaster or civil war is but months away and there is nothing we can do forestall it. Issa Kassissieh says that the West has taken a "kill quickly" decision regarding Hamas in hopes that an aid cutoff will lead to a quick collapse of the newly elected government. He blames the West for Hamas's election, noting that during the year in which Abbas led the Palestinian Authority, he was not able to negotiate the removal of a single Israeli checkpoint.

There is a consensus for a two-state solution with Palestine, a consensus that includes most Hamas voters, but Hamas has been given no room to climb down from its historic positions, no time to explore ways in which it can come to terms with the reality of Israel.

Kassissieh tells us the Palestinian Authority has begun discussing the option of simply dismantling itself: the PA has no intention of managing an Israeli occupation of a non-sovereign and non-viable Palestine. One can see how this choice—something akin to going limp when facing arrest at a civil-rights demonstration—would have an appeal after other avenues have been cut off. Israel as the occupying power would have responsibility for the humanitarian crisis it has created, and the Palestinians could begin to agitate for voting rights in the country that governs them. It is not clear whether this option was being presented as a rhetorical point for our benefit or is a serious alternative. But it clearly has the appeal of a real reset, a way of abruptly reversing the tempo of a losing game.

Midway through our trip, we spent a hurried hour with Victor Batarseh, mayor of Bethlehem, a courtly Catholic of about 70. He was, as almost all Palestinians were, eager to see us, as if he believed that Americans—if we could somehow convey to our countrymen what was going on—could tear down the gates that imprison the Palestinians. And, typically, just as the conversation was getting going, it was time for us to move on to our next appointment. My wife dawdled in the mayor's antechamber as the group filed out, and I waited with her. She approached him and said, "My father worked for the United Nations, in the Office of Peacekeeping, for many, many years. He was here in 1967, and in 1973, and many other times—it was his life. He retired in 1987, and just a couple of years ago, he was dying. He was Chinese, and had no religion really, but my mother, who is English, thought he ought to have a minister come.

"When the minister came, my father, who was very lucid and knew what was happening, was very polite. He chattered for a while and then turned serious and said to the minister, 'If there is a God and I meet him, I am going to ask him why he has been unjust to the Palestinians.' That night, he died." Margaret started to choke up as she finished, and Mayor Batarseh also began to cry. They embraced each other; he said he was very glad that she had told him the story.

There are many wrongs in the world, most with complicated histories. But the Israeli–Palestinian impasse is a special one for Americans, in part because of Jerusalem, holy to Christians, Muslims, and Jews, and in part because of the role the conflict plays in generating Muslim hostility to America and the West, but mostly because it is a wrong that the United States has done so much to create and perpetuate, a wrong that the United States has the power to set to right—not by bombing anyone but simply through the normal tools of aid and diplomacy.

It is not a question of the creation of the state of Israel, a country born in tragedy and hope and one with numerous extraordinary accomplishments to its credit. It is a question of the continued dispossession of the Palestinians, an unnecessary act and yet one that Americans sustain every day with their tax dollars. Unlike many other injustices, it is one of the easiest in the world to put right: everyone knows the parameters of a just solution, what the shape of a fair settlement would be.

My fear, and it is the fear of everyone who went on the trip and a great many of the people we met with, is that the failure to achieve a just peace will come back to haunt us in terrible ways.

The American Conservative
July 3, 2006

The Lobby Strikes Back

One prism through which to gauge the impact of John Mearsheimer and Stephen Walt's *The Israel Lobby and American Foreign Policy* is a September incident involving Barack Obama. His campaign had placed small ads in various spots around the internet designed to drive readers to its website. One turned up on Amazon's page for the Walt and Mearsheimer book. A vigilant watchdog at *The New York Sun* spotted it and contacted the campaign: Did Obama support Walt and Mearsheimer?

The answer came within hours. The ad was withdrawn. Its placement was "unintentional." The senator, his campaign made clear, understood that key arguments of the book were "wrong," but had definitely not read the work himself. In short, Walt and Mearsheimer had reached a pinnacle of notoriety.

Though *The Israel Lobby* was on the way to best-sellerdom and has become perhaps the most discussed policy book of the year, the presidential candidate touted as the most fresh-thinking and intellectually curious in the race hastened to make clear he had not been corrupted by the toxic text.

The episode illustrates one of the book's central arguments: the Israel lobby is powerful, and American politicians fear its wrath. Any Democrat running for president—drawing on a donor stream that is heavily Jewish, very interested in Israel, and perceived as hawkish—would have reacted as Obama did.

In their book's introduction, Walt and Mearsheimer summarize the consequences of this power. In an election year, American politicians will differ radically on domestic issues, social issues, immigration, China, Darfur, and virtually any other topic. But all will "go to considerable lengths to express their deep personal commitment to one foreign country—Israel—as well as their determination to maintain unyielding support for the Jewish state." The authors find this remarkable and deserving of analysis, which they provided first in a paper, posted last year on Harvard's Kennedy School website and published in the *London Review of Books*, and now expanded into a book.

This is not the first time prominent Americans have taken on the subject. George Ball, undersecretary of state in the Johnson and Kennedy administrations, and the government official most prescient about Vietnam, a bona fide member of the Wall Street and Washington establishments, called for the recalibration of America's Israel policy in a much noted *Foreign Affairs* essay in 1977, and at the end of his life co-authored a book on the subject with his son. Eleven-term congressman Paul Findley, defeated after a former AIPAC president called him "a dangerous enemy of Israel," wrote a book that became a bestseller, and there are others.

But no one with the combined skills and eminence of Walt and Mearsheimer has before addressed the subject systematically. These two are mandarins of American academia, having reached the top of a field that attracts smart people. They have tenure, job security, and professional autonomy most journalists lack. They have the institutional prestige of Harvard and the University of Chicago behind them. Most importantly, they bring first-rate skills of research, synthesis, and argument to their task.

One might wish that their book had been different in some ways—more literary, more discursive, more precise in some of its definitions, deeper in some areas, and (my favorite, from blogger Tony Karon) more "dialectical." But *The Israel Lobby* is an extraordinary accomplishment, completed with great speed—a dense, factually based brief of an argument that is often made but rarely made well.

In public appearances discussing their book, Walt and Mearsheimer are tremendously effective: measured, facts at their fingertips, speaking with the fluency of men accustomed to addressing demanding audiences. Most of all, while treating a subject where hyperbole is common, they are moderate. They are respectful of Israel, admiring of its accomplishments, and extremely aware that criticism of Israel or the Israel lobby can turn ugly and demagogic. As might be expected of top scholars in America, they are fully conscious of what Jews have suffered in the past and how much anti-Semitism has been a moral blot on the West as a whole. So while they have none of the excessive deference, guilt feelings, and reluctance to engage so typical of the remaining WASP elite, they are very well-modulated. Their detractors would have preferred loose-tongued adversaries, Palestinians whose words are raw with loss and resentment, a left-wing anti-Zionist like Noam Chomsky, or genuine anti-Semites. Instead, with Walt and Mearsheimer, they are encountering something like the American establishment of a vanished era at its calm, patriotic best.

It is obvious that *The Israel Lobby*, both the article and the book, would be extremely unwelcome to those pleased with the status quo. Under the current arrangement, the United States gives Israel $3-$4 billion in aid and grants a year—about $500 per Israeli and several orders of magnitude more than aid to citizens of any other country. Israel is the only American aid recipient not required to account for how the money is spent. Washington uses its Security Council veto to shield Israel from critical U.N. resolutions and periodically issues bland statements lamenting the continued expansion of Israeli settlements on the Palestinian land the Jewish state has occupied since 1967. When Israel violates U.S. law, as it did in Lebanon by using American-made cluster bombs against civilian targets, a low-level official may issue a mild complaint. These fundamentals of the relationship go unchallenged by 95 percent of American politicians holding or running for national office.

Walt and Mearsheimer's goal was to ignite a conversation about the lobby—which they define expansively as an amorphous array of individuals, think tanks, and congressional lobbying groups that advocate Israeli perspectives—and its consequences, which they believe are damaging to America's core strategic interests in the Middle East. They support Israel's existence as a Jewish state, and while they readily summarize Israeli blemishes, drawing on Israeli sources and the arguments of the country's revisionist "new historians," they are fully aware that no modern state has been built without injustices. They seek a more normal United States relationship with Israel, rather like we have with France or Spain, and an Israeli–Palestinian peace settlement that can start to drain the poison out of American relations with the Arab world.

At least in a preliminary sense, they have started a discussion. The initial working paper on the Kennedy School website was downloaded 275,000 times, throwing Israel's most ferocious partisans into a panic. Deploying a McCarthyite tactic, *The New York Sun* quickly sought to link the authors to white supremacist David Duke. *The New Republic* published a basketful of hostile pieces. Several pro-Israel congressmen initiated an embarrassing effort—ignored by the institution's president—to get the Naval War College to cancel scheduled lectures by the two. In a column about "the Mearsheimer-Walt fiasco," neoconservative writer Daniel Pipes summed up his dilemma: it would have been better, Pipes said, to have ignored the essay by "two obscure academics" so that it disappeared "down the memory hole" instead of becoming "the monument that it now is." Pipes was wrong about this. Hostile reaction to the piece hadn't inspired a quarter of a million downloads. With the United States mired in a quagmire in Iraq, increasingly detested in the Muslim world, and wedded to an Israel policy that, beyond America's borders, seems bizarre to friend and foe alike, Walt and Mearsheimer had touched a topic that was crying out for serious analysis.

And the book could do more than the article. Arguments could be filled out, footnotes could be easily read. The 2006 Lebanon War—which saw the American Congress endorse the Israeli bombardment by the kind of margin that would satisfy Nicolae Ceauḍescu while seeming genuinely puzzled that moderate Arab leaders did not join their applause—was analyzed as a test case. A book could continue the discussion and deepen it. But the book's enemies (how odd that a book could have enemies, but there is no better word for it) had time to prepare their ideological trenches, and within a month or two of publication, one could see the shape of the defense.

By the end of October, two months after *The Israel Lobby* appeared in stores, there had not been a single positive review in the mass-market media. For a long time it seemed that no editor dared trust the subject to a gentile, causing blogger Philip Weiss to ask cheekily, "Do the Goyim Get to Register an Opinion Re Walt/Mearsheimer?" By then, *The Wall Street Journal* editorial page, *The New York Sun*, and *The New Republic* between them must have printed 25 attacks on Walt and Mearsheimer, virtually all of them designed to portray the authors as beyond the pale of rational discourse.

Anti-Semitism was not a credible charge. The authors make clear that the lobby isn't representative of the views of all or even most American Jews, and they support an Israel within recognized boundaries. Their recommendation that the United States treat Israel like a normal country is hard to demonize. Ditto their repeated assertions that lobbying is a perfectly normal part of the American system and that conflicted or divided loyalties have become commonplace in the modern world. But what many did was to discuss the book in a context of anti-Semitism to convey the impression that *The Israel Lobby* was a deeply anti-Semitic book without explicitly saying so. Thus Jeffrey Goldberg, in a 6,000-word *New Republic* piece, introduced Walt and Mearsheimer after a detour through Osama bin Laden, Father Coughlin, Charles Lindbergh, and, of course, David Duke. He eventually called the book "the most sustained attack ... against the political enfranchisement of American Jews since the era of Father Coughlin."

Samuel G. Freedman in *The Washington Post* opened his discussion of the book by invoking the New Testament concept of original sin, whose burden one can escape only through acceptance of Jesus Christ. A passage from Romans, Freedman claims, framed the book's argument—"if unintentionally." When was the last time *The Washington Post* introduced a serious foreign affairs book with Bible talk that had no bearing on the work in question?

One of several *Wall Street Journal* attacks on the work claimed, "it is apparently the authors' position that ... [in the face of Arab lobbying efforts] American Jews are obliged to stay silent." This statement is more than a misrepresentation of Walt and Mearsheimer's argument, it is a flat-out lie. Did the editors who assigned and published the piece know this? Was discrediting the book so important that normal American journalistic standards had to be waived?

Another track of the demonization campaign was the repeated effort to cancel the authors' appearances or to demand that opposing speakers be invited to "rebut" their noxious views, a format hardly typical for authors on book tours. Unfortunately, these initiatives sometimes succeeded, as when the Chicago Council for Global Affairs cancelled an event at a venue where the two professors had spoken many times before. Some efforts to marginalize the book were more like parody, as when Congressman Elliot Engel complained that Professor Mearsheimer had been invited to participate in a Columbia University forum on academic freedom.

It would be naïve to think that the campaign waged against the authors had no impact. It managed to muddy the debate about the book. Even on some of the wonkier Washington blogs, where there was manifest interest in contending with the book's arguments, the focus got shifted to whether *The Israel Lobby* was anti-Semitic. As one frustrated commenter on Ezra Klein's blog wrote, "[P]art of the theory is that the power of the 'lobby' is to effectively remove certain topics from the debate. And the closest we come to debating those topics is a meta-discussion of whether debating those topics is appropriate or some evidence of anti-Semitism/self-hating Jewry." Klein rued that "marginalizing the authors as anti-Semitic is more effective than arguing back their viewpoint."

The barrage also had an intimidation effect, a sort of "shock and awe" for the political journalism set. What humble book review editor could fail to be impressed by the sheer volume of rhetoric painting the book as disreputable or avoid wondering what bombs might explode under his own career if he asked former national security adviser Brent Scowcroft or Palestinian-American professor Rashid Khalidi to review the book. Television producers took note as well. While Mearsheimer managed an amiable 10 minutes on "The Colbert Report," the authors got nowhere near the regular public affairs discussion shows. Scholars and writers got the message: if men as esteemed in their field as Walt and Mearsheimer were subject to the Coughlin/Duke treatment and had their appearances cancelled, surely those less cushioned by tenure and eminence had good cause to keep silent. This probably explained the sheer ferocity of the campaign against *The Israel Lobby*.

Not all the negative reviews were as egregious as those cited above. But those that tried to address the substance of the book tended to land weak blows. Les Gelb's critique in *The New York Times* was representative. His central point was that if the Israel lobby—actually, he incorrectly claimed that Walt and Mearsheimer called it a "Jewish lobby"—was indeed so powerful, why has every American president over the past 40 years "privately favored" the return of the Palestinian territories and the establishment of a Palestinian state, and why has Washington consistently "expressed displeasure" at Israel's settlement expansion? This is precisely the question to which Walt and Mearsheimer provide an answer. If, as is indeed the case, most American presidents have "privately" sought Israeli withdrawal, and since Israel is extraordinarily dependent on American largesse, why has the United States never seriously put pressure on Israel to stop the settlements and give back the land? How did Israel manage to move 400,000 settlers into the West Bank in 40 years, often using American funds, if this was contrary to the wishes of every president? Gelb goes on to acknowledge that Walt and Mearsheimer were prescient in their opposition to Bush's Iraq folly, but asserts that the Israel lobby had nothing to do with the decision to go to war. Bush and Cheney needed no lobbying on this point, and they don't about Iran either.

This last area is easily the most disputed point between Walt and Mearsheimer and those reviewers who sought to answer their book rather than smear it. The Israel lobby, the two assert, helped drive the United States into Baghdad. It couldn't have done it by itself—that required 9/11 and Bush and Cheney. But, argue Mearsheimer and Walt, "absent the lobby's influence, there almost certainly would not have been a war. The lobby was a necessary but not sufficient condition for a war that is a strategic disaster for the United States."

This is a powerful polemical charge, if only because tens of millions of Americans who could care less who has sovereignty over the West Bank recognize that the Iraq War has been a painful failure on every level. But is it true? *The Economist* says the argument about Iraq "doesn't quite stand up," but might make sense if "neoconservatives and the Israel lobby were the same thing." Leonard Fein, who writes on the dovish Americans for Peace Now website, called the charge "monstrous" and accused the authors of treating the lobby and neoconservatives "as if the two are interchangeable." Are they?

On one aspect of the argument, the historical record is clear. The two authors do valuable service by documenting the near hysterical "attack Iraq now" recommendations made by various Israeli politicians to American audiences during the run-up to the war. Benjamin Netanyahu, whom the U.S. Congress customarily treats with the kind of deference it might reserve for a Lincoln returned from the dead, warned senators and congressmen that Saddam was developing nukes that could be delivered in suitcases and satchels, and Shimon Peres told Americans that Saddam was as dangerous as bin Laden. The lobbying was so blatant that some political consultants warned Israel to cool it, lest Americans come to believe that the war in Iraq was waged "to protect Israel rather than to protect America." AIPAC, too, pushed for the invasion. It is clear that the Israel lobby, as everyone understands it, was part of the rush-to-war atmosphere that swept the capital in 2002.

But the critics do have a point: AIPAC and similar groups played a comparatively minor part in the frenzy. But what of the neoconservatives, who had openly pushed for war against Saddam since the late 1990s and who held several key posts in the Bush administration?

For Walt and Mearsheimer, neoconservatives are an integral part of the lobby, and indeed, for their argument to make sense, the lobby has to be defined broadly. Of course there is AIPAC, which exists to influence Congress, and its myriad associated groups that raise money for candidates. The recent emergence of Christian Zionism as an electoral force is an important addition, adding ethnic and social diversity and increased political weight to the lobby. This is a sociologically and psychologically rich area, which the authors don't explore as deeply as they might. What currents in American Protestantism suddenly made Israel so compelling? It is interesting to learn, for example, that in 1979, Menachem Begin gave Jerry Falwell a private jet as a gift and soon after bestowed upon him the Jabotinsky Medal for "outstanding achievement." (Other recipients include Elie Wiesel and Leon Uris.) But such facts, intriguing as they are, don't entirely speak for themselves. And whatever enhanced political clout Christian Zionism brought to the lobby, it did not include access and influence to inner decision-making sanctums of the Pentagon and White House or the ability to start a war.

That required the neoconservatives. The path that took the United States from 9/11 to Iraq has yet to be precisely documented, but it is generally accepted that Bush, Cheney, and other key policymakers became converts to neoconservative views after the attack, if they weren't already sympathetic. This is important because neoconservatism has a broad gravitational pull that more focused lobbying groups, no matter how effective, can never match.

It is one thing to motivate a senator or congressman to vote for "pro-Israel" legislation—and AIPAC does that well. The recent Kyl-Lieberman bill labeling Iran's military "terrorist" was reportedly first drafted by AIPAC, and an AIPAC aide's boast that he could have the signatures of 70 senators on a napkin within 24 hours was altogether believable.

But that kind of lobbying has obvious limitations. How many of those 70 senators would vote the lobby's way while discretely rolling their eyes, disliking the pressure they are subjected to but willing to go along because it is the course of least resistance? People don't start wars for such reasons.

Neoconservatism is something far more than advocacy of the interests of a foreign country. It is a full-blown ideological system, which shapes the way people interpret events and view their own society and its relation to the world. Yes, its foreign policy views are strongly pro-Israel. The main shapers of neoconservatism would readily argue that their foreign policy positions were good for Israel while those they opposed imperiled the Jewish state. No one who has spent time with major neocons would doubt the centrality of Israel to their worldview or their attachment to the no-compromise-with-Arabs parts of the Israeli political spectrum. But such attitudes come embedded in a larger set of viewpoints, which are now fairly disseminated among the American elite. While it is one thing for a lawmaker to accommodate the Israel lobby over something like the Kyl-Lieberman bill, it is quite another for an executive-branch policymaker to see the world through a neocon perspective, to have fully internalized slogans like "moral clarity" and "Islamofascism" and "the lessons of appeasement" and elevated them as lodestars.

Neoconservatives did play a crucial role in preparing the Iraq War—in the press, in generating dubious intelligence conclusions and piping them into the executive branch, and in framing an argument that George Bush would be "surrendering" to terror if he didn't attack Iraq. It was a performance that more conventional lobbying organizations like AIPAC or the Zionist Organization of America couldn't match in their wildest dreams. Walt and Mearsheimer don't go into this history deeply. (In *The Assassin's Gate*, *New Yorker* writer George Packer gives one of the most nuanced portraits of the attitudes of the Bush administration's intellectuals, exploring the difficult to pin down matter of how intellectuals' attitudes seep into policy choices.) But in view of their convictions and pivotal positions inside the executive branch and ability to shape policy at the very top, to say that neoconservatives "overlap" with the Israel lobby hardly does them justice: the faction might more properly be described as, to borrow the well-known phrase, the highest stage of the Israel lobby.

Moreover, as an ideological movement, neoconservatism has a reach that more focused pro-Israel advocacy could never duplicate. Does one call Donald Rumsfeld a neoconservative? Few do. While obviously quite capable, he isn't known as an intellectual, isn't Jewish (though of course not all neocons are Jewish), isn't an ex-liberal or leftist. He is usually described as a Republican "nationalist," though he pretty much delegated Iraq policy to men—Paul Wolfowitz, Douglas Feith, and others—who fit most classical definitions of "neoconservative." But there are connections: in the 1980s Rumsfeld was enlisted by Midge Decter to chair the neoconservative Committee for the Free World, so certainly the neocon cast of mind was not unfamiliar to him.

In short, just as the boundaries of the Israel lobby are blurry, so are those of neoconservatism. The revival of terms like "fellow traveler" would probably be helpful.

The most striking aspect of the reception of *The Israel Lobby* was the distance between the reviews in the U.S. and those abroad. In England, reviewers for the major papers (including the Murdoch-owned *Times*) treated the book's argument as self-evidently true. Geoffrey Wheatcroft, author of a prize-winning book on Zionism, noted in *The Guardian* that it must be obvious to a 12 year old that the Israel alliance, "far from advancing American interests, gravely damages them and has hindered every American endeavor in Arab countries or the whole Muslim world." Israel's most influential paper, *Haaretz*, ran a review by Daniel Levy, who was involved in the last serious round of Israeli–Palestinian negotiations. He told his readers that Walt and Mearsheimer's most shrill detractors either had "not read the book, are emotionally incapable of dealing with harsh criticism of something they hold so close, or are intentionally avoiding substantive debate on the issue." Like others, Levy draws a line between the neocons and the Israel lobby proper and explains the Iraq War as a sort of perfect storm: Bush and Cheney, 9/11, many neoconservatives in the executive branch, and for the first time a Republican administration with Christian Zionists as a substantial part of its electoral base. He regrets that mainstream parts of the lobby have been co-opted by the neocons and closes with a plea for moderate Israelis to take American politics seriously and devote as much attention to forming American alliances as the Israeli Right does. This is very welcome advice, for Americans as well, because, as Walt and Mearsheimer stress (and Levy helpfully repeats), it is not Israel per se but Israel as an occupier that constitutes a major strategic liability for the United States.

But it should be noted that casual newspaper readers in Israel, in Britain, and soon in the rest of Europe, where the book is being translated into seven languages, are being treated to far more nuanced and serious discussion of *The Israel Lobby* than Americans have been.

At least there has been the blogosphere. One wouldn't know it from the major American newspapers or magazine reviews, but a fresh breeze is beginning to blow. *The Israel Lobby* did receive more attention on the serious blogs than any other book this year. M.J. Rosenberg, the director of policy analysis for Israel Policy Forum and a prominent "two-state solution" advocate, describes the influence of the book as enormous: "Capitol Hill staffers are talking about the book, everybody is arguing about it, people are intrigued. ... it has opened up discussion."

Despite, or perhaps because of, ferocious attacks in *The New Republic* and *The Wall Street Journal*, *The Israel Lobby* made it onto *The New York Times* bestseller list. It remained there only a couple of weeks, soon displaced by Alan Greenspan's memoir and Laura Ingraham's latest. But the book's influence is still early in its trajectory. International sales will be large, there will be paperback editions, and the book will be assigned in course readings. *The Israel Lobby* will be around a long time, perhaps longer than AIPAC itself. Israeli peace activist Uri Avnery has already compared the work to *Uncle Tom's Cabin*, Philip Weiss to Rachel Carson's *Silent Spring*. To build upon Tony Karon's analogy that *glasnost* is breaking out in the American Jewish community, and that younger Jews are questioning Israel like never before, *The Gulag Archipelago* didn't receive good reviews in Russia when it came out either.

Walt and Mearsheimer haven't written the last word on American–Israeli relations. Other books, more psychologically probing and more discursive, are in the works or waiting to be written. But in clearing the first path since the pivotal date of 9/11, these two authors have done their country a great service.

The American Conservative
December 3, 2007

The Special Relationship with Israel: Is It Worth the Costs?

In December 1962, President Kennedy hosted Israeli Foreign Minister Golda Meir at his family home in Palm Beach. Mrs. Meir opened their conversation by speaking of Jewish history and the threat of another Holocaust. The president responded with an effort at reassurance. "The United States," he said, "has a special relationship with Israel really comparable to what it has with Britain over a wide range of issues." Perhaps Kennedy was engaging in diplomatic flattery; he would go on to stress that America's ties to the Arab world were of critical importance as well. Still, his words marked a landmark of sorts. The Eisenhower administration would not have used "special relationship" to describe its generally chilly ties with Israel. And Kennedy would inaugurate the sale of advanced weapons to Israel, an important early step in the development of a strategic relationship between the two countries.

The British comparison had then, and retains, a powerful and favorable resonance with Americans. Britain was our closest ally in America's last "good" war. Recently, former Israeli ambassador Dore Gold would resurrect Kennedy's statement in an effort to dismiss John Mearsheimer and Stephen Walt's essay, "The Israel Lobby." Look, Gold was saying, this is what one of the most beloved American presidents thought about Israel. The implication is that the relationship is intimate, based on powerful bonds of shared values and interests.

But if one delves deeper into the special relationship, a more complex portrait emerges. The Anglo-American tie was based on the readiness of much of America's ruling establishment reflexively to take Britain's side, and more: to see the world through Britain's eyes. If this sensibility was laudable in a world with an aggressive Nazi Germany, it had been seeded by Britain long before, in the decades preceding World War I. Americans were the audience for Kipling's call to "take up the white man's burden." Rhodes Scholarships prepared Americans for leadership. Before America was Britain's ally, it was Britain's pupil. Or, as Christopher Hitchens would describe it in *Blood, Class and Empire*: "[T]his relationship is really at bottom a transmission belt by which British conservative ideas have infected America."

Two generations later, the special relationship with Israel has almost completely supplanted the British tie. But like the earlier special relationship, the new one is at bottom a transmission belt, conveying Israeli ideas on how the United States should conduct itself in a contested and volatile part of the world. To a great extent, a receptive American political class now views the Middle East and their country's role in it through Israel's eyes.

An early step in the relationship's evolution was the development of an American taste for Israeli political intelligence. As the Franco-Palestinian scholar Camille Mansour puts it in *Beyond Alliance: Israel and U.S. Foreign Policy* (a book published nearly 20 years ago when the relationship was less mature than today):

> The Israelis are seen as the experts, the "Orientalists" of the Middle East in the sense defined by Edward Said: they are at once knowledgeable about the terrain and imbued with Western civilization. They are the ones who can claim to understand Arab mentalities, their political processes, their "irrationality."

When the Cold War ended, traffic on the transmission belt grew apace. Radical Israeli strategies for dominating the Middle East, which might once have been scoffed at, were repackaged by newly empowered American neoconservatives and eventually found a receptive audience in a White House reeling from the shock of 9/11. As Israel's list of potential enemies grew to include wider and wider swaths of the Muslim world, Islamophobia made inroads into the United States, nudged along by pro-Israeli funders and intellectuals.

A new level of the special relationship was signaled only days after 9/11 when Congress invited former (now current) Israeli Prime Minister Benjamin Netanyahu to speak. The Israeli leader presented guidelines for what should be America's strategy in the "war on terror." No statesman from any other country was similarly honored, and it is unimaginable that another could have been. In terms of political symbolism, the Netanyahu address signaled that the special relationship had reached a plateau that John F. Kennedy (and Golda Meir) could not have imagined.

How did the relationship reach this height? America's tie with Israel has grown through three relatively distinct stages. During the first, roughly from Israel's founding to 1967, many Americans were fond of Israel, admired its achievements, wished it well. But Israel wasn't really considered an ally, and whatever strategic ties existed were of little consequence. The second stage ran between the Six-Day War in 1967 and the end of the Cold War when American military and financial aid to Israel accelerated sharply, and the country came to be considered by Washington, in the context of a battle for regional influence with the Soviet Union, as a valuable regional ally. The third stage began to germinate in the years following the collapse of the Soviet Union and came into full bloom after 9/11. Built upon the foundation of the relatively beneficial strategic relationship of the second stage, it was often justified by similar rhetoric. But it is actually a more profound and consequential relationship than existed between 1967 and 1990.

Realists and Wise Men

Washington's early discussions about the strategic value of Israel took place before the state was founded in the years after World War II. Foreign policy professionals could see no benefit from it. They were focused on the beginnings of the Cold War, on finding their bearings in a postwar world that was both fluid and menacing. Then, as now, they saw America's major strategic interest in the Middle East as unfettered access to oil from the Gulf, which was essential to the rebuilding of Europe and to the supply of American armed forces globally. No foreign policy professional believed a Jewish state in Palestine would do anything but complicate that goal. They regretted that President Truman seemed to be making his Palestine decisions with an eye to domestic politics. Secretary of State George Marshall, Under Secretary of State Robert Lovett, Policy Planning Staff head George F. Kennan, the regional specialists from the department's Near East Division and Secretary of Defense James Forrestal all feared the creation of Israel would prejudice and harm American interests throughout the Muslim world. They worried that Israel would require American military forces to protect it—troops America couldn't spare. Even worse was the prospect of a U.N. or international peacekeeping force, giving the Soviet Union an entry point into the region. Some worried that Israel itself might lean towards the Soviet bloc.

The "wise men" of Truman's cabinet, most of whom were WASPs, the American elite at that time, were correct in many of their predictions, though off the mark in others. The CIA predicted correctly that Israelis would not be satisfied with the 55 percent of Palestine allotted to them by the 1947 U.N. partition resolution and would seek to expand its borders. The agency foresaw that Islamic reaction against Zionism would eventually become a major force in Mideast politics. It also predicted that, in the short run, the Israeli forces, better armed and trained, would hold their own against the Arab armies. But in the long run, their consensus was that the Jewish state couldn't hold out against forty million Arabs. Marshall was so angered by his perception that President Truman was going to disregard the professional foreign policy consensus and grant diplomatic recognition to Israel on the grounds of political expediency that he told the president he wouldn't vote for him in the next election.

The Washington establishment underestimated Israel's fighting capacity, however. By the time Kennedy met Golda Meir in Palm Beach, Israel had already won two significant wars against Arab armies and had demonstrated in several skirmishes that it was comfortable throwing its military weight around. Nonetheless, Israel has never gotten over the sense that American policy makers did not see it as a potential ally, but rather as an encumbrance forced upon them by domestic politics. In 1954, in an episode that came to be known as the Lavon Affair, Israeli intelligence officers plotted to blow up American and British facilities in Egypt with the idea that Egyptians would be blamed. The purpose was to short-circuit a possible American opening toward Egypt's Nasser. The plan went awry, but its existence is a testament to Israel's perception that its utility as an ally of the West was far from self-evident. In his memoir, Moshe Dayan relates a conversation he had with Henry Kissinger in 1973. "Though I happened to remark that the United States was the only country that was ready to stand by us, my silent reflection was that the United States would really rather support the Arabs."

Dayan was mostly wrong about this. By the late 1960s, Israel's military prowess had changed Washington's thinking. Presidents Johnson and Nixon were bedeviled by the endemic weakness of South Vietnam, which seemed incapable of making effective use of American arms. One strategic consequence of the Vietnam quagmire was the Nixon Doctrine, which posited that U.S. allies would ensure regional stability by using American arms to fight their own battles. Israel, by then the victor in three wars, fit the bill perfectly.

Those who tout Israel as a strategic asset invariably point to the two decades between 1970 and 1990. After tracking the rapid rise of American military and financial aid to the Jewish state after 1970, the political scientist A.F.K. Organski concluded, "when the United States did not see Israel as supporting U.S. interests in stemming the expansion of Soviet influence, it did not help Israel." Relations warmed with Kennedy and Johnson, and "when U.S. leaders, beginning with Nixon and Kissinger, decided that Israel could be an asset in the U.S. struggle with radical Arabs they perceived as Soviet clients, they helped Israel."

How did Israel benefit the United States? Its advocates point to the PLO-Jordanian faceoff in 1970 during which Israeli threats thwarted a possible Syrian intervention and perhaps saved the throne of Jordan's King Hussein. They cite the success of American arms deliveries during the October 1973 war, which helped persuade Egypt to abandon its Soviet orientation for an American one and make a separate peace with Israel. They note the decisive victory of Israel's American-supplied air force over Syria's Soviet Migs in 1982, which demonstrated to the world the superiority not only of Israeli pilots, but of American technology. They point to the captured Soviet weaponry Israel turned over to the United States for examination. They note Israel's permission for the U.S. Navy to port in Haifa, Israel's technological advances in drone warfare, and myriad other matters. Proponents of the alliance make the broader argument that Israel has kept the peace in the region. As Martin Kramer, a former Israeli academic who is now a leading advocate for Israel in the United States, puts it, Israel "underpins the Pax Americana" in the Eastern Mediterranean. When the United States kept Israel at arm's length (from 1948 to 1973), there were four wars; with the onset of the special relationship and with universal acknowledgement of Israeli regional military superiority, the wars have been small and easily contained. If only, Kramer concludes, the United States could be so fortunate as to have another Israel to protect its interests in the Gulf, its strategic position would be rosy indeed.

If these arguments are not airtight, they shouldn't be dismissed. As Stephen Walt and John Mearsheimer—hardly staunch advocates of the special relationship — acknowledge, a strong case can be made that Israel was, on balance, a useful ally for the United States to have during the Cold War. It is not an open and shut case. How and why, one might ask, were the so-called "radical Arabs" whom Israel helped to contain and defeat radicalized to begin with? Would Arab states have sought Soviet support absent their conflict with Israel? Speaking before a private group in 1975, Henry Kissinger said that it is "difficult to claim that a strong Israel serves American interests, because it prevents the spread of communism. It does not. It provides for the security of Israel."

The idea that Israel was a good ally was never decisively refuted by actual events. Camille Mansour, whose *Beyond Alliance* is an extremely nuanced exploration of the American–Israeli relationship, writes (in 1992) that the mere fact that the alliance endured for 45 years is evidence enough that it did no "indisputable damage to American interests."

The argument that Israel is a good friend to the United States was straightforward and simple to make. It was reinforced by a cultural affinity and buttressed by the messages of the Israel lobby. As a result, politicians tended to proclaim Israel's strategic value even if they were skeptical about it. Mansour cites the example of Jimmy Carter's welcome of Menachem Begin to Washington in 1979. Carter stated that whatever the United States did for Israel was more than balanced by what Israel did for the United States. Carter didn't believe that, and key officials in his administration didn't either. They did think that Israel had the potential to be a far better ally, indeed a genuine strategic asset, if it pursued a compromise peace with the Palestinians and other Arabs. But that was a complex case to make, and nuanced arguments generally fare worse in the political arena than simple ones. In the end, virtually every president treated Israel as an ally deserving unconditional aid, whether he and his aides believed it or not. If the primary American strategic interest in the Middle East was oil, alliance with Israel, save for the brief embargo after 1973, seemed to cause no insurmountable problem. When Lyndon Johnson proposed shipping advanced fighter planes to Israel in the winter of 1968, an assistant secretary of state, Lucius Battle, demurred. The President replied: "You have to give me more reason not to do it." Mansour concludes that detractors of the alliance could never "prove positively that other choices would have been preferable from the point of view of American interests."

From Asset to Burden

However, during the third and most intense period of the special relationship, the costs to the United States began to mount. The third stage was inaugurated by the Soviet Union's collapse and withdrawal from active engagement in the region. Without Moscow to counter, America could act unilaterally in the region without fear of a larger confrontation. The collapse of Soviet power left both Israel and the United States relatively much stronger. More ambitious ideas of how to shape the region made their way from Israel to Washington. This proved to be a very mixed blessing.

These new costs were hardly visible in the 1990s. A hint of what was to come arrived with a shock in the form of the 9/11 terror attacks. Part of the bill for the Iraq War can be attributed to Israel, as can the cost still to be determined of a possible confrontation with Iran. Finally, there is the cost to America's domestic tranquility, both the loss of freedom that is a consequence of becoming a terror target and the rise of bigotry associated with Islamophobia. Perhaps ironically, as the costs rose, American politicians became more fervent than ever in expressing their devotion to Israel and the special relationship.

The initial post-Cold War test of Israel as a strategic asset came in 1991 during the first Iraq War. As a regional ally, Israel proved worse than useless. Washington had to beg Tel Aviv not to attack Iraq, because Israeli involvement would have torpedoed the coalition President George H. W. Bush was building against Saddam Hussein. The United States diverted Patriot missile batteries to Israel to keep it on the sidelines, leaving its own forces more vulnerable. Some of Israel's closest friends acknowledged as much. Bernard Lewis, the prominent Middle East historian and Israel supporter, wrote, "whatever value Israel might have had as a strategic asset, that value obviously ended when the Cold War came to a close."

By the mid-1990s, however, Israel and its American boosters were seeking new rationales for the special relationship. Even in the first optimistic years of the Oslo peace process, Israeli Labor party politicians had begun to talk up "the clash of civilizations" and the threat Iran posed to the "equilibrium" between Islam and the West. The Clinton administration initiated a policy of "Dual Containment," seeking to isolate Iran as well as Saddam's Iraq, which was "influenced and stimulated" by Israeli thinking.

When Benjamin Netanyahu was chosen as Israel's prime minister in 1996, a handful of prominent American neoconservatives prepared for him a policy document entitled, "A Clean Break: A New Strategy for Securing the Realm." The authors, several of whom would obtain influential posts in the George W. Bush administration, recommended an aggressive stance towards Syria, confrontation with Arafat, an effort to "wean" the Lebanese Shia away from Hezbollah, and the removal of Saddam Hussein from power. In his recent book *Israel and the Clash of Civilizations*, Jonathan Cook traces these recommendations to themes worked up by several right-wing Israeli strategists in the 1980s. The Israelis were proposing that Jerusalem cement its status as the Mideast's dominant power by fomenting sectarian and ethnic strife in the surrounding states. As Oded Yinon, an Israeli journalist and former senior Foreign Ministry official, put it in a 1982 essay:

> The total disintegration of Lebanon into five regional localized governments is the precedent for the entire Arab world including Egypt, Syria, Iraq, and the Arab peninsula, in a similar fashion. The dissolution of Egypt and later Iraq into districts of ethnic and religious minorities following the example of Lebanon is the main long-range objective of Israel on the Eastern Front. ... [I]n the long run the strength of Iraq is the biggest danger to Israel. ... Iraq can be divided on regional and sectarian lines just like Syria in the Ottoman era. There will be three states in the three major cities.

Cook contends that strategists such as Yinon did not simply sell their vision to the neoconservatives and seek its implementation. The neocons interpreted these strategies as not only good for Israel, but good for America. Israel's regional dominance and America's control of oil could be assured through the same means, the fomenting of chaos in the Middle East and the break-up of its large states. Shortly after "A Clean Break" was published, its authors wrote another paper, predicting that, after Saddam Hussein was deposed, Iraq "would be ripped apart by the politics of warlords, thieves, clans, sects and key families." Of the three authors who made this prediction, David Wurmser would four years later become Vice President Cheney's top Middle East adviser, Douglas Feith would be Paul Wolfowitz's chief deputy at the Pentagon, and Richard Perle would chair the president's intelligence advisory board. Cook contends that these men understood full well that Saddam's ouster would cause Iraq to collapse, and that chaos was not an accidental or unanticipated result of the invasion, but the intended one.

Jonathan Cook's argument is obviously not conclusive. However, as an examination of a public record, where ideas emerging from both Israeli and neoconservative discourse reflect and build on one another over time, it is extremely suggestive. It helps to explain the seemingly inexplicable: the American decision to allow Iraq to fall into chaos after the invasion.

Tallying the Bill

Counting in a more comprehensive manner, the price the United States pays for the special relationship with Israel has become one of across-the-board friction with much of the Muslim world, friction that would be greatly attenuated without the special relationship and might not exist at all. Whereas in the Soviet Union, the United States had one strategic enemy in a relatively stable contest for global dominance, it now faces opponents on many fronts. None possesses more than a fraction of America's military strength, and none possesses nuclear weapons. But collectively, the conflict with Islam, now considered a given by Israel and Israel's friends in America, exacts a substantial price in American blood, treasure and overall well-being.

First, there is the price of terrorism. American backing of Israel has been a major, if not the sole, factor in making the United States a target of Muslim terrorists. This is invariably what such terrorists say, whether in custody or at liberty, and no one has explained plausibly why they would misrepresent their motivations. Ramzi Yousef, mastermind of the 1993 attack on the World Trade Center, mailed a letter to several New York newspapers demanding that the United States cut off aid to Israel. After his arrest, he told agents that he felt guilt over American civilian deaths but his desire to stop the killing of Arabs by Israeli troops was stronger. Osama bin Laden began inserting references to Palestine into his public statements in 1994. The 9/11 Commission Report notes that Bin Laden tried to move up the date of the attack to tie it more directly to Ariel Sharon's provocative visit to the Temple Mount in Jerusalem (site of the al-Aqsa Mosque) accompanied by hundreds of heavily armed riot police. The commission also noted that Khalid Sheikh Mohammed, the principal architect of the 9/11 attack, was motivated primarily by U.S. support of Israel. He claimed the purpose of the attacks was to focus the "American people on the atrocities America is committing by supporting Israel against the Palestinian people." Of course, the percentage of Muslims who have been moved to carry out terrorist attacks is miniscule. But America's prestige in the Middle East is abysmally low, and Arabs and Muslims consistently hold America's position on Palestine responsible. According to the University of Maryland's Shibley Telhami, a long-time student of public opinion in the Muslim world, "no other issue resonates with the public in the Arab world, and many other parts of the Muslim world, more deeply than Palestine. No other issue shapes the regional perception of America more fundamentally than the issue of Palestine."

Prominent commentators like Robert Satloff, director of the Washington Institute for Near East Policy, acknowledge such sentiments while dismissing their importance. In a recent debate with Chas W. Freeman, Jr., at the Nixon Center, Satloff scoffed at Arab "harangues," which, he said, don't match up to "Arab actions." The oil flows freely. Arab governments will support U.S. policies in the region anyway. Satloff's comments are a window into the dominant sensibility of contemporary Washington. They are voiced without fear of ridicule, the instant response that would have greeted a claim that the political feelings of Czechs or Poles or Chinese or anyone else living under politically un-free conditions could be discounted as inconsequential.

In its third stage, the Israel alliance has drawn the United States into the Middle East in a particularly violent way. Over the last decade, cities in Iraq, Lebanon and Gaza have been ripped apart by U.S. weaponry. While America's freely elected leaders bear the ultimate responsibility for the decision to invade Iraq, it should not be forgotten that Israeli officials were pressing for the invasion every step of the way, giving speeches before Congress, writing op-eds, appearing on television.

Let us note some of these urgings, which are but a fraction of those documented in Mearsheimer's and Walt's *The Israel Lobby*. Netanyahu warned *Washington Post* editors of Saddam's supposed nuclear-weapons program in April 2002, and Sharon's spokesman Raanan Gissin touted the Saddam nuclear threat a week later. The following month, Shimon Peres said on CNN that Saddam was as "dangerous as Bin Laden" and told Americans they "cannot sit and wait." Later that spring, Ehud Barak warned *Washington Post* readers to remove Saddam "first of all," and in August, Sharon told the

Knesset that Saddam was "the greatest danger facing Israel." When Vice President Cheney kicked off the go-to-war campaign in August of that year, many newspapers reported that Israel was urging America not to delay. Peres repeated the "don't delay" message on CNN later that month.

Meanwhile, American networks reported that "Israeli intelligence" was warning that Saddam was "speeding up" his WMD programs. In the run-up to the war, Prime Minister Sharon stated, "Strategic coordination between Israel and the U.S. has reached unprecedented dimensions." In September, Barak told *New York Times* readers that the United States needed to hurry up with the war, adding, "I believe I speak for the overwhelming majority of Israelis in supporting a pre-emptive strike against Saddam's regime." In the winter of 2003, the press was full of reports of Israeli concern that diplomacy might delay the attacks. While mass antiwar protests broke out across Europe, there were none in Israel, where 77.5 percent of Israeli Jews said they wanted the United States to invade Iraq. The Israeli columnist Gideon Levy concluded, "Israel is the only country in the West whose leaders support the war unreservedly and where no alternative opinion is voiced."

The Israeli support for the war would not, in itself, be decisive in pushing the president to order the attack, but deference to Israeli sensibilities is what is unique about the special relationship. When Israelis talk, Americans listen. When Israelis want to circulate their views, they have an access to the opinion pages of elite newspapers and slots on network news shows that leaders of no other foreign country can dream of. Several of America's European and Arab allies objected cogently and clearly to the idea of attacking Iraq. If Israeli leaders had voiced similar sentiments, it is inconceivable the invasion would have taken place.

Of course, there turned out to be no Iraqi weapons of mass destruction, and the invasion of Iraq is now widely considered the most costly foreign policy blunder in America's history. In its wake, Israelis and American friends of that country have worked overtime to rewrite history and absolve Israel of any responsibility for the disaster. Making an argument that would have hundreds of imitators in media platforms throughout the United States, the editor of *The Jerusalem Post* wrote about "the false notion that Israel encouraged the U.S. to fight the Iraq War." Martin Kramer now claims that, time and again, Israel disagreed with the United States, always believing that Iran was the greater threat. It is now repeated incessantly that the connection of Israel to the Iraq War is a "canard" with no factual basis. But, even if it were likely that Israel preferred the United States to attack Iran, Israeli leaders lobbied energetically for a war against Iraq. The weak Saddam regime was low-hanging fruit, after all.

Today, Iran is Israel's preferred target, and Americans are witnessing an energetic campaign on the part of Israeli officials and Israel's American backers to instigate an attack on that country. This marks an interesting turnabout. A top selling point of the special relationship has long been that Israel did not need U.S. troops to fight on its behalf. Provided with America's best weapons, Israel could take care of its own defense needs. Now that doctrine, implicitly abandoned with the Israeli campaign for an American war on Iraq, has been tossed out the window. While Israel rattles sabers at Iran, everyone understands that it doesn't have the capacity to destroy Iran's nuclear program by itself. Hence, it is calling on its only real ally, the United States, to do the job.

Polls indicate that Americans remain reluctant to fight Iran over any cause other than an Iranian attack on U.S. forces. Even fears of Iranian development of a nuclear weapon haven't produced the desired war fervor. Nuclear deterrence, after all, worked with Mao's China, once considered the archetype of an "irrational oriental" regime. Hence, the campaign against Iran includes not only depiction of the Teheran government as noxious and repressive (which is indisputable) but an irrational "apocalyptic cult" or "martyr state" ready to pursue its foreign policy goals with "messianic fervor." Several of these articles contain seemingly scholarly references to a Shiite longing for the return of the "Hidden Imam," an element of Muslim theology that allegedly renders its adherents impervious to reasonable cost-benefit calculation. The point is that if Iran managed to develop one or two nuclear weapons, they wouldn't use them to deter an attack on themselves, but would immediately strike Israel. Their messianic ideology makes Iranian leaders ready to sacrifice one half of their population, Israeli "experts" are said to believe.

Andrew Grotto has examined some of the scholarship that underlies these claims as an analyst at the Center for American Progress. His findings are instructive. The articles claiming a religious basis for the Iranian desire for apocalyptic martyrdom frequently cite one another in a kind of circular footnoting that gives the impression of serious scholarship. One oft-cited source for the wilder claims about Iran as a "martyr state" is an essay by Shimon Shapira and Daniel Dicer published by the Jerusalem Center for Public Affairs. Grotto found that the two authors either misinterpreted or misrepresented the conclusions of the scholars they cite on Shiite theology and its role within the internal politics of Iran's government in order to create a more menacing or "irrational" picture of Iran than their sources actually depicted. Another frequent source for the wilder claims about Iran is a work by an MEK member (an anti-Iranian regime group labeled terrorist by the U.S. State Department) and an unnamed "Israeli Ministry of Defense analyst."

There is more sophisticated Israeli scholarship about Iran, though perhaps less than one would expect from Israel's robust university system. Columbia University Professor Richard Bulliet visited Israel for three weeks last spring, helping to evaluate the country's Middle East Studies programs: "To my recollection," Bulliet told a Columbia audience in October, "there were five professors who were specialists on Iran." Bulliet named one, Ben Gurion University's Haggai Ram, author of *Iranophobia: The Logic of an Israeli Obsession*. He added that none of the five believed Iran was an imminent threat: "Not a single one of them was a hawk on Iran."

Nevertheless, that is not the view Americans are receiving. Instead, such prestigious publications as *The Atlantic*, *The Washington Post*, and *The New Republic* are helping to disseminate a tendentious misrepresentation of Shiite theology shared by neither Israeli nor Western experts. The misrepresentations then bounce around the American media echo chamber, acquiring the status of received wisdom. Iran's so-called "martyr complex" makes a preemptive attack seem almost prudent. Precisely as in the run-up to the Iraq War, an element of right-wing Israeli discourse has managed to carve for itself a privileged spot in the American political dialogue.

What began as a struggle between Zionist settlers and Palestinian Arabs became in 1948 a conflict between Israel and the neighboring Arab states. It has now been transformed into a battle between Israel and the larger Muslim world. The surrounding Arab states now pose no serious military challenge to Israel. Iraq has been shattered and may not recover for a generation. Iran, long an ally of Israel, is now a foe. So, apparently, is Turkey. Turkish leaders, long allied with Israel and the United States, have expressed public solidarity with the Palestinians in Gaza. Almost instantly, Israel's friends in the Congress have turned against Ankara, though they are not yet suggesting war. One important consequence of a "special relationship" with Israel is that Israel will work to ensure that its enemies become enemies of the United States. To the extent it succeeds, the United States will have fewer friends and more enemies.

Finally, we must consider another cost, one not easily measured in terms of blood and treasure. It is hard to miss that anti-Muslim bigotry is becoming embedded in American political culture, and Israel and its supporters are playing a substantial role in generating it. Some rise in anti-Muslim sentiment may have been inevitable after 9/11, as U.S. troops became engaged in fighting two insurgencies in Muslim countries. But bigotry has not had a mainstream sanction in the United States since the civil rights movement. There was relatively little domestic anti-Asian racism during the Vietnam

War, and attacks against Muslims in the United States after 9/11 were few and invariably the work of marginal figures. That is no longer the case.

The controversy over the Park 51 Islamic cultural center, the so-called "Ground Zero mosque," signals that anti-Muslim bigotry has been mainstreamed. The American political environment now contains several well-funded institutions devoted to painting everything having to do with Islam in the worst possible light. As Matt Duss put it recently in *The Forward*, "Groups like The Israel Project, the Middle East Media Research Institution, and Middle East Forum seem to exist for no other reason than to spotlight the very worst aspects of Muslim societies." It is no longer surprising to see racist language in elite journals such as Martin Peretz's *The New Republic*, or from Harvard's Martin Kramer. It comes from conservatives like the prominent Republican Newt Gingrich, and from liberals like Alan Dershowitz. Much of it is purely Zionist in motivation: as Israel has come to be seen as less likeable to Americans, one response has been to blacken the reputation of the Palestinians and Arabs who challenge it. As Duss puts it, "Smearing Islam is seen as a legitimate expression of Zionism."

It remains American conventional wisdom that Israel is a major ally and a strategic asset. This is quite different from seeing a moral justification for the creation of Israel or admiring the country's considerable economic, scholarly, technological and artistic accomplishments, a view which I share. But unlike that idea, the notion that the United States benefits from Israel seems extraordinarily far-fetched. What is in the special relationship for Americans? It is obvious what is in it for Israel. First, large amounts of foreign aid, though Israel is by any standard a rich country. Second, privileged access to the arsenals of the most advanced armed forces in the world. Third, the support of American diplomacy to spare Israel from the brunt of international condemnation or sanctions for its actions. In return, the United States receives, principally, the enmity of Israel's seemingly ever-expanding circle of foes, a small percentage of whom resort to terrorism. And, as an added bargain, it gets a powerful domestic lobby that now pursues as its main activity the incitement of wars between the United States and Israel's enemies.

Some of the minor, but far from trivial, milestones of the relationship—the Lavon Affair, the sinking of the USS Liberty, the Jonathan Pollard case—make it evident that Israeli leaders do not regard the United States as an ally at all. The affection implicit in the special relationship flows in one direction only. *The Washington Post* reported recently on a poll of CIA officers. They ranked Israel dead last among allies for intelligence cooperation with the United States. The same story noted that American counterintelligence officials, pointing to aggressive Israeli spy operations on U.S. soil, ranked only Russia and China as more serious intelligence threats.

No Exit

So why does the United States stay in the relationship? Surely domestic politics accounts for a good deal of the explanation. But there is another strategic reason that is seldom mentioned publicly. It was expounded clearly by Ariel Roth, a professor at Johns Hopkins University and an Israeli army veteran. In an essay in *International Studies Perspectives*, Roth argued that the key U.S. interest in the Middle East is stability and unfettered access to the region's oil. This is indisputable; it is the point James Forrestal made to President Truman more than sixty years ago. And what is the greatest threat to stability? Well, says Roth, it is Israel itself. Because of its unique history and the heavy weight of the Holocaust in the consciousness of Israeli leaders, Israel is uniquely terrified of being "alone" in the international arena. As a result, any suspicion on the part of its leaders that the United States is backing away from it might incite Israel to behave more aggressively than it already does. Those who decry the special relationship "are blinded to how Israel's sense of vulnerability causes. ... behaviors that have the potential to undermine American interests." Israel needs constant "reassurance" that it "does not stand alone." Supporting Israel through "constant affirmation" and generous arms shipments is the best way to pursue American interests "without the fear of a panicked and unrestrained Israel bringing a cataclysm to the Middle East."

This claim is at once alarming and compelling. Roth is asserting that the principal ally of the United States in the twenty-first century—its main source of strategic advice, the nation whose leaders have an unequaled access to American political leadership—is not a rational actor. The United States is in the position of a wife whose spouse is acting erratically. A "panicked and unrestrained Israel," armed with an estimated two hundred nuclear weapons, could do an extraordinary amount of damage. The only conclusion one can draw is that the special relationship would now be very difficult to exit, even if Israel had no clout whatsoever within the American political system, even if the United States desired emphatically to pursue a more independent course.

I submit that this argument has long been internalized by those U.S. officials who recognize that the special relationship brings the United States far more trouble than benefits. It is the principal reason no major American figure has ever advocated simply walking away from Israel. Even those who argue that America should make its aid conditional on a more forthcoming Israeli attitude toward peace with the Arabs invariably recommend that the necessary Israeli territorial withdrawals be rewarded by iron-clad American defense guarantees and other sweeteners. Most intelligent people understand there is something uniquely evil about the Holocaust and the circumstances under which Israel came into existence, even as they are uneasy with the current special relationship. For those who recommend a U.S. security guarantee following a peace settlement, the overture made by the Arab League—offering full recognition and normalized relations with an Israel that relinquished its 1967 conquests and allowed a viable Palestinian state—is a development of enormous promise. Regrettably Israel has ignored this opening.

Can the costs of America's special relationship with Israel be quantified? Is it, as A.F.K. Organski put it in his 1990 book, *The $36 Billion Bargain*? That figure, derived from military and financial assistance to Israel from 1951 to 1983, led Organski to conclude, not surprisingly, that Israel's net value as a Cold War ally is blindingly obvious. Or is the figure closer to $3 trillion, as economist Thomas Stauffer estimated after factoring in the rise in the price of oil, the financial assistance to neighboring states, the cost of the agreements to guarantee Israel's oil supplies and myriad other factors? I believe the answer is nearer to Stauffer's figures, but it is plainly a judgment call. The essence of the relationship is not its dollar cost, but the fact that the United States has come to perceive its interests in the Middle East through Israel's eyes. This is what renders it special. One can debate how important Israel was in encouraging the United States to invade Iraq, but there is no doubt that, if Israel had opposed the invasion, no American politician would have supported it. The same can be said about the possibility of an attack on Iran.

This is also the case with the outbreak of Islamophobia in the United States. The editor of a major liberal magazine—a high-profile intellectual— has written that he doesn't feel First Amendment protections should apply to Muslims. Would Martin Peretz have arrived at this independently of his feelings for Israel? It would be hard to find a knowledgeable person who believes so. Peretz is hardly alone. Thus, one can likely chalk up a portion of America's retreat from its own liberal principles to Israel.

In the coming years, as the prospect of a two-state solution disappears, it is likely that Israel will continue its inexorable march toward becoming a state between the Jordan River and the sea, with one set of laws for Jews, who will have the rights of citizens, and another for Arabs, who will be denied full citizenship. What will it cost America's broader relationship with the Muslim world to maintain a special bond with a state based on this kind of ethnic discrimination? That also would be difficult to quantify. And yet this scenario may be impossible to escape. The threat of Israel's turning itself into a nuclear-armed desperado striking at will at the oil states in the Gulf cannot, alas, be entirely dismissed. That may be, as Ariel Roth argues, a compelling reason to maintain the special relationship pretty much unchanged.

If this is what the future holds, it would make the "wise men" who advised Roosevelt and Truman in the post-war era—the top officials in the Pentagon, the State Department and the CIA who opposed American support for the Zionist project—seem not overly pessimistic so much as woefully limited in their imaginations.

Middle East Policy
Winter 2010

Normalizing Relations

President Obama has probably studied the first President Bush's standoff with Israel. Then as now, the issue of contention was Israeli settlement-building in the West Bank and Jerusalem. George H.W. Bush was hopeful about moving toward a comprehensive peace between Israelis and Palestinians. In the last days of the Reagan presidency, the Palestine Liberation Organization had finally laid down the only significant diplomatic card in its possession, accepting U.N. Resolutions 242 and 338, recognizing Israel's right to exist within its 1967 borders and limiting its aspirations to a Palestinian state on the West Bank and Gaza. In May 1989, Secretary of State James Baker addressed AIPAC's annual Washington conference. After praising Israel's commitment to democracy and role as a strategic partner, Baker went on to say, "Now is the time to lay aside, once and for all, the unrealistic vision of a greater Israel. ... Forswear annexation. Stop settlement activity. Allow schools to reopen. Reach out to the Palestinians as neighbors who deserve political rights."

AIPAC's delegates gave Baker a chilly reception. Relations between Israel's Likud Party Prime Minister Yitzhak Shamir and President Bush were frosty as well. Bush believed Shamir had lied to him about settlements in East Jerusalem, which the United States (and every other country) considered occupied territory. The embryonic peace process stalled.

But after driving Saddam Hussein from Kuwait, Bush and Baker returned to the Palestine issue. In May 1991, Israel asked the administration for a $10 billion loan guarantee. The funds were to be used to settle immigrants from the former Soviet Union. At the time, Israel was building settlements at breakneck pace, and Baker and Bush both labeled them an obstacle to peace. Shamir was confident Israel's clout in Congress would force the president to relent and turn over the money. Bush worked to ensure no funds could be used for construction beyond Israel's 1967 borders. When AIPAC held an "education day" in Congress to press for the loans with no strings attached,

Bush went public with a denunciation, depicting himself as "one lonely little guy" battling thousands of lobbyists. Some American Jews were bothered by the language, but the country was supportive, backing the president by two- and three-to-one margins. Bush stuck to his guns through the following summer when Israeli voters tossed out Likud and elected Yitzhak Rabin's Labor Party by a decisive margin. He then released the loan guarantees. The peace process, which came tantalizingly close to producing a two-states-for-two-peoples agreement by the end of Bill Clinton's presidency, would begin.

A principal lesson is that an American president can prevail in a showdown with Israel over settlements. But the Bush-Shamir dispute also highlights the centrality of the settlement issue. Pro-Israel commentators have gone into overdrive apologizing for Israel's "gaffe" of announcing that 1,600 new homes for Jews would be built in East Jerusalem while Vice President Joe Biden was visiting the country. Bibi Netanyahu decried this "regrettable incident, done in all innocence, which was hurtful and certainly should not have occurred." (The "hurtful" part is especially rich, as if the injury was to Biden's self-esteem and not to America's national interest.)

But, of course, the issue is one of substance, not timing, just as it was in 1991. It can be difficult for outsiders to grasp what is at stake in these seemingly endless battles over the building of neighborhoods in a few contested acres. But the 22 percent of Palestine that remained for the Palestinians after the 1948 armistice has, since 1967, been sliced and diced by Israeli settlements, by roads connecting the settlements to one another and to Israel proper, and by checkpoints and roadblocks designed to hinder Palestinian commerce and normal life. Israel's East Jerusalem settlements supplement a policy of slow-motion bureaucratic population removal—Palestinians are routinely denied residency permits, permission to live with a spouse, authorization to build. Palestinians in Bethlehem have a difficult time visiting a Jerusalem-based doctor or lawyer or parent 10 minutes away. Quite apart from its sacred status to Islam, Jerusalem is the center of bourgeois Palestinian life, a place where the majority of professional families have their roots. A Palestinian state without a capital in East Jerusalem is as much an absurdity as a Jerusalem stripped of an official Jewish presence.

In recent months, the battle of neighborhoods has been intensifying. In January, an Israeli court evicted several Palestinian families from their homes in Sheikh Jarrah, another East Jerusalem Arab neighborhood, and Jewish settlers were moved in. Thousands of Arabs and Jews have marched together in weekly demonstrations to protest this ethnic cleansing by housing court. Likewise, there have been regular demonstrations in Bil'in, where the route of Israel's "separation wall" severs the Arab village from its farmland.

Settlement-building has been incessant; 10 percent of Israelis now live in the occupied territories, four times the number that did so in 1993.

But if new settlements with their roads and checkpoints and the separation wall have transformed the physical geography of the West Bank since the first George H.W. Bush confronted Shamir, the moral geography of the region and how it is perceived in the United States may be changing more rapidly—and not in Israel's favor.

One of the most interesting developments—not to my knowledge ever quantified—is the dramatic growth in the number of Americans who have become well-informed about Israel from a critical perspective. This group, far too diffuse to be called a coalition, includes some anti-Zionists, but its vast majority favors a two-state solution. It is composed of Christians and Jews and an increasing number of Muslims. It includes congressmen who tour the region under non-Israeli auspices, young people who volunteer on the West Bank, a talented coterie of bloggers, and a proliferation of Jewish peace groups, stretching from the establishment-oriented J Street leftward. Whereas informed skepticism about Israeli claims was once limited largely to American diplomats who served in the region, today its base may be ten times larger. For the first time in U.S. history, the pro-Palestinian side has a competitive voice in the public discourse—far smaller than the Israel lobby's but growing every day.

In December 2008, Israel initiated a war against the Palestinian population of Gaza, then under the rule of Hamas. For over a year prior, there had been an uneasy but viable ceasefire, which Israel broke with some "targeted killings" in November. Hamas responded with rocket fire. Gaza was without serious military defense during the three-week campaign, and the IDF had its way, killing 1,400 Palestinians, using white phosphorous against civilian targets, and destroying much of Gaza's infrastructure while suffering a handful of casualties. Several American congressmen who visited Gaza in the weeks after were appalled at the destruction and disturbed by Israel's use of American weaponry to carry it out.

Shortly thereafter, Judge Richard Goldstone was named by the United Nations Human Rights Council to investigate Israeli and Hamas actions during the Gaza war. A highly accomplished international jurist, Goldstone has been described as nothing less than an archetype of Jewish liberalism, a believer in the rule of law and in human rights, a Zionist with a daughter living in Israel. His scathing report about Israeli conduct in the war opened up the possibility that the war's initiators, the leaders of Israel's centrist Kadima Party, could be arrested and charged with war crimes if they traveled abroad. The United States used its power in the U.N. to constrain the writ of the report, but in public-relations terms, the stain on Israel was there for the world to see.

At the same time, Israel began to be increasingly linked in the public mind with the term "apartheid." Jimmy Carter used it in his bestselling book, *Palestine: Peace Not Apartheid.* In interviews, he explained carefully that Israel itself was not an apartheid state, and Palestinian Arabs living in Israel proper possessed civil rights. But for 40 years, Israel has been ruling over Arabs on the West Bank, and the growth of settlements and Jews-only roads and checkpoints has created a *de facto* apartheid system. Some Israeli leaders have used the term to warn of their country's fate in the absence of a two-state solution. And indeed there are parts of Israel now visible to anyone with internet access that resemble South African apartheid conditions or worse. *The New York Times* website recently posted a video of Israeli settlers, newly moved into an Arab neighborhood in East Jerusalem, singing songs in praise of the mass murderer Baruch Goldstein. It is hard to know how much such scenes have altered American perceptions, but clearly the racist settlers are a world away from the *Exodus* performances of Paul Newman and Eva Marie Saint.

A milestone in this shifting moral climate was the face-off between Andrew Sullivan and Leon Wieseltier. Gay, Catholic, and eclectically conservative, Sullivan is an extremely popular political blogger. Combining moral seriousness and whimsy, he manages to post on dozens of topics every day. After initially supporting the Iraq War, he revised his view and in the last few years has become increasingly critical of Israel and occasionally of the role of the Israel lobby. Leon Wieseltier—the longtime literary editor of *The New Republic* and Sullivan's colleague when the latter edited the magazine in the early 1990s—is known for prose drizzled with displays of philosophical erudition and is author of the award-winning book *Kaddish*, an exploration of Jewish liturgy.

Generally centrist, Wieseltier is a staunch defender of Israel. "We're the cops," he once said of his magazine's role in policing the Washington debate on the Mideast. In February, Wieseltier posted a long essay accusing Sullivan of displaying "venomous hostility toward Israel and the Jews." The "rants" Wieseltier cited in evidence were in the main Sullivan's expressive critiques of Israeli policies—the "pulverization of Gaza," the "daily grinding of Palestinians on the West Bank"—and the assertion that "standing up to Netanyahu's provocations" would help the U.S. "advance its interests in the region and the world."

What happened next invites a point of comparison. In the mid '80s, the editor of Commentary, Norman Podhoretz, launched a campaign against Joe Sobran, then a senior editor at *National Review*. Sobran was a less judicious and far more reactionary writer than Sullivan, but there was nonetheless a fair degree of overlap between what he was writing about Israel then and what Sullivan is writing now. Under pressure from Podhoretz, NR founder William F. Buckley wrote an editorial affirming that "the structure of prevailing taboos respecting Israel ... is welcome" and that Sobran, in full "knowledge of the reigning protocols," had transgressed them, giving rise to "suspicions of anti-Semitism." NR henceforth disassociated itself from Sobran's syndicated columns. This was the first step along the way to the severance of Sobran from the magazine. Outside the *National Review* orbit, Sobran's career unraveled. Apart from a few paleoconservatives, few took time to lament the hit.

In Sullivan's case, almost the opposite occurred. Much of the liberal blogosphere rose to his defense. Wieseltier was widely mocked, most effectively perhaps by Matthew Yglesias, who observed that a former Bolshevik minister of justice had said that "execution of the innocent will impress the masses even more" than execution of the guilty. Yglesias added, "flinging baseless charges of anti-Semitism is the essence of [*The New Republic*'s] commentary on Israel." In the Washington intellectual blogosphere at least, the "structure of prevailing taboos" concerning Israel had eroded nearly out of existence.

The newest and potentially most decisive development in this American conversation about Israel, the settlements, and the Palestinians arose, by chance or design, at almost precisely the moment that the vice president and secretary of state were denouncing Israel's settlement policy. Mark Perry reported in *Foreign Policy* that Gen. David Petraeus of Central Command had dispatched a team of officers last year to the Middle East to take a reading of America's position. In January, they reported to the Joint Chiefs that the conduct of Israel toward the Palestinians was causing Muslims throughout the region to conclude that the administration was weak. The message was delivered in dramatic terms and reportedly shocked the White House. Petraeus reiterated the finding in testimony before the House Armed Services Committee: "The enduring hostilities between Israel and some of its neighbors present distinct challenges to our ability to advance our interests. The conflict foments anti-American sentiment. ... Arab anger over the Palestinian question limits the strength and depth of U.S. partnerships with government and people in [the region]."

Such analysis is hardly new: one could have heard variations on it from almost any American Mideast specialist over the past forty years. But it has usually been discounted by political Washington, a murmur from the foreign affairs bureaucracy that could be ignored.

But Petraeus is no mid-level Arabist or anonymous retired general. He is the military's best-known commander, admired for apparently turning around the conflict in Iraq and touted by conservatives as a potential president. While his statements were a frontal challenge to the Israel lobby's claims that America's and Israel's interests are identical, his stature seemed to render him immune to the defamation typically showered on those making this argument.

The Petraeus intervention may prove a case study in the role of unintended consequences in history. Both he and Vice President Biden stressed the increased danger American troops now face because of perceptions that the U.S. is anti-Muslim and weak because of its deference to Israel. Ironically, it was in great part because of Israel and its American lobby that U.S. soldiers were in this position to begin with. A parade of Israeli leaders had professed to American audiences that Saddam Hussein was the new Hitler whom the United States had to take out, and it is well documented that pro-Israel voices within the administration worked relentlessly to ignite the Iraq War. Of course, Bush, Cheney, and Rumsfeld had to be inclined to listen to them. But as Stephen Walt has pointed out, it is inconceivable that the United States would have attacked Iraq had Israel and its American friends argued against such an invasion.

And so the United States is now there, and the security of its troops depends considerably on cooperation with Arab friends and the effective neutralization of those less friendly. As a society, the United States is thus much more engaged with Arab perceptions than it was before March 2003. The patronizing generalizations of Israeli "Orientalism" about the "Arab mind" have lost much of their cachet in Washington, as the United States has had to expand its base of specialists to deal with the Arab world. A fair number are in the military and report to General Petraeus.

The result is that two streams of anti-settlement, pro-peace process discourse have begun to merge and reinforce one another. The realist argument about Israel—which can be traced from President Truman's Secretary of State George Marshall through Kennedy and Johnson aide George Ball to Stephen Walt and John Mearsheimer—now appears to have the patronage of American's most respected military commander. The pretense that America's and Israel's interests in the Middle East coincide completely is being challenged at the highest level and may never recover.

At the same time, the humanitarian argument, rooted in observation of Israeli oppression and Palestinian suffering, is disseminated more widely than ever. It reaches Americans through the internet, through congressional visits, through the work of Israeli peace and human rights monitoring groups, through the burgeoning communities of international solidarity workers, through church groups, through Richard Goldstone. Expressions of unconditional solidarity with Israel—such as Joseph Lieberman's claim that we must not quarrel in public, because Israel is "family"—are of course as common as ever. But they often give off the musty scent of Soviet bloc boilerplate in the 1970s and '80s—words that many recite ritualistically but fewer and fewer say with conviction.

A gap in the line has been opened, but no one yet knows whether Obama will push through it. Chas Freeman, the veteran diplomat whose appointment to chair the National Intelligence Council was scuttled by objections from Israel lobbyists, says, "The president gets it"—that his appreciation of the centrality of these issues was manifest in his Ankara and Cairo speeches. Freeman views the showdown as an historic juncture: "The first time anything resembling an assault on an entrenched interest that many have recognized is contrary to American interests" has taken place. The moment has the potential to unite "Obama as the commander in chief with the visionary who spoke in Cairo." But Obama's track record is not reassuring, Freeman admits. He notes that the president has a "pattern of laying out a sensible strategic doctrine followed by delegating its implementation to people who may work to subvert it or who have their own agendas."

Progress does not seem possible with the current Netanyahu government. But Israeli governing coalitions last, on average, eighteen months, and some fall more quickly. (Netanyahu was sworn in a year ago.) George H.W. Bush had the leverage of Israel's extraordinary request for a $10 billion loan guarantee, which Obama lacks. But there are many steps short of a cut-off of American aid that the administration could use to prod Israelis toward the two-state solution the majority of them say they want.

Biden and Clinton's condemnations of East Jerusalem settlement-building were a start. The U.S. could choose not to veto a U.N. resolution condemning the occupation. It could suspend or downgrade military or intelligence cooperation with Israel as Ronald Reagan did after the invasion of Lebanon. It could end tax deductions for U.S.-based organizations that fund settlements.

In a broader sociological sense, the United States and Israel are plainly moving in different directions: America has been striving to become less racist and is inexorably becoming more multicultural. So are all the Western democracies. Israel, founded on the idea that Jews, like other peoples, should have their "own" state, is animated by an ethno-nationalism that seems, in the Western world at least, increasingly anachronistic. Meanwhile, Israeli racism is on the upswing. I know no one on the Israeli Right who has proffered a suggestion for what Israel might do with the Palestinians in the absence of a two-state solution: the choices would seem to be either to grant them democratic rights in what would then become a bi-national state or solidify the current West Bank apartheid and rule over a growing Arab population while denying it equal rights.

The moment for decisive action is seldom obvious, but the first polls could hardly be more favorable to Obama: there is roughly a fifty-fifty split in Israel over whether settlement-construction in Jerusalem should be stopped, and Americans approve Obama's position on the settlements by nearly a five-two margin (likely more than their approval of any other presidential initiative). With the Biden trip and the Petraeus report, the Obama administration has crossed its Rubicon in dealing with Israel. What remains to be seen is whether the president recognizes this.

The American Conservative
May 1, 2010

FIVE YEARS AGO TODAY, WALT AND MEARSHEIMER GAVE AMERICANS THE VOCABULARY TO DISCUSS A CENTRAL ISSUE

What stood out from the first page was the tone—measured but firm, uncompromising but not strident. Every assertion seemed precisely weighed, put forth without exaggeration, flamboyance, or polemical excess. Also striking was the absence of gratuitous deference toward the opponent. There was no pulling of punches, no telltale signs of anxiety about the consequences of an argument taken too far, or indeed made at all. Such was my first reaction to reading John Mearsheimer and Steve Walt's *Israel Lobby* paper, posted five years ago today on the website of Harvard's Kennedy School and published in shorter form in the *London Review of Books*. It had arrived at the opening of business one morning in an email from Michael Desch, then a professor at Texas A&M's George H. W. Bush School of Government. I sent it across the hall to my colleague Kara Hopkins, a woman a generation my junior, somewhat less engaged than I by the Middle East, and certainly less persuaded that a coterie of neocons had gotten George W. Bush on a leash and were leading him this way and that. Three minutes later, I walked into her office, where she had the paper up on her screen. "This is exactly what I believe," said Kara, words that I had never heard from her before on any subject, much less this one.

American Christians who are neither ignorant nor bigots have a difficult time finding the right words to discuss Israel and its special relationship to the United States. Anyone with knowledge of European history knows of the connection between discourses about Jewish power and anti-Semitism. Inevitably this history has intruded on American discussions of Israel and its lobby. Save a handful of exceptions, mainstream dissent from the special relationship with Israel has taken the form of the dry aside or the understated sentence or two published amidst a lot of other stuff, almost as if the author hoped it would not be noticed. Occasionally public figures at the end of their careers made remarks that more resembled outbursts, the parting shot of the 75-year-old senator or aging general. But more often than not, ever sensitive to the perils of anti-Semitism, Americans let their fears of contributing to injustice shut off necessary debates. People rolled their eyes or took refuge in wry remarks: "What's the matter with the rest of them?" said a friend upon seeing a *Washington Post* story about the 360 members of Congress who had showed up to pay homage at one of AIPAC's annual gatherings.

The reasons differed for every individual, and were composite. There was the worry about offending close Jewish friends or colleagues, concerns over possible adverse professional consequences, or the general inhibitions associated with the Jewish power/leading to anti-Semitism/leading to the Holocaust nexus.[1] The result was that critical analysis of the special relationship was shoved to the margins of American political discourse. The discussions may have been richer and more involved on the Marxist and anti-imperialist Left than on the quasi-isolationist Old Right, but in neither case did they much influence the political mainstream. Even in the wake of the Iraq disaster, with the looming prospect of more American wars in the Middle East, Israel's role was alluded at most in passing, but seldom really pursued.

The evasions could be almost comical.

In the second issue of *The American Conservative*, in the fall of 2002, we published an outstanding 8,000 word essay by Paul Schroeder, a distinguished diplomatic historian, who argued that Americans had a great stake in preserving an international system that inhibited preventive wars of the sort Washington was preparing to wage against Iraq. After being granted 8,000 words, Schroeder added some footnotes, the fourth of which stated, *inter alia*, "It is common for great powers to try to fight wars by proxy, getting smaller powers to fight for their interests. This would be the first instance I know where a great power (in fact, a superpower) would do the fighting as the proxy of a small client state."

To Schroeder's consternation, this footnote was the only item from his argument mentioned a few months later in a *Washington Post* op-ed, where it was cited among other examples of the supposed anti-Semitism of Iraq War critics who had deigned to notice that the push for war was connected to Israel.

---

[1] These inhibitions included the fear of offending other non-Jews. My wife, whose father was a U.N. official with extensive responsibilities for Middle East peacekeeping, grew up with a far more critical attitude toward Israel than I had. It was not until my own (previously neoconservative) views began to change in the mid '90s, fifteen years into our marriage, that she acknowledged to me some of her pro-Palestinian sympathies.

Five years ago, John Mearsheimer of the University of Chicago and Stephen Walt of Harvard stepped directly into these bogs of understatement, circumlocution, and the relegation of major points to footnotes. Here are some of the points the two made in the first pages of their paper:

> For the past several decades ... and especially since the Six-Day War in 1967, the centerpiece of U.S. Middle East policy has been its relationship with Israel. The combination of unwavering U.S. support for Israel and the related effort to spread democracy throughout the region has inflamed Arab and Islamic opinion and jeopardized U.S. security.

> More importantly, saying that Israel and the United States are united by a shared terrorist threat has the causal relationship backward: rather, the United States has a terrorism problem in good part because it is so closely allied with Israel, not the other way around.

> This situation has no equal in American political history. Why has the United States been willing to set aside its own security in order to advance the interests of another state?

In the essay that followed, the two backed up these and other equally forceful assertions with tightly-argued, factually-based paragraphs and extensive footnotes. They were not, of course, the first pioneers in pursuing this subject from an establishment vantage point: on at least two occasions, the Israel subject had been addressed by Americans of comparable eminence. George W. Ball, probably the wisest figure to hold high positions in the Kennedy and Johnson administrations, had late in life co-authored with his son an important book on America's "entangling alliance" with Israel —a book whose antecedent was in an article written for *Foreign Affairs* in the late 1970s, proposing that America "save Israel from itself" by stopping its incipient campaign to colonize the West Bank. A few years earlier, Senator William Fulbright, probably the leading foreign policy intellectual among Americans who held elective office in the postwar era, bemoaned the Israel lobby's influence, and pushed for an American security guarantee for Israel within the 1967 borders.

Both Fulbright and Ball came to the subject at the close of long careers. In contrast Mearsheimer and Walt published their paper during their professional primes. Their argument had none of that "Now I can finally say it" quality; instead the authors arrived with every intent of carrying their argument forward. They had tenure at two of the country's top universities. They had reached the top of a profession that rewards clear writing and thinking, and possessed the argumentative eloquence that comes from years of lecturing before the nation's brightest students. They were political moderates—whose careers had placed them squarely in the "vital center" of American academic foreign policy discourse. They were fully prepared to go larger, and in 18 months turned the paper into a best-selling book.

Of course, it mattered somewhat that the Israel lobby used every tool at its disposal to smear the authors and bury their argument. Every journal and newspaper that had ever felt the need to stress its "pro-Israel" credentials published a negative review of the book. (*The Israel Lobby* received generally far more favorable reviews in Europe and, in fact, in Israel.) But the sheer volume and intensity of the attacks on the paper may have been self-defeating. By April 2006, it seemed that everyone with an interest in foreign policy had read the article and was eager to talk about it. (I would note that in that month, I went on a trip with a church group to Syria, Israel, and the occupied West Bank, on a schedule that included five or six meetings a day for 10 days. Excepting the purely religious figures, it is no exaggeration to say that every single Arab intellectual, government or NGO official we met with mentioned the Mearsheimer and Walt paper. It was also the very first topic raised by Owen Harries, the very wise retired editor of *The National Interest*, at a private dinner I gave in his honor when he was visiting from Australia that May.)

Like the original essay, the book itself was a blend of precise analysis and exact documentation. As a resource, it is unparalleled. If someone confidently asserts that Israel and its backers had nothing whatever to do with encouraging the United States to invade Iraq (a "canard" is the usual dismissal phrase), one can find in *The Israel Lobby* five or six pages of quotes from television appearances and op-eds by leading Israeli political and military figures, who utilized their untrammeled media access to convey their war-mongering points to the American public. The same holds true for dozens of other subtopics of their broader subject: precise generalizations, supported by facts, authoritatively and contextually presented in a rhetoric that neither overheats nor backs down.

There are several different frames of reference in which to discuss Israel, the Palestinians, and the United States. One potentially critical new front is now being opened by some Jewish liberals, who charge that Israel's longstanding occupation policies contravene Jewish values. But important as this argument is, it initiates a debate in which the vast majority of Americans have no standing to participate.

This underscores the achievement, and the yet unrealized potential, of Mearsheimer and Walt's essay and book. As international relations scholars and centrist "realists," the two examined the American relationship with Israel through the prism of American national interests and values—or at least the non-racist and democratic values America has aspired to for most of the past century. They found the Israel relationship deficient on both counts. In doing so, they not only wrote a milestone paper and book— what political work in the past decade comes close to The Israel Lobby in importance? They provided the tens of millions in the vast American political center with a vocabulary and a conceptual frame to discuss a subject of critical importance to them. Non-Jews especially, for the reasons discussed above, desperately needed such a vocabulary, for without it they were all but mute. No matter that this potential remains, as yet, relatively underutilized: it is still there, ready to be deployed. In the long run, this may prove the greatest contribution of the two scholars, one which far surpass what the book has achieved thus far.

Mondoweiss
March 23, 2011

NETANYAHU'S MACHINE

The Crisis of Zionism opens with Peter Beinart watching a video on his computer sent by an Israeli friend. It depicts an incident on the occupied West Bank: Israeli military police arrest a Palestinian man for trying to siphon water from the pipes that feed an Israeli settlement after he had made repeated efforts to secure permission. As he is taken away, his 5-year-old son, Khaled, cries plaintively after him, "Baba, Baba."

For those familiar with the occupation, the context is clear. The settlers, with the legal rights of citizens of Israel, have privileged access to the aquifers in this arid land and use water at five times the rate of the Palestinians. This inequality is secured by Israeli military law, which governs the stateless inhabitants of this occupied territory.

Beinart describes the emotions the video set off in him:

> As soon I began watching ... I wished I had never turned it on. For most of my life, my reaction to accounts of Palestinian suffering has been rationalization, a search for reasons why the accounts are exaggerated or the suffering self-inflicted. ... But in recent years, for reasons I can't fully explain, I had been lowering my defenses, and Khaled's cries left me staring in mute horror at my computer screen.

It is a powerful passage in a book filled with them, one that encapsulates and personalizes the inequity of the occupation, the apartheid-like legal distinctions between Jewish settlers and Palestinians, and the grotesque disparity between two people's access to natural resources and civil and political rights. It captures with precision the rationalizing process of many American Jews, most of whom would decry such injustice were it to occur in America or elsewhere in the Western world. Finally it touches on the ineffable mystery of how sophisticated people change their minds—"I had been lowering my defenses"—a puzzle even for those at the top rungs of opinion journalism.

Peter Beinart is a young (early forties) and precocious former editor of *The New Republic* and "liberal hawk" who had once been a prominent voice promoting the Iraq War. For several years now, he has been recasting his views, first on American foreign policy and now on the questions of Israel and the Palestinians. He remains a liberal Zionist, committed to a Jewish state that practices the democratic values proclaimed at its founding: "complete equality of social and political rights for all its inhabitants, irrespective of religion." He is aware that the plausible window for creating such an Israel—with a viable Palestinian state alongside it—is closing rapidly and may be already shut.

The Crisis of Zionism is in part a meditation on the present "golden age of Jewish power," a critique of the American Jewish establishment, and a less than optimistic view of the increasingly Orthodox religious attitudes that will replace it; in part a history and analysis of Israeli Prime Minister Benjamin Netanyahu's tactical success in undermining the Oslo Accords and his shocking humbling of President Obama. While most of Beinart's arguments are not novel, they are presented with unerring precision. His book is full of keen insights into the contradictions and self-deceptions of his former side. It would not surprise me if this book became a lodestar for American Jews and non-Jews alike who are finding Israel's policies increasingly difficult to defend.

Beinart throughout blends themes of Judaism and Zionism: Israel and the attitudes of American Jews toward it are each the product of Jewish ideas, often contradictory ones. While this is in many ways obvious, it violates a quite useful, usually unspoken liberal taboo: the idea that Israel is a foreign state; it does not speak for American Jews. One can see the utility of this formulation for almost everyone. When radical anti-Zionists like the ex-Israeli Gilad Atzmon emphasize the inseparability of Israel from Jewishness, they make a lot of people uncomfortable. Beinart is neither anti-Zionist nor radical, but he is playing on the same field: for him the debate about Israel is not simply between competing political choices but about competing moral attitudes within Judaism.

While Jews have experienced an astonishing ascent in America in the past 70 or so years, this rise has not, he argues, changed attitudes at the top of major Jewish organizations. There, Jews are still eternal victims, the targets of primordial anti-Semitism. Jewish strength might be reveled in privately, but it is never publicly acknowledged, much less discussed. Soul-searching over how power can be used responsibly is more or less non-existent. The leading organizations are beholden to a relatively small number of rich elderly donors, Palm Beach retirees who write checks based on appeals about "Iran, anti-Semitism, and something bad someone said about Israel." Anyone who criticizes Israel can be smeared as an anti-Semite.

Interestingly, Beinart points out that many Jews know such charges are more often than not ridiculous but rationalize them anyway. "Jews assume that gentiles, because they are powerful, can take it, and that Jews, because of our history of persecution, can play fast and loose in the Israeli government's defense."

The Palm Beach retirees will pass on. But Orthodox Jews will increasingly move to the forefront of Jewish organizational life, and Beinart provides ample grounds for pessimism here: modern Orthodoxy is diverse and many-layered, but leading Orthodox institutions promote attitudes that are insular or simply racist—"the soul of the Jew and the non-Jew are made of different material," says Yeshiva University's Hershel Schacter, an influential Orthodox rabbi. So there is every possibility that Jewish organizational life in America will move in lockstep with an increasingly right-wing Israel. Beinart notes with alarm that Israeli high school students are far more intolerant than their elders. Occupation—the practice of it, the justification of it—breeds racism.

The principal political beneficiary of such trends is Netanyahu, Israel's most powerful figure. Netanyahu grew up in the shadow of Vladimir Jabotinsky; his father Benzion was a close associate of the charismatic founder of Revisionist (right-wing) Zionism. Jabotinsky believed that Zionism must purge Jews of their "childish humanism" and the justice-seeking Judaism of the prophets and toughen them for struggle against the Arabs. Compromise with the Palestinians was unthinkable. As late as 2009, Netanyahu's father told an interviewer that the Arabs ought to be encouraged to flee their land by denying them food, electricity, and access to education. His son's primary political goal has been the prevention of a Palestinian state.

While some right-wing Israelis pine openly for ethnic cleansing of the West Bank, Netanyahu's more limited vision is to sequester the remaining Palestinians in four disconnected cantons bisected by Israeli roads and checkpoints and deprived of any agricultural areas, a bantustan plan for 40 percent of the territory. The settlers would keep the rest. When he first came to office in 1996, he exploited a loophole for military bases in the Oslo Accords and declared the entire Jordan River Valley a "military zone."

As a young man, Barack Obama had been influenced by several of Chicago's leading liberal Zionists, but as a presidential candidate he began to defer to the Jewish establishment. Even so, he retained his commitment to a two-state solution. (As Beinart relates, after Obama's election, a worried

Netanyahu tried to open a secret channel to White House chief of staff Rahm Emanuel, an effort that was rebuffed.) But Obama found he could not prod Tel Aviv into serious negotiations without facing massive political retaliation from the Israel lobby. In 2010, he asked Israel to stop building settlements on territory that would become part of a Palestinian state, if there were to be such a state, but he was forced to retreat.

A year later, when Obama stated that the 1967 borders should be the starting point for renewed two-state negotiations—an American position for more than a generation—Netanyahu delivered what Beinart describes as "one of the most extraordinary humiliations of a president by a foreign leader in American history." Fresh from speaking at AIPAC's annual conference, Netanyahu replied that there was no chance of Israel withdrawing to "indefensible lines." Then Netanyahu went before a joint session of Congress. Each member of Congress had a single gallery pass to give out, and most gave theirs to their largest AIPAC donor. With the hall packed with supporters, Netanyahu received one thundering ovation after another. Congresswoman Debbie Wasserman Schultz, who as head of the Democratic National Committee plays a key role in party fundraising, used arm motions to signal to her colleagues when to stand and applaud, and they rose and clapped at Netanyahu's most controversial statements.

Concluding from this that America was unlikely to help, the Palestinian Authority tried to secure United Nations backing for a state within the 1967 borders. Palestinian leader Mahmoud Abbas claimed before the General Assembly that he wanted not to delegitimize Israel but to coexist with it. Though this vision of a two-state settlement was more or less identical to his own, Obama ordered the State Department into a full-court press to thwart the Palestinian initiative. One State Department official, after lobbying 150 foreign diplomats against the Palestinian effort, told Beinart, "sometimes I feel I work for the Israeli government." The liberal Zionist American president had been brought to heel.

Beinart's detailed history of these episodes is the best reported and most incisive one in print. It should put to rest any notion that Israel's current government has the slightest interest in allowing the Palestinians a state or that Obama can be counted on to move Israel towards fruitful negotiations.

The author probably has sufficient establishment ties to ensure his book a fair hearing. For months now, Likud-camp Zionists have worried that Beinart has aimed a Walt and Mearsheimer-sized bombshell in their direction. In contrast to the two professors, Beinart, who is Jewish, may avoid having his arguments falsely represented and being smeared as having authored an anti-Semitic book.

Formidable as it is, however, *The Crisis of Zionism* is not without flaws. It may not be clear exactly at what point the relentless settlement project that all Israeli governments have encouraged will render the two-state solution a political impossibility. But if that point has already been reached, or is about to be, a plea for a democratic Jewish state, no matter how persuasive, is simply no longer relevant. One can understand Beinart's reluctance to address this question, which could only complicate his argument, while nonetheless wishing he had tried.

The Crisis of Zionism also has a problem of agency. Though few writers are more clear-eyed about the hurdles American Jews face in changing the way their community relates to Israel, Beinart nonetheless writes as if they are the sole audience that matters for a serious argument about Zionism. Perhaps that is simply realism: it can seem that, apart from the Christian Zionists shepherded to support Netanyahu's agenda, the Mideast opinions of American gentiles simply do not count.

But can such a circumstance endure? America's engagement with the Middle East once centered on the construction of schools and universities, an outgrowth of the Protestant missionary presence in the region. The first generation of Western-educated Arabs often studied in such schools, so the American presence in the region was associated with science, the education of girls and women, a modernity untainted by colonialism—in short, a genuine program of liberation. A century later, the centerpiece is Israel, and America is best known in the region through such events as its anti-Palestinian vetoes in the Security Council, the fracturing of Iraq by war, and an entire Congress standing to applaud oppressive Israeli policies. One can trace this transformation to many sources, perhaps none more decisive than the slow, silent abdication of the Protestant establishment from its positions of power and responsibility.

Yet this landscape too is beginning to shift, and it has the potential to change more rapidly than Beinart acknowledges. Just as "the question of Palestine" resonates far beyond the borders of the Palestine Mandate, so in American politics its significance has begun to be felt beyond the confines of American Jewish opinion. If American Jews are to help forge a democratic and non-racist Israel, they are unlikely to succeed without allies. It would not be without irony were such allies to be found, among other venues, among the politically active Muslim students in the American universities and those mainline Protestants who are now, finally, finding their voice to say "Enough!" to America's unconditional support for Israel.

The American Conservative
March 26, 2012

I Like and Respect Israel, But It's Not America

There's a new neocon catchphrase going around. I heard it first on Chris Hayes's show a couple of weeks ago, when Eli Lake turned to Phyllis Bennis and said something like "Okay, we get it, you don't like Israel"—after Bennis mentioned the amount of aid Israel receives from the U.S. Then Danielle Pletka, a major player at the American Enterprise Institute upped the ante, devoting a blog post to Obama's "hate" for Israel.

Honestly, anyone who has written or spoken in public about the Israel-Palestine question is subject to this, whether openly or behind their back. It is a stark charge, often used to insinuate anti-Semitism. But rather than being simply defensive, it might be helpful to explore one's feelings more deeply. I've been to Israel twice, have met dozens of Israelis who were outstanding in terms of wisdom, vision, compassion, eloquence. There are several I know better who I'd count as among the most impressive people of my acquaintance.

Israel in a general sense has a great deal going for it: its science and medicine are first rate, and it produces many great scholars. All things being equal, it would probably rank high on my list of favorite countries—the way I feel about Switzerland perhaps, or Spain—a place where I would happily spend a year, root for their teams when playing countries I don't particularly care for, etc.

But of course all things aren't equal. As an American, one is never asked simply to like or respect Israel as a foreign country—one is asked to more or less worship the place. *TAC* contributor Michael Desch has an excellent short-form summary in Foreign Affairs. Some key points:

> When it comes to Israel, American security guarantees are far less hedged and legalistic, leaving little doubt that the United States seeks to protect it from almost any imaginable threat. In a 1994 address to the Knesset, U.S. President Bill Clinton waxed poetic on the subject. "Your journey is our journey," he told the Israelis, "and America will stand with you now and always." In a 2008 speech in Jerusalem, President George W. Bush was similarly expansive: "When you confront terror and evil," he said, "you are 307 million strong, because the United States of America stands with you." So when President Barack Obama declared that the U.S. commitment to Israel's security is "unshakable," or as he recently put it, in more colloquial terms, that the United States will "always have Israel's back," he was following in a long tradition.

> Of course, the commitment to Israel's security goes well beyond rhetoric. The United States has provided Israel with more than $160 billion in bilateral aid since 1948, most of it for military purposes.

About 60 percent of all U.S. aid to foreign militaries now goes to Israel, constituting around 20 percent of the Jewish state's annual military spending, according to the Congressional Research Service. Washington requires other recipients of its military aid to spend the money in the United States, but allows Israel to use a significant part of its aid allotment to buy weapons from its own defense industry rather than from U.S. suppliers.

The United States also takes steps to ensure Israel's ready access to American arms. The United States prepositioned ammunition and equipment in Israel in the 1980s as part of its war reserve stocks for allies program, and now regularly allows the Israel Defense Forces to replenish their supplies from them, as they did after the 2006 conflict between Israel and Hezbollah. Israel also benefits more than any other country from the U.S. Excess Defense Articles program, a veritable military flea market open to "major non-NATO allies" of the United States, a designation that Israel obtained in 2001.

Desch was responding in part to Netanyahu's insistence that Obama adopt Israel's "red lines" for dealing with Iran and start a war that might conceivably be in Israel's interests but is certainly not in America's. But in fact the special relationship is broader than that. Netanyahu, a rabid ethnic nationalist who has done everything he could to squelch the Oslo peace process, and whose real views about America are aptly summarized by his quote "America is a thing you can move very easily"—a bit of candor caught off the record when Netanyahu was speaking to some right-wing Israeli settlers—is treated quite literally like royalty on Capitol Hill and in American newsrooms. Congress grants him 30 standing ovations. David Gregory refers to him as "leader of the Jewish people." This "special relationship," with all that it implies about my country, its relationship to the Middle East and the entire world, and its ability to look sensibly after its own affairs, I genuinely do detest.

The American Conservative
September 26, 2012

Why Americans Don't Understand Palestine

If a man from Mars descended to observe Israel's attack on the Gaza strip, he would have seen one group of humans trapped in a densely populated area, largely defenseless while a modern air force destroyed their buildings at will. He might have learned that the people in Gaza had been essentially enclosed for several years in a sort of ghetto, deprived by the Israeli navy of access to the fish in their sea, generally unable to travel or to trade with the outside world, barred by Israeli forces from much of their arable land, all the while surveyed continuously from the sky by a foe that could assassinate their leaders at will and often did.

This Martian also might learn that the residents of Gaza—most of them descendants of refugees who had fled or been driven from Israel in 1948—had been under Israeli occupation for 46 years, and intensified closure for six, a policy described by Israeli officials as "economic warfare" and privately by American diplomats as intended to keep Gaza "functioning at the lowest level possible consistent with avoiding a humanitarian crisis." He might note that Gaza's water supply is failing, as Israel blocks the entry of materials that could be used to repair and upgrade its sewage and water-treatment infrastructure. That 10 percent of its children suffer from malnutrition and that cancer and birth defects are on the rise. That the fighting had started after a long standing truce had broken down after a series of tit-for-tat incidents, followed by the Israeli assassination of an Hamas leader, and the typical Hamas response of firing inaccurate rockets, which do Israel little damage.

But our man from Mars is certainly not an American. And while empathy for the underdog is said to be an American trait, this is not true if the underdog is Palestinian.

Among the chief milestones of Washington's reaction to Israel's military campaign were: President Obama stated from Bangkok that America supported Israel's right "to defend itself" and "no country on earth would tolerate missiles raining down on its citizens" while national-security aide Benjamin Rhodes added that, "the reason there is a conflict in Gaza is because of the rocket fire that's been launched at Israeli civilians indiscriminately for many months now." Congress took time off from partisan wrangling about the fiscal cliff to pass unanimously two resolutions, in the Senate and House, expressing its "unwavering commitment to the security of the State of Israel" and backing its "inherent right to protect its citizens against acts of terrorism." Its members could further inform themselves by attending a closed briefing by Israel's ambassador Michael Oren on November 28, the only figure invited by the House Foreign Affairs Committee to testify.

As the fighting continued, Walter Russell Mead, a prominent political scientist, conveyed impatience that the just-war tradition seemed to inhibit Israeli air attacks, which by then had killed and wounded scores of people. Mead asserted that Americans would back an Israeli response of "unlimited ferocity."

When Republican governor of Virginia Bob McDonnell, not known for his foreign affairs opinions, issued a statement backing Israel's response to "unwarranted and random violence," he was assumed to be signaling his presidential aspirations. The polls seemed to back him up: Americans told pollsters they supported Israel's actions against the Palestinians in Gaza by

57 percent to 25 percent, though the percentage of backers were somewhat lower among Democrats (41 percent), and the young (45 percent).

One explanation for such sentiments is that most Americans take foreign policy cues from political leaders, and no prominent American politician is willing to publicly express sympathy or compassion for Palestinians at the expense of Israel. Since roughly the time of John F. Kennedy, the politically ambitious have understood that expressing a wish for even-handedness between Israel and Palestine would threaten one's career. Whatever their private views might be, by the time they get to Congress, legislators learn that uncritical support for Israel is the "smart" political choice.

The spectrum of Congressional debate is shaped by the American Israel Public Affairs Committee, whose leaders vet potential candidates from across the political spectrum for their willingness to promote AIPAC-sponsored views on the Middle East, and ensure the access of those who agree to the lobby's superb national fundraising networks.

Those who stray are punished. Among notable victims was Illinois Senator Charles Percy, a moderate Republican once considered by many a possible future president. But after Percy refused to sign "the letter of 76" senators opposing President Ford's call for a reassessment of U.S. Middle East policy, and described Yasser Arafat as relative moderate among Palestinians, he faced well-funded opponents in the primary and general elections, and an outsider from California spent more than $1 million in negative ads against him. As J.J. Goldberg, editor of *The Forward*, noted a decade ago, "there is this image in Congress that you don't cross these people or they take you down." Given the absence of any publicly Palestine-sympathetic politicians at the national level, it may be surprising that support for Israel's strikes is not higher than 57 percent.

There are of course reasons beyond AIPAC's campaign-finance heft for Congress's Israel support. Christian Zionism is a significant factor, particularly in the Bible Belt. Former House Republican leader Dick Armey declared that his "number 1 priority in foreign policy is to protect Israel" while Tom Delay, his successor, described himself as "an Israeli at heart."

Other factors count as well. After 1967, Israel earned respect as a Cold War ally, with a military that could dominate Soviet allies in the region. Its creation in 1948 was widely viewed as partial moral compensation for the enormity of the crimes of the Holocaust—a view probably held by most Americans, including those opposed to many of Israel's current policies.

Furthermore, Palestinians have often had poor leadership in their national struggle. When success required international support, their use of terrorism rendered that problematic. Palestinians are hardly the first national-liberation movement to use terror as a tactic, but neither the

Zionist Irgun and Stern Gang, nor the Algerian FLN, nor the IRA seemed as dependent on terrorism to gain attention. This made it easier for its enemies to define the Palestinian national movement as "terrorist" tout court and allowed Israel's backers to tie their denial of Palestinian aspirations to America's "war on terror"—however dissimilar the two projects were.

A free and responsible press could challenge this political monoculture. But while there was more varied commentary about this Middle East war than previous ones, major journalistic organs failed dramatically at providing Americans information to understand the conflict. On November 19, *The New York Times* published an editorial outlining its view of the Gaza war. Its core passage described the outbreak of conflict:

> Hamas, which took control of Gaza in 2007 and is backed by Iran, is so consumed with hatred for Israel that it has repeatedly resorted to violence, no matter what the cost to its own people. Gaza militants have fired between 750 to 800 rockets into Israel this year before Israel assassinated one of its senior leaders last week and began its artillery and air campaign.

This summary mirrors precisely the oft-voiced Israeli *hasbara* point: "We withdrew from Gaza, and they started firing rockets." But the *Times* ignored entirely the virtual occupation of Gaza that Israel has maintained over the territory since its withdrawal, an occupation that intensified after Hamas won a Palestinian election, then prevailed in a struggle against the PA for control of the strip. The *Times* "balanced" its assessment with mild extraneous criticism of Israel for "marginalizing" the Palestinian Authority and isolating itself diplomatically. But the Israel-dominated reality Gazans had faced for the prior six years is left out.

Yes, it is true that Hamas is hostile to Israel and that its charter is anti-Semitic. It is also true that Hamas leaders have expressed interest in a long-term negotiated truce—a concession many observers feel is prelude to accepting a two-state solution. By failing to acknowledge that Israel had been blockading Gaza and its people, the *Times* gave its readers no way to understand why the people under Hamas rule might support resistance against Israel, including firing rockets, or why millions of people throughout the Arab and Muslim world support them.

On the same day in *The Washington Post*, Richard Cohen accused Hamas of not caring about human life, including that of Gazans. He too dwelled on the anti-Semitism in the Hamas charter, and mentioned the 2005 Israeli "pullout" from Gaza. He chided Israel for building settlements, but also could not bring himself to mention the blockade Israel has imposed on Gaza.

Neither, writing a few days hence, could his *Post* colleague David Ignatius. Like Cohen, Ignatius is a centrist, sometimes critical of Israeli actions. But about Gaza, he hewed tightly to Israeli propaganda guidelines:

> The Israelis withdrew from Gaza in 2005, only to have Hamas fire about 12,000 rockets and mortars at the Jewish state. The Israel Defense Forces invaded in 2008 (Operation Cast Lead) and a ceasefire followed. But in the years since, Hamas and other militias fired more than 3000 rockets and mortars, despite periodic cease-fires. On November 14, the Israelis got fed up and retaliated. . . they assassinated Hamas military leader Ahmed Jabari.

Again, no mention of the blockade, no reference to Israel's denial of Palestinian access to everything from the fish off their seacoast, to the opportunity to go to universities run by their compatriots on the West Bank, to their best arable land, to the equipment that would allow them to mend their broken water system. Palestinian resistance to the occupation is presented as simple bloody-mindedness. It is less surprising that *Post* columnist Charles Krauthammer, whose views track more closely with Israel's right-wing government, would take the identical line: Israel withdrew, got rockets in return.

Does not publishing this kind of narrative, again and again, constitute a kind of journalistic malpractice, an abrogation of a major newspaper's responsibility to inform? To imply that the Palestinians have no cause to resist, when rather plainly they exist in circumstances no people on earth would tolerate, is not really different from an actual lie. Israel can lie about Gaza if it wants, as governments do. But should major U.S. newspapers do so in their editorial and opinion pages?

It is hardly as if such journalistic distortions come without cost to Americans. Faced with a vast region of critical strategic importance, American readers are being deprived of information essential to understanding what is going on. The Arab world is radicalizing rapidly, often in anti-American ways, and one stream feeding the radicalism is U.S. diplomatic and moral support for Israel's cruel blockade of Gaza.

This is not to say that media coverage of the Israel-Palestine issue has not improved. Now, perhaps for the first time, Palestinians appear on network talk programs (MSNBC's Chris Hayes) and major radio outlets (NPR). It is important that Yousef Munayyer can be heard telling *Democracy Now* radio host Amy Goodman that to claim Israel is not occupying Gaza is like saying your goldfish are not under your control if you are not actually in the tank swimming with them.

The internet also has transformed the U.S. media landscape, on no issue more than Israel-Palestine. Nevertheless, most Americans do not seek news from specialized platforms. At a time when American politicians labor under all the constraints discussed above, the media's omission of critical contextual information violates its mission to inform and educate.

In the very recent past, Americans paid a heavy price for ignorance about the Arab world—many of its leaders having been led to believe that an Iraq invasion force would be welcomed with rose petals. There are now ample reasons to fear that they are being misled again.

The National Interest
November 27, 2012

Will Israel Go Fascist?

Max Blumenthal's sprawling portrait of contemporary Israel is far more a work of journalism than political theory. It largely avoids sustained argument or analysis, allowing its main points to be inferred through the words of Israelis and Palestinians, and short contemporary or historical descriptions, presented in several dozen vignette-like chapters. This is nonetheless a bold and shocking book, presenting persuasively a major theoretical and polemical argument about Israel almost completely at odds with the image most Americans have of it.

In *Goliath*, America's foremost partner in the Middle East is not the humanistic and ever resourceful "David" using guile to vanquish surrounding brutes, but a militaristic and racist state whose electoral majorities have set it on a trajectory towards fascism, if it isn't there already. Even those generally well-informed about Israel, and its occupation of the Palestinian territories, will have their views challenged by Blumenthal's sharp eye and deadpan factual presentations.

Goliath eschews the standard liberal Zionist position that a relatively virtuous and democratic Israel was driven off course by some combination of the post-1967 occupation of territory won in the Six-Day War, the burgeoning political power of the settlers, the authoritarian political culture of Russian immigrants, or the swelling political clout of Jews from North Africa and the Arab world. For Blumenthal, Israel's 1967 victory was not a turning point so much as a new opportunity to implement the ethnic-cleansing ideology present at the state's creation.

To a degree that has no clear equal among American journalists who cover the Mideast, Blumenthal is versed in the history of the 1948 war that created Israel, with its multiple expulsions of Palestinians from their towns followed by wiping those towns off the map. His narrative makes regular connections between this past and the present. For instance, a section on security procedures in Ben Gurion Airport is introduced by a description of the massacre of civilians in the Arab town of Lydda in 1948 that was followed by a forced march of 55,000 survivors to Ramallah, the so-called Lydda Death March. Lydda was then Hebraicized to "Lod," site of the international airport where visitors to Israel and the occupied territories are now sorted by ethnicity before interrogation, their electronic devices often searched or seized.

Another episode: during the 1970s, the Jewish National Fund planted fir trees to cover the ruins of three Palestinian towns Israel had bulldozed in the aftermath of the 1967 war. The trees were nonindigenous to the region, though they reminded some Israelis of Switzerland. Three years ago, they burned in a huge forest fire Israel could not control. Some who fled the conflagration came from nearby Ein Hod, which once was an Arab town built of stone houses. In the 1950s, an Israeli artist lobbied for Israel to preserve the houses as studios instead of bulldozing them as planned, and the town was turned into a tourist destination. When Blumenthal visited, a young woman acknowledged that the bar in which they were sitting was in fact a converted mosque. "Yeah, but that's how all of Israel is ... built on top of Arab villages. Maybe it's best to let bygones be bygones."

Such a sentiment may have some practical utility and might be spoken in good faith, but from a citizen of a country where so much national culture is derived from remembrance of wrongs done to Jews, its lack of self-awareness is remarkable.

Not all the past memories are bitter. Blumenthal tells the story of Benjamin Dunkelman, a Canadian officer who volunteered to lead troops in Israel's War of Independence. After signing a local peace pact with the notables of Nazareth, a cultural and economic center of Palestinian Christians, Dunkelman received a general's orders to expel the inhabitants. He refused. When the general sought a formal written order to override Dunkelman, David Ben-Gurion, who had given such orders before with a wave of the hand, balked at putting them in writing. So Palestinian Nazarenes, both Christian and Muslim, continue to live in Israel today.

A story of one of them, Hanin Zoabi, is told in one of *Goliath*'s pivotal chapters. Blumenthal arrived in Israel shortly before the Mavi Marmara affair, when a flotilla of boats sailed from Turkey with provisions to alleviate the blockade Israel had imposed on Gaza, the strip of territory it had evacuated settlers from in 2005 and then pulverized three years later. Israeli officials joked that Gazans, a majority of whom were suffering from what the United Nations called "food insecurity," were having "an appointment with a dietician" and emailed to journalists sarcastic remarks about the menus of Gazan restaurants. As the flotilla approached, the Israeli military and Hebrew-language press ginned up a great panic about the boats, with their crews of aging European peace activists and a few Palestinian politicians. While the organizers assumed that Israel would relent and allow the provisions through, Israel sent commandos on helicopters and attack dinghies to storm the ship.

When some passengers resisted by throwing bottles and debris at the boarders, Israeli commandos replied with live ammunition. Nine passengers were killed, including a 19-year-old Turkish-American, shot in the face execution-style while lying wounded on the deck. Israel eventually apologized to Turkey for the incident and will probably pay compensation. But Blumenthal recounts with some astonishment that an overwhelming majority of the Israeli public felt their country's brutal treatment of unarmed peace activists on the high seas was perfectly justified.

In the aftermath, the IDF went into public-relations mode. Israeli soldiers gathered up knives from the boat's kitchen and laid them out in a photographic display with several Qurans, supposedly evidence the Mavi Marmara was leading an Islamist terror convoy. Israel jailed the surviving passengers and confiscated their laptops and electronic equipment. The IDF doctored a sound clip to make it appear that flotilla organizers were crazed anti-Semites. Outside the Turkish embassy, Israeli demonstrators railed against Turkey. Blumenthal interviewed several of them, who ranged from self-described peaceniks to Meir Kahane supporters. "The longer I spoke with the demonstrators," he relates, "the more likely they were to merge their nightmare visions of the flotilla activists as hardcore agents of the Islamic Republic of Iran and al Qaeda with Holocaust demons. 'Everything is against the Jews and we have the right to defend ourselves.' 'No matter what we do everything is against us—everybody. And we know we're right.'"

This sentiment was echoed in the Knesset, when Hanin Zoabi, a 38-year-old Palestinian representative from Nazareth, elected by one of the Arab parties, instigated a virtual legislative riot by challenging Israel's right to board the Mavi Marmara on the high seas. Zoabi holds a master's degree from Hebrew University and had been a feminist activist prior to her election in 2009. She was on the boat, and after the assault began, she grabbed a loudspeaker and used her Hebrew to try to get soldiers to stop killing unarmed passengers. Returning to the Knesset two weeks after the incident, she was interrupted by shouts of "terrorist" and "go back to Gaza" while the Likud speaker of the legislature tried in vain to restore order.

A member of Yisrael Beiteinu, one of Israel's governing right-wing parties, presented Zoabi with a mock Iranian passport. Michael Ben Ari, a follower of the late Rabbi Meir Kahane—whose party had been banned for racial incitement in the 1980s—initiated a measure to strip Zoabi of her parliamentary privileges. It passed with minimal opposition. The next week Zoabi was deprived of her diplomatic passport. The Knesset then passed a bill, called the "Anti-Incitement Act," promising to criminalize speech that could be characterized as disloyal.

These maneuvers reflected a broader popular spirit: an Israeli grocer offered free groceries for life to anyone who would assassinate the Nazarene legislator, while an "Execute Zoabi" Facebook page was created, attracting hundreds of supporters. No one in the Knesset and few in the media protested. Blumenthal sardonically concludes, "shouting down Arab lawmakers had become a form of electioneering."

Sadly, the episode was in sync with Israel's broader political culture. Was the verbal violence against a Knesset member more troubling than the regular chants of "Death to the Arabs" shouted out at Israeli soccer stadiums? More menacing than legislation designed to impede marriages between Israeli citizens and West Bank Palestinians? More detestable than the Jerusalem celebrations of the life of Baruch Goldstein, a Jewish-American doctor who murdered 29 Muslim worshipers in Hebron in 1994? Or the provocation parades through Arab neighborhoods in Jerusalem, where hundreds of young Israelis and American Zionists join together to march the narrow streets of Jerusalem's Old City, booming the Hebrew slogans "Muhammad is Dead!" and "Slaughter the Arabs"? Or the mob violence young Israelis carried out against Arabs in the center of Jerusalem? Or the fact that followers of Kahane sitting in Parliament boast that the late rabbi's vision is now widespread in Israel's governing parties?

Since the 1920s there has been a word in Western discourse for this style of politics. The Israeli leftists and dissidents who became Blumenthal's friends have now taken it up. "'Fascism' was a word the leftists used almost invariably," writes Blumenthal, "as they told me about having their homes defaced with graffiti, death threats by right-wing thugs or about being summoned to interrogation." Speaking with journalist Lia Tarachansky on a Tel Aviv bus, Blumenthal probed what Israelis meant by the word. How could she claim fascism was in the air when anti-Zionists like her were permitted to conduct their journalistic and political activities freely?

The Israeli replied:

> To explain fascism in Israel, it's not that easy ... it's so depressing I usually repress my thoughts about it. But if you really want me to define it, then I'd tell you it's not just the anti-democratic laws, it's not the consensus for occupation, it's not the massive right-wing coalition government, it's not watching the people who ask questions and think critically being interrogated by the Shabbak. What it really is, is a feeling that you have sitting on a bus being afraid to speak Arabic with your Palestinian friends.

A young woman who had overheard their conversation interrupted to ask Blumenthal, "You with Israel or Turkiya?"

Blumenthal and his Israeli friends were not the first to broach the subject of fascism; the word has some history in Israel as a term of denigration against the right by the Zionist Left. But is there substance behind the charge today? Or is this simply another variant of the promiscuous use of "fascist" as an epithet, in the style of the American New Left of the 1960s?

One scholar who has at least tangentially addressed this is Robert Paxton, an eminent Columbia historian and one of the world's leading scholars of fascism, the author of a prize-winning work on Vichy France's murderous persecution of Jews. In his last book, *The Anatomy of Fascism*, published in 2003, Paxton speculated on fascism as a continuing menace beyond Europe and the interwar era. "If religious fascisms are possible," he wrote, "one must address the potential—supreme irony—for fascism in Israel." He noted that Israeli national identity is associated with human rights, long denied to Jews in the Diaspora. But he also observes Israel's demographic shift away from European Jews to Jews from North Africa and the Mideast (and today Russia), where democratic traditions are far weaker.

"By 2002," Paxton continued, "it was possible to hear language within the right wing of the Likud Party and some of the small religious parties that comes close to the functional equivalent of fascism. The chosen people begins to sound like a Master Race ... that demonizes an enemy that obstructs the realization of the people's destiny."

Surveying the "mobilizing passions" of fascism, Paxton lists among others "the primacy of the group, toward which one has duties superior to every right, whether individual or universal, and the subordination of the individual to it" and "the belief that one's group is a victim, a sentiment that justifies any action, without legal or moral limits, against its enemies both internal and external." A reader of *Goliath* will find a people thoroughly marinated in such sentiment.

Blumenthal closes his book with a short chapter on Israeli expatriates: fully 13 percent of Israelis now reside abroad. The United States and Germany are the most favored destinations. "The Exodus Party," he calls them. In Brooklyn, Blumenthal encounters several Israeli expats, including Rafi Magnes—the grandson of Judah Magnes, a famous Reform rabbi who was a founder and former president of Hebrew University in Jerusalem— along with his wife, Liz. The latter relates, "We could have stayed, of course, but the fascism had gotten to be too overwhelming."

Is the situation really so dire? Blumenthal arrived in Israel shortly after the election of Israel's most right-wing Knesset ever. Those inclined to optimism can assert that that this election represented a high tide; more recent election results were somewhat more centrist.

The Israel *Goliath* depicts would probably not be denied by liberal Zionists like Peter Beinart or the leaders of J Street. But they would argue that the proto-fascism is neither as widely nor deeply entrenched, nor as truly representative of the essential Israel as Blumenthal maintains, and that a fair settlement with the Palestinians could break the fever of racism and allow more sensible leaders to re-emerge as Israel's dominant voices. They could point out, as well, that Israel remains a functioning democracy for its Jewish citizens and at least guarantees some rights to others, while true fascist regimes—if popular at the outset, as they always were—eventually dispense with competitive elections and legal norms.

It is by no means obvious to me, however, which interpretation of the Israeli reality will appear, 10 years hence, to have been closer to the truth.

The American Conservative
November 6, 2013

John Kerry Walks Up to the Truth

A Washington gaffe, as Michael Kinsley once observed, occurs when a politician states an obvious truth he isn't supposed to say. John Kerry's closed door remark before a Trilateral Commission (an elite establishment group) gathering, where he said that without a two-state solution, Israel will become an apartheid state, reaches the important gaffe category. The remark is largely true (though it would have been truer if he had said that Israel already subjects most Palestinians in the territories it controls to apartheid conditions); it concerns a matter of great importance to American foreign policy, as Israel colors our relationships with the entire Arab and much of the Muslim world; and it breaches a dam on American internal discourse which the Israel lobby has fought hard to construct and defend.

Israel plays an extraordinary role in the American political system. Its leaders flood the important Sunday talk shows when any Mideast topic arises; Israelis lobbied hard for an American war against Iraq, as they do now for an American war against Iran. Americans, by and large, receive them with deference and rapt attention. They also honor Israel by subsidizing it: Americans give more foreign aid to Israel, a rich country, than to all of sub-Saharan Africa combined. So for Kerry to suggest, even with a heavy heart, that Israel is headed for apartheid in the absence of a two-state solution is to tread into Emperor's New Clothes territory. It may be true, indeed, of course it's true. But for a high ranking American politician to actually say so falls somewhere between lèse-majesté and blasphemy.

Kerry was rapidly denounced by Israel lobbyists in their multiple guises. *Commentary* called the comments a "calumny" against Israel. One of Bill Kristol's groups, the Emergency Committee for Israel, called for Obama to fire Kerry and for Hillary Clinton to repudiate his remarks. AIPAC called the remarks "offensive" and "inappropriate," comments echoed by the ADL and the American Jewish Committee. The National Jewish Democratic Committee, a major arm of Democratic Party fundraising, expressed its "deep disappointment" with the remarks, rejecting the idea that racially based governance "in any way describes Israel." Kerry was asked to apologize.

Kerry stated that if he could "rewind the tape" he wouldn't use the A-word while reminding everyone that current Israeli Justice Minister Tzipi Livni, and former prime ministers Olmert and Barak, had explicitly claimed Israel was headed toward apartheid if it didn't come to an agreement with the Palestinians. Some saw this statement as a grovel, but it could as easily be read as a non-apologetic "explanation."

The facts under discussion are clear enough. In his *Commentary* article, Peter Wehner laid out some standard talking points: Palestinians within the 1967 borders benefit from the full range of citizenship rights. One can quibble with this, as Israel has many laws and customs that limit real civic participation to Jews, but it is largely true that Israel's million or so Palestinian Arabs possess civil rights. The over-the-top expressions of hatred leveled at the Palestinians who get elected to the Knesset, reported in lurid and sometimes terrifying detail in Max Blumenthal's *Goliath*, indicate that many Israelis are far from reconciled to Palestinians having these rights and making use of them. But it is to Israel's credit that Israeli democracy is at least partially functional. Ditto the apologists' claim that Israel is the "only democracy" in the Middle East. This too is arguably the case. South Africa was, at least for its whites, a well-functioning democracy as well—and in this realm compared favorably to the other states in Africa. Apartheid is not incompatible with democracy for the privileged ethnic group.

The point—Kerry's and Livni's and Barak's and Olmert's—is that Palestinians in the West Bank and Gaza don't have these rights. They don't have self-determination either. The West Bank is effectively cantonized into half a dozen townships by Israeli checkpoints. Palestinians can't come or go without Israeli permission. They have no control over their water resources or their internet. They can't travel anywhere and return without Israeli say so, which is given or denied arbitrarily. They are effectively stateless, controlled by a government over which they have no say. And this has gone on for nearly fifty years. Peter Wehner and the others who are shouting "calumny" know these facts and don't try to rebut them. The standard talking point is that Israel made generous offers of Palestinian statehood, but that is a talking point, not a reality: Israel's famous Camp David "offer" in 2000 was never formally proposed in writing, and what was suggested by Israeli negotiators was something far less than a sovereign Palestinian state. The insincerity of Israel's interest in Palestinian statehood can be inferred by the fact that Israel approved building permits for 14,000 new settler apartments in the West Bank while the most recent talks were ongoing. The current Israeli government has no desire to help midwife a Palestinian state, a fact that John Kerry, if he didn't fully recognize before, surely does now.

We are left with the question of why did Kerry say this. He is, by all appearances, a man who measures his words with care, one given, if anything, to diplomatic doublespeak. He supported the Iraq War, perhaps against his better judgment. He may have once have been an outspoken Vietnam war opponent, but from this background he gradually become a consummate establishment politician, a cautious figure with little record of saying original or daring things.

In short, it is highly unlikely Kerry used the apartheid word casually or by accident. He knew full well that top Israeli politicians have used it, that former President Jimmy Carter had used it (about the West Bank, not Israel proper). He almost certainly knew that most serious foreign policy observers not just in the United States but throughout the world realize that Israel, once revered as a redeeming and admirable achievement, is now widely perceived as an oppressive, racist force. It stunts the lives of millions of Palestinians through a combination of brute power and racially based bureaucratic entanglement. Its current, democratically-elected, leaders have no intention of changing that. If Kerry once doubted this, he knows it now, after nine months of futile shuttle diplomacy. As does former Mideast mediator George Mitchell, as does Obama, as do the top Mideast experts on Kerry's staff. What Kerry said may be a gaffe, but it is one that most people know to be true. And look around: more and more are ready to take the flak and abuse hurled at those who speak the truth out loud.

Now even the careful John Kerry has tiptoed up to the truth before performing a slight, well-modulated semi-walk back. Kerry won't resign; Obama won't ask him to, and the calls for his resignation will soon peter out. At some point, speaking the truth about Israel will no longer be a "gaffe"— and we're getting nearer to it every day. Perhaps that's even what Kerry intended.

The American Conservative
April 30, 2014

THE PRESBYTERIAN VICTORY

The invective is telling. The Presbyterian Church USA's razor thin vote to divest from three American companies that aid the Israeli occupation is, opponents of the move tell us, irrelevant, because Presbyterians are irrelevant. The language used to make this point is not particularly ecumenical: here, Rabbi Shmuley Boteach inveighs against the PC-USA's vote by referring to the "rotting corpse of the Presbyterian church." One suspects that if a prominent Presbyterian cleric used comparable language about a branch of Judaism, it would attract some negative attention.

To influence the general assembly vote of this allegedly "dying" and "irrelevant" denomination, Zionist groups mobilized like mad, chastising the resolution and coordinating with Presbyterian groups created to oppose it, like the misnamed "Presbyterians for Middle East Peace." Opponents of the resolution more often than not claimed that while they didn't like Israel's policies either, they balked at taking even symbolic action to oppose them. Amorphous threats were cast by leading Jewish establishment figures. Presbyterians would become isolated as anti-Semites, some charged. The interfaith dialogue between Presbyterians and Jews would be "called into question." (One wonders about the value of dialogue with people who consider you a "rotting corpse.") The Israeli embassy implicitly accused the Presbyterians of supporting terrorism.

Prior to the vote, Rabbi Rick Jacobs, an organizer against the resolution, offered the Presbyterians a meeting with Israeli Prime Minister Benjamin Netanyahu if only they would vote it down. Presbyterian delegates would be able to tell Bibi himself, in person, why they opposed Israel's West Bank settlement and occupation policies. How this was supposed to be a blockbuster negotiating sweetener somehow escapes. Did Rabbi Jacobs imagine that the Presbyterians believed that Netanyahu was unaware that many Americans opposed the occupation—and his readiness to give forty-five minutes of his time to the Presbyterians might indicate an open mind? Please, there are no Presbyterians so stupid.

Internal Presbyterian politics move at a glacial pace, with an almost ponderous attention to procedure and internal democracy. The divestment resolution, crafted to target only three American companies, which directly aid Israel's illegal occupation, has been in the works for years. Two years ago, it came up short by two votes. Presbyterian concern about the suppression of Palestinian rights is of longer duration, the fruit of fact-finding missions and study groups dating to the aftermath of the 1967 war. Because endorsing even symbolic measures against Israel was such an emotionally wrenching step, it took a very long time for any measures to be taken.

Among the occupation's defenders and apologists, the most common strategy was to mock Presbyterians as an irrelevant church. Few tried to defend Israeli policies, knowing that they would not be persuasive. But calling attention to the numerical decline of the Presbyterian church touches on interesting subjects. All mainline Protestant churches are in decline since their heyday, which could be loosely dated at sometime between the 1920s and the 1950s. Protestantism, or to be more precise, liberal establishment Protestantism, used to be something of a state religion in America. Protestant clerics were widely quoted, featured on the covers of news magazines. *Time* magazine (itself widely read) ran a weekly "religion" feature, which more often than not circulated Protestant ideas and covered the comings and goings of mainline church luminaries. Presidents sought their advice, or at least claimed to.

That day is past: since then, America has elected a Catholic president, and a substantial part of its financial and cultural establishment is Jewish. Multiculturalism has triumphed. Within Protestantism, the evangelicals have the numbers—if mainline denominations once roughly equaled them in size, the children of the mainline were far less likely, after the 1960s, to become active church members. Mainline women had fewer children than their evangelical counterparts. Then came the ideological earthquakes of the 1960s, which undermined the self-confident assumptions of mainline Protestantism. Prominent liberal Protestants commenced a process of often excoriating self-criticism, often spurred by efforts to come to terms with America's racism. The unleashed energies spilled over into the anti-Vietnam war and eventually to the women's and gay liberation movements.

Meanwhile, fundamentalists and evangelicals, the other side of Protestantism's historical divide, were able to move into the breach as the "patriotic" God, flag, and country sort of Protestants, defending the familiar in the face of upheaval. As always, nationalism was a potent force, and the denominations that embraced it thrived more than those that questioned it.

No one should feel sorry for Presbyterians. As David Hollinger has cogently argued (and from whose work much of this short summary is derived), by persisting to raise discomforting questions about American racism and American smugness, liberal Protestants had a major impact both on the 1960s and the subsequent development of America as a liberal multicultural polity. But more often than not, they (or their children) exerted their influence as individuals, not as Presbyterians, or Methodists, or Episcopalians. Their children often absorbed some of their values, increasingly universalist and self-critical, without becoming active church members. So Presbyterians and other mainline denominations lost to the evangelicals the battles for dominance within American Protestantism while winning those over the broader shape of American culture.

This history makes a point to those who think that it doesn't matter much when a small but historically significant Protestant denomination decides that the Israeli occupation has gone on long enough. Presbyterian leaders in America have a richly textured history of political cooperation with Jews; they made common cause in opposition to Vietnam, over civil rights, over issues of church-state relations. They are fewer than two million now, but they are generally well educated, and have both activist skills and a strong penchant to combat injustice. They are a smaller group than two generations ago, but the Israel lobby obviously cared enough about them to make a major effort to defeat the divestment vote. The Israel lobby failed, suffering a significant public defeat. Presbyterians made themselves more visible and relevant than they've been in decades.

The American Conservative
June 25, 2014

History

In history graduate school, or even before, one learns how to write history from primary sources. I've done some of that, but the pieces below are not that kind of history. They are instead fragments of either personal history or memoir, or essays grounded in historical personages and events, written in an attempt to better illuminate the present.

The two longer ones concern a turning point in Jimmy Carter's presidency and de Gaulle's success in ending the Algerian war. It is probably not a coincidence that the two one-term presidents in my lifetime, George H.W. Bush and Jimmy Carter, both fell afoul of the Israel lobby. Encouraged by the example of a Columbia professor I much admired, Zbigniew Brzezinski, I worked for Carter's campaign in 1976. Though the Camp David agreement was perhaps the zenith of his presidency, Carter aspired to do much more—to set the stage for a genuinely lasting framework for Israeli–Palestinian peace. Of course, he failed.

I now tend to think of de Gaulle as the twentieth century's most admirable figure, both as conservative opponent of Nazism, giving hope to France in its darkest hours in 1940, and then ensuring through his charisma and the respect he inspired a modicum of stability in what might have been a catastrophic postwar period. And then, more than a decade later, emerging from retirement to steer France out of its seemingly impossible Algeria morass. America certainly has produced no comparable figure, but I often feel it needs one. And certainly a reappearance of Gene McCarthy in the Senate would be welcome as well.

The Good Strategist

George F. Kennan was more than the architect of America's Cold War victory, he was the last of a line of gentlemen statesmen

When he died in March at the age of 101, George F. Kennan was remembered principally as America's leading Cold War strategist, one of the "Wise Men" who took control of American foreign policy in the pivotal years after World War II and molded the institutions that shaped the world for the next 50 years. The containment doctrine most associated with him—espousing the need to confront Soviet postwar expansion with an American "counterforce" and holding out the prospect that a Soviet communism denied significant military or political expansion would eventually wither and die—was the central skein of American strategy for two generations after World War II.

Kennan later observed that if the famous "Long Telegram," which he sent to Washington while a Moscow-based diplomat in February 1946, had been delivered six months earlier, it would have fallen on deaf ears. Six months later it would have simply expressed conventional wisdom. Whether that is so, it is a fact that this 8,000-word missive caught Washington's attention the way no diplomatic cable had before or since. In it, Kennan explained that the pursuit of "peaceful co-operation" with Stalin's government was a chimera and that the then-widely held view that maintaining the spirit of the anti-Hitler alliance and turning a blind eye to brutal Soviet behavior in Eastern Europe was the only alternative to war was equally false. Stalin's was a hard-edged, unsentimental government that would not be swayed by the West's concessions or professions of friendship but was highly sensitive to "the logic of force."

The cable's author was summoned home shortly thereafter and made the State Department's first policy-planning chief, under Secretary of State George Marshall. There Kennan became the intellectual architect of the Marshall Plan, which sent billions of dollars to a prostrate Western Europe and helped set up a political-warfare unit, the precursor of the CIA. With the publication a year later of his "X" article in *Foreign Affairs*, Kennan became known as the principal American foreign-policy strategist.

Kennan viewed the Soviet Union primarily as a political and psychological threat, not a military one and by 1948, with the economic reconstruction of Western Europe proceeding, he was convinced the worst of the danger was passed. By 1950, he was already on the dovish side of the Washington establishment and for much of the next decade opposed what he called the militarization of the containment doctrine.

If Kennan had been simply a foreign affairs expert and an exemplary public servant, a diplomat who formulated a successful strategy to deal with unprecedented danger in a world in great flux, he would merit an important place in American history. But he was far more than that. After leaving the State Department in 1950, he developed an outstanding second career as a scholar, memoirist, polemicist, and moral philosopher. He was probably the last great American WASP intellectual, the last American man of letters whose thought and instincts were consciously rooted in the American WASP past and who was able to take full advantage of that past's lessons and habits of mind. For Kennan, this history was not a source of guilt or a hurdle to be overcome but a springboard for self-understanding and acting in the world. Indeed, in his work one can see (as one could find virtually nowhere else in America of the 1960s and after), Protestantism as the driving and disciplining cultural force it once was, an inner fire that could push a highly gifted individual to transform himself into a great man.

Kennan came from a middle-class family in Milwaukee and never felt socially comfortable with the richer students from the East he met at Princeton in the 1920s. He joined the Foreign Service after graduation, undertook Russian language training, served in the embassies in Prague, Berlin, and Moscow, and rose steadily in its ranks.

He was a Presbyterian by background who, as he once wrote, regarded himself as a Christian, although others "would question my right to that status." But whether he was devout in any orthodox sense, he certainly possessed the inner fire, which left traces throughout his work, as, for instance, when he describes leaving the Department of State in 1950 to become a scholar at Princeton's Institute for Advanced Study. Kennan writes of a momentary euphoria: "The hours and days of liberty seemed to stretch forward abundantly into a future too remote to be considered finite. There would now, it seemed, be time for everything." He wanders into the Princeton bookstore, "intoxicated with the illusion of freedom" and purchases Calvin's Institutes, sits down on a bench outside and reads "with pleasure and profit." But the illusion of happiness could not last, and spiritual strain soon makes its appearance. As he writes, "the private diaries now began to contain more in the way of self-reproaches, complaints of the vanity of current preoccupations, protests about the aimlessness of one's existence, yearnings for a greater unity and seriousness of purpose."

Thus, a glimpse into the inner life of a man of middle age—one who had just completed a stint in government during which he played a pre-eminent role in shaping the strategic posture of the United States, and hence the West, towards Stalinist Russia, and who would in the ensuing decade publish four volumes of highly regarded scholarship about the history of America's relations with the Soviet Union and two more about American foreign policy—lamenting his "aimlessness" and exhorting himself to greater "seriousness of purpose."

Kennan's writing covered a vast ground, including the publication of two volumes of memoirs that won him the Pulitzer Prize, a spirited polemic with 1960s radical students and their fellow travelers, numerous essays on nuclear weapons and Soviet-American relations, and a semi-philosophical iteration of his general worldview published when he was 89.

He was more or less the founder of the realist school in American foreign policy thought, wary of the role ethnic lobbies and congressional enthusiasms played in the formulation of foreign policy and of the country's seemingly irrepressible need to view conflicts with other nations as black and white moral crusades. His bestselling book *American Diplomacy* introduced the term "national interest" into the foreign policy lexicon. In Kennan's view, the term was a brief not for selfishness but modesty, for recognition that "our own national interest is all that we are really capable of knowing and understanding."

Over a wide range of subjects, Kennan could produce passages that were remarkably free of the whole bundle of multiculturalist concessions and guilt that had managed to overwhelm the WASP sense of self in the 1960s. His writing could sometimes sound like a voice from a distant past, and yet it enabled him to address the range of subjects around the intersection of the United States and other civilizations like no other American in the second half of the 20th century.

At the opening of his memoirs, Kennan wrote of his own family:

> Its members were neither rich nor poor. They never owned an appreciable amount of capital. There was not one who did not work long and hard with his hands. They were, on the other hand, as devoid of self-consciousness with regard to their poverty as they were of social bitterness over the fact that it existed... [W]hen times were hard, as they often were, groans and lamentations went up to God, but never to Washington ... No family could have been more remote from the classic social predicament to which Marx, outstandingly, had drawn attention and to which his followers tended to ascribe so overwhelming a significance.

Thus Kennan credits his background for inoculating him against taking Marxism too seriously, an inoculation that the majority of intellectuals of his era plainly did not receive. It served him well in the 1930s and especially the 1940s when he became, in effect, the United States' most important interpreter of Marxist ideology and its role, or lack of one, in Stalin's foreign policy.

But this frugal pioneer-stock background could be wielded to make other, more polemical points. For instance, in *The Cloud of Danger*, a foreign policy treatise published in 1977, Kennan touches on the then-extremely volatile subject of Third World development and the relations between the "rich" and "poor" countries. He wrote, "I have before me ... a faded snapshot, recently sent to me by a relative, of the log house in which my great-grandparents lived when they first came, in 1851, to the Green Bay region of Wisconsin: a crude almost windowless structure, standing in a dreary treeless field. And I am moved to recall that the Wisconsin of that day was very much of what we today would call an underdeveloped country."

He then proceeds to describe the growth of the state's governing institutions, the development of tolerance and respect for majority opinion, how its inhabitants made use of developmental capital acquired at normal rates of interest, all which made Wisconsin today "the seat of a high prosperity—too high, I sometimes think, for the good of its own inhabitants." And then there follows, in a broadside at the pervasive and cacophonous discourse about the rapacious North and the noble South then emanating from the United Nations and virtually every establishment newspaper and major university president, "Had we Wisconsinites been a lazy, violent, improvident people, devoted more to war than to industry ... and had we therefore remained undeveloped instead of developing our resources— would we today be seen as possessors of a peculiar virtue vis-à-vis the more developed countries, entitling us to put claims on their beneficence and to demand of them that they exert themselves to promote our development?" The West, Kennan concluded, needed to divest itself of its guilt complex in its dealings with the Third World.

Throughout Kennan's memoirs are insights that would have tested the boundaries of political correctness, had the concept a name at the time, and some which transgressed the sensibilities that actually did exist. In 1950, for instance, Kennan, still an employee of the State Department, was sent on a multi-country tour of Latin America, culminating in an American ambassadors' conference in Rio de Janeiro. In his diaries, he recalls being haunted by the huge gaps between the rich and poor and dismayed most of all by the despairing opulence of the "hopelessly rich."

Upon his return, he filed a report that the head of State's Latin American division promptly locked away from view, saying it did not belong in the department's archives. In his memoirs, published 16 years later, Kennan quoted from it. Latin America, he wrote, was disfavored by geography and climate and weighted down by its history, permeated by a "heavy, melancholy force." Noting the "inordinate splendor" and "pretense" of Latin American cities and the "squalor" of their hinterlands, he wrote, "[I]n the realm of individual personality this subconscious recognition of the failure of group effort finds its expression in an exaggerated self-centeredness and egotism—in a pathetic urge to create the illusion of desperate courage, supreme cleverness, and a limitless virility where the more constructive virtues are so conspicuously lacking."

One can see why the State Department might shield Foreign Service officers from these observations without concluding Kennan was wrong in making them. In his memoirs, Kennan added a sort of amendment, writing that despite the tragic aspect of Latin American civilization, "in another sense" it might be humanity's best hope for the future. In phrases that reflected his increasingly critical view of the United States, he wrote that he might well prefer the human ego in its Latin American manifestations, "spontaneous, uninhibited, and full-throated," to the "carefully masked and poisonously perverted forms it assumes among the Europeans and the Anglo-Americans."

Noting that no Latin American country possessed nuclear weapons or was even thinking of acquiring them, he concluded that the region "may prove some day to be the last repository and custodian of humane Christian values that men in the European motherlands and in North America— overfed, over-organized, and blinded by fear and ambition—have thrown away."

Of comparable interest was Kennan's view of China. He was never a Sinophile of any stripe, neither an enthusiast of China's Maoist revolution nor of the powerful China lobby of the 1950s, which sought to enlist Washington's support for restoring Chiang Kai-shek to power on the mainland. Kennan thought that little good could come from too close relations with the Chinese, whom he considered masterful at manipulating American perceptions of them. Mao's revolution and the expulsion of Westerners from China meant for the first time, China held no more American "hostages" whose views were inevitably corrupted by their own affections. Of the Chinese themselves, Kennan wrote that they were "probably the most intelligent, man for man, of the world's peoples." But "admirable as were many of their qualities—their industriousness, their business honesty, their practical astuteness ... they seemed to me to be lacking in two attributes of the Western-Christian mentality: the capacity for pity and the sense of sin. I was quite prepared to concede that both of these qualities represented weaknesses rather than sources of strength in the Western character. The Chinese, presumably, were all the more formidable for the lack of them."

Two generations after these discursions on Latin America and China were published, it is far from clear they are anachronistic or irrelevant. One could meaningfully debate whether they are correct. What is more certain is that today no American official, in or close to government, would dream of committing such thoughts to paper—or even be capable of entertaining them. However many self-professed devout Christians may now inhabit the upper echelons of the present administration, are there any who could conceive of their own country having a "Western-Christian" mentality in a nuanced fashion or use such vocabulary? It is far easier to imagine a contemporary Christian nationalist advocating that Washington attack or invade non-Christian countries, a prescription more based on ignorance of the targeted countries than knowledge of them.

"Isolationist" is not the right word for Kennan, and "realist" is too freighted with calculations of power politics to be quite correct either. Perhaps the perspective of these passages can be described by a term like "civilizational"—a point of view that combines understanding and attachment to one's own tradition, awareness of its differences with others, and alertness to the possibility that distance can be a wise thing for the diplomat to cultivate. It is a conservative viewpoint in the true sense, which makes it the antithesis of contemporary neoconservatism and neoliberalism, as well as all universalist ideologies. Needless to say, it is a kind of voice that is no longer heard at all in the top echelons of official Washington.

In the last decades of his life, Kennan was increasingly critical of American society, its ecological waste, its commercialism, in some sense its superficiality. In the 1980s, he emerged as a vociferous critic of the American defense strategy, based as it was on the possible first use of nuclear weapons. In the last book he wrote, *Around the Cragged Hill*, published in 1993, he welcomed the Cold War's end as providing the United States a chance once again to cut a more modest figure in the world, arguing that the greatest service this country could render would be to put its own house in order and make of American civilization an example from which others could take inspiration.

He thought the United States had grown too large for successful self-government, urging that it consider dividing itself into smaller constituent republics. He questioned the whole point of an economy based on constant growth, wondering if there was not "something diseased, something cancerous, something open-ended and unstable" about an economy that had always to expand to be seen as adequate. He would have preferred a nation that traveled by train, with denser, more concentrated cities, a citizenry that read more and spent more time outdoors and watched less television. He opposed mass immigration, saying that a society that depended on cheap outside labor was like the Romans, who became dependent on barbarians to fill the ranks of their armies. He found it absurd that Washington, "while not loath to putting half a million armed troops into the Middle East to expel armed Iraqis from Kuwait, confesses itself unable to defend its own southwestern border from illegal immigration." He recognized, of course, that his speculations were idle—that there was no possibility of the political system accommodating his views and that a man who questioned some American shibboleths was simply regarded with "gasping horror."

Kennan's point of view—that of a Russell Kirk conservative with Green tendencies, elitist in tone, infused with serious experience in government and knowledge of the world—is today far outside the mainstream. The United States did not turn inward at the end of the Cold War, showed not the slightest inclination to abandon the quest for bigness, and has pursued foreign policies exactly the opposite of what Kennan recommended.

But none should doubt that a century or two hence, whatever fate has befallen the United States in its immodest and belligerent quest for world "democratic" empire, George F. Kennan's voice will be seen as of the peak of dissident wisdom, and historians will note that the United States would have been extremely fortunate to have had men like him with the president's ear in 2002, as it did in 1946.

The American Conservative
June 6, 2005

PEACE CANDIDATE, '68 VINTAGE

TAC's publishing schedule did not allow for a timely obituary of Eugene McCarthy, but the late senator deserves notice in these pages: his views—and particularly his long frustration with the limitations of two-party hegemony—have a great deal of common ground with this magazine.

There are inevitably some personal ties as well. In the winter of 1968, I was a student at a New Hampshire boarding school and with dozens of my classmates went out to canvass for McCarthy on the weekends. His strong New Hampshire primary performance against incumbent Lyndon Johnson—running almost entirely on an anti-Vietnam War plank—was enough to persuade Johnson to withdraw from the race and to entice Bobby Kennedy to throw his own hat into the ring. I recall little about the campaign besides the buttons and a large billboard in Manhattan showing McCarthy's face and windblown hair, proclaiming something like "a breath of fresh air." But I knew—or thought I did—enough about the Vietnam War to support any candidate who would stand against it. If you opposed the war in 1967 and early 1968, it was tremendously frustrating that there was almost no established politician who would stand up against it, seemingly no chance that it could be ended or even combated through electoral means, and that much of the vocal opposition to the war was monopolized by the hard Left. That would change over the next few years, but it was certainly McCarthy's campaign that broke the establishment logjam.

Much has been written about McCarthy's quixotic, almost diffident campaign, his seeming reluctance to be a leader in the normal political sense. The world of campaigns is rife with anecdotes about his "laziness"—his late rising, his refusal to say the same thing again and again, his general lack of doggedness and stamina as a candidate. I assume these charges were true, and yet it cannot be denied that he and only he among established political figures was willing to take the first plunge and take up the antiwar banner against Johnson in late 1967.

In his later years, his views—if not his political style—were rather Buchananite. He was long a believer that the United States should control its borders, writing in the 1990s an immigration-control polemic entitled *A Colony of the World: the United States Today*, taking issue with the bipartisan establishment idea that the U.S. should serve as a kind of drainage vessel for the surplus populations of other nations, and serving as an advisory-board member of the immigration-control group FAIR. He was a trade protectionist as well and naturally was skeptical about the Iraq War.

In the winter of 2000, when Pat Buchanan was running for president on the Reform Party ticket, Kara Hopkins and I had dinner with Gene McCarthy at Washington's Jockey Club. He had spoken favorably of Buchanan's presidential bid to a reporter from the *L.A. Times*, and it was our intent to feel out whether Gene would publicly endorse Pat or perhaps even sign on to an important advisory role in the campaign.

During the course of a delightful dinner, he commented—generally favorably—on the language and rhythm of Pat's speeches and urged the campaign to do something to address "the issue of time." He meant the way people are overscheduled in the modern world and don't have time to savor life's experiences. He was right, though it was hard for us to think of a four-point plan that might speak to the issue. He deferred a decision on the endorsement question, letting us know that Jesse Ventura, his home state's governor and a player in the complicated and invariably vicious internecine wars of the Reform Party, had been extremely gracious to him recently. What was unsaid was that Ventura and the Reformers who were then backing Buchanan were on opposing sides. It was too bad—I think Gene could have connected in a public way the various strands of Buchananism, which is far more than a right-wing phenomenon, much better than the campaign was able to do on its own.

McCarthy was old then, but his mind was sharp. After the dinner, Kara drove him home to his Washington apartment and helped him up the outer steps, terrified that he would fall and that she would forever go down in history as the person on the scene at Gene McCarthy's death.

1968 is supposed to be a sort of devil year in the conservative calendar, akin almost to 1789 and 1917. But there was something special and deeply democratic about a poetic, intelligent senator stepping forward to mobilize and give political focus to all that unrepresented sentiment. Pat Buchanan has written recently that a Gene McCarthy for our day will emerge soon. We should be so fortunate.

The American Conservative
January 30, 2006

ALGERIA, THE MODEL

When contemplating Iraq, Americans look into a murky crystal ball. History naturally presents itself as a tool to clarify the choices and possibilities that lie before us. But what history? Before the invasion, neoconservatives soaked the capital in the rhetoric of Winston Churchill and the "lessons" of the 1930s. Later, after Saddam was found to have no weapons of mass destruction, they sought to rebrand the Iraq War as a part of the long struggle against totalitarian "Islamofascism" and thus a successor to the Cold War. For many Americans, the natural comparison is the Vietnam War, which ended with evacuation choppers on the Saigon embassy's roof and several more years of bloodshed in Indochina.

The French war in Algeria, never well known in the United States, has its own claims to stake. Before the Iraq War commenced, some Pentagon special operations officers attended a screening of Gillo Pontecorvo's classic 1966 docudrama, *The Battle of Algiers*. More recently, reporters were told that George W. Bush was reading Alistair Horne's exhaustive *A Savage War of Peace*—a book that, Horne stated in the preface to the recent paperback edition, was Ariel Sharon's favorite bedtime reading. (Israeli dove Amos Elon remarked that Sharon must have completely misunderstood the work.)

What lessons might Americans draw from the Algerian war? They are not obvious. The brutal conflict, which gave rise to an extraordinary memoir literature in French, impinged on France's national life far more than Iraq has yet touched America. But some common features are clear. The Algerian war was more or less part of our own historic era, influenced by international air travel and mass communications. A Western democracy was facing off against Arab Muslims; terrorism against civilians—first employed by the Arab guerrillas and later by the French far Right—was a central aspect of the war; and the use of torture to root out the terror networks produced a moral upheaval in France. Indeed, the war very nearly cost France its democracy.

In the end, it required the extraordinary political leadership of Charles de Gaulle, who turned against some of his most devoted supporters to extricate France from the mess and move the country forward. Losing the war proved far more painful for the Algerians who had aligned themselves with France than for France itself. If one is looking for an example of a comparatively rich and technologically superior Christian country trying to dominate an Arab land against substantial local and international opposition, Algeria surely fits the template.

Still, different people will draw different conclusions about the conflict: *The Weekly Standard*'s Irwin Stelzer reports (with great satisfaction) that the lesson George W. Bush has apparently imbibed from Alistair Hornes's book is that France didn't stay long enough!

Of course, the parallel doesn't fit perfectly. France was tied to Algeria through the presence of 1 million European settlers, who saw themselves as French, though they came from throughout the northern tier of the Mediterranean. Prosperous landowners, small industrialists, holders of lower middle-class city jobs, shopkeepers, (a few) manual laborers, the *pied noirs* were united by attachment to a privileged status that French control over Algeria gave them. They had a powerful lobby in Paris, through which they exercised great influence on the appointed colonial government. A local legislature—originally created as a liberalizing reform—was designed with separate wings, one for Europeans and one for Muslims, so that any Algerian democratic initiative would be stillborn. The *pied noirs* secured for themselves the colony's best land and had access to the best jobs. France devoted more resources to schooling the children of the 1 million *pied noirs* than it did to those of 9 million Muslims. The two communities had little social contact and virtually no intermarriage.

The accelerating disparity between the groups' birthrates reached into every aspect of the colony's social system. At the time of the French conquest in 1830, the Muslim population was less than 2 million; it was 9 or 10 million at the outbreak of the insurrection—and growing fast. Any program of real integration between the two communities—one that gave every Algerian an equal right to a European to vote for representatives in Paris—would have led to Muslims becoming a powerful voting bloc in France proper. This was a fact few partisans of French Algeria were willing to face.

In May 1945, the *pied noirs* conceit that Algerian Muslims were content with second-class status was contradicted by a violent Muslim riot: a V-E march in the town of Sétif took on nationalist overtones, the police fired shots, and the Muslim crowd turned on the Europeans. The unrest spread quickly to neighboring towns: 103 Frenchmen were killed, often brutally. In punitive retaliation, the French used dive bombers, naval shelling, and Senegalese troops to destroy several villages, producing a Muslim death toll in the thousands. The Sétif riot and its aftermath passed almost unnoticed in France but set a pattern that would be repeated as the rebellion gathered steam: the Muslims would riot or stage an attack, and the French would answer with massive and relatively indiscriminate reprisals. At the end of each round, nationalist sentiment would grow.

Months after the French defeat at Dien Bien Phu in 1954, the Algerian rebels—the FLN—then numbering fewer than a thousand, launched their first organized attacks, setting off bombs, striking isolated barracks. The ringleaders were young men of modest education, with no real ideological program beyond getting the French out. But they succeeded in igniting a war and capturing the imagination of Algeria's youth, who in the tens of thousands proved willing to kill, suffer, and die for Algerian independence.

France responded as a sophisticated liberal Western power might be expected to. The Fourth Republic's leaders were humanist, temperate democratic socialists, convinced that France's ideals of liberty, combined with increases in economic and technological aid, could surmount the acknowledged evils of colonialism and bind Algeria to France. They sent Jacques Soustelle, an ethnographer first prominent as a left-wing intellectual, later a key organizer of the Resistance and an associate of de Gaulle, to govern the colony. Soustelle was determined to make France's rule enlightened and not reactionary, to break the social and economic monopolies of the *pied noirs*, to make "Algérie Française" something progressive France could be proud of.

Meanwhile, the military set about to clean up the guerrillas in the countryside, and France began to pour in troops. Within a year, most of the initial FLN leadership was killed or captured. But still the rebellion managed to survive. In 1955, a handful of guerrillas incited the Muslims of Philippeville to set upon the town's European majority with knives and axes. In an orgy of violence, the Muslims killed women and children, slitting throats, disemboweling pregnant women. The death toll was 123, including 53 Muslim "collaborators." The French responded in kind, but more widely. The *pied noirs* went on a countrywide rampage, shooting Muslims in the street. American diplomats estimated the death toll of the French retaliation at 20,000.

Philippeville brought a practical end to "integration" as a concept, though it lingered on in French rhetoric. The massacre also brought a quick end to Soustelle's liberalism; at the funeral of one slain Frenchmen, he spoke of revenge and of the "totalitarian fanaticism" of the rebels. He would end his career as a backer of the terrorist far Right trying to hold on to French Algeria at all costs.

Military means could never definitively smother the rebellion, even after France stationed half a million troops in the colony. As a character in Jean Lartéguy's war novel *The Centurions* put it, the guerillas were "like the algae which always comes back in aquariums." Their chief targets were the Muslims who cooperated with the French and the most liberal representatives of the French effort, teachers, and engineers. Killing was not enough. The guerrillas preferred mutilation, severing the noses, lips, and sexual organs of their victims. The purpose was to make the middle ground untenable. "France is at home here," Soustelle had announced to the Algerian Assembly when he arrived at his post. Following Philippeville, this claim sounded ridiculous.

After one battle in which a platoon of French reservists was ambushed and wiped out, the rhetoric escalated as France sought more grandiose justification for a conflict it couldn't face losing. French Resident Minister Robert Lacoste described the war in Algeria as "but one aspect of a gigantic global struggle, where a number of Muslim countries, before collapsing into anarchy, are trying through Hitlerian strategies to install an invasive dictatorship. ... The war we are waging ... is that of the Western world, of civilization, against anarchy, democracy against dictatorship." By the third year of the war, language like this was commonplace among diplomats and intellectual partisans of Algérie Française, who increasingly depicted the conflict as "terror" against "liberty." To justify the sacrifices of the war, much of the French political class essentially talked itself into believing that defeating the rebels in Algeria was a matter of national life and death, which of course made a negotiated withdrawal that much more difficult to contemplate.

The war reached the city of Algiers in the spring of 1956. The FLN recognized that killing French civilians in the capital was worth more, propaganda wise, than killing soldiers in the field. The memorable scenes in Pontecorvo's docudrama tell the story well enough: attractive young Muslim women getting dressed up in Western clothes, flirting with the French soldiers, and placing bombs in the social hangouts of the gilded youth of Algérie Française. After a few months, the city yearned for martial law. Gen. Jacques Massu and a division of paratroopers were put in charge. The paras began torturing. Contrary to liberal conventional wisdom, the torture did its job, and the secret organizations of bomb makers and placers began to give up their secrets. Electrodes to the genitals—"la machine qui fait parler"— was the most effective method.

The paras won the Battle of Algiers. By the fall of 1957, the city was free of violence and would remain so for four years. And the legend of the paras in their colorful regimental berets grew: many Frenchmen would come to see them as their country's most legitimate political force.

But elite metropolitan France—or at least its liberal intellectuals—was not willing to accept torture done in its name. Repugnance at the paras' methods waxed during 1957, inciting an uproar in the Parisian journals.

Then it waned, the mood of indignation proving impossible to sustain. By 1960, an American writer in Paris noted that among the intelligentsia, torture had become a bore—perhaps the worst fate a moral cause could suffer. Nevertheless, the debate lingered. France officially disavowed the methods that seemed necessary to defeat the guerrillas, and mainstream French political opinion began to shift toward finding the costs of staying in Algeria heavier than defeat.

Much as France sought to depict the battle as a decisive conflict between "Western civilization" and "Islamic fanaticism," few elsewhere in the West shared the view. The Eisenhower administration remained publicly understanding toward its ally. Forging NATO and a strong Western Europe were central to its diplomacy. But when the war swelled France's budget deficit, forcing it to seek emergency aid from Washington, Secretary of State John Foster Dulles hinted that withdrawing from Algeria would help matters. The young Sen. John F. Kennedy called openly for Algerian independence in 1957, and the chic French weekly *L'Express* put him on the cover. Americans of both parties feared that if the war dragged on, Communist infiltration of the North African nationalist and independence movements would become inevitable.

It was in this context that the Fourth Republic stumbled. In February 1958, a French air strike along the Tunisian frontier killed scores of civilians, and British and American diplomats offered their "good offices" to calm matters. This was widely seen as a prelude to dreaded American interference, and the army and the *colons* sniffed a "sellout." A mob in Algiers, eventually backed by several key generals, seized the government buildings and put the city under the rule of a Committee of Public Safety. Rumors flew around Paris that the army would take power there too; it was not clear that in a crunch any regiments would defend the Fourth Republic against a military coup.

Charles de Gaulle was well informed of these plots through his own network—perhaps encouraging them while holding himself aloof as an arbiter between the elected government and a rebellious military. In May 1958, he was asked to form a government by Fourth Republic politicians who knew they might otherwise be swept away by a few regiments of angry paratroopers.

He was 67, too old for the job by his own reckoning. Six feet, five inches tall, his regal style was evident in both spoken and written word. His call to national resistance after the 1940 armistice had salvaged France's honor in World War II—he had won a place for France among the war's victors by the force of his own personality more than by France's military contribution to the victory—and his presence in the first postwar liberation government was a critical brake on the ambitions of France's largest organized political force, the Communists. He resigned in 1946, perhaps expecting to be summoned back. By the 1950s, his mystique still lingered, and he maintained a powerful network of devoted followers among the French political class. The first volumes of his memoirs were huge bestsellers; even without his remarkable second act, de Gaulle would have been one of the political giants of the 20th century.

But the key aspect of de Gaulle's return as the first president of the Fifth Republic—about which most of the country was unaware—was that he was prepared from the outset to flout the wishes of the very generals and colonels who had eased his return to power. From 1946 onward, one can see a clear line in de Gaulle's thinking: the era of colonies was finished. It could end sooner or later, gracefully or abruptly. France could retain cultural and economic ties to its ex-colonies or not. But the end of colonial rule was inevitable. And yet de Gaulle allowed many Gaullists who were fierce partisans of Algérie Française to interpret his Delphic utterings as they wished.

Having ascended to power in the slipstream of a *pied noir* riot, within weeks of his investiture in Paris, he visited Algeria. Standing on an Algiers balcony with his commanding general Salan and the hawkish Soustelle, he addressed a crowd very much like the one that set the coup in motion weeks before. Introduced amid oceanic cries "long live Algérie Française," he replied, famously, "Je vous ai compris"—"I have understood you." He would later write that those words, "seemingly spontaneous but in reality carefully calculated," would fire the crowd without committing him to any further action. In the same speech, he spoke of "10 million French citizens of Algeria" who would decide their own destiny. Already he was using a formulation too liberal in its implications for any French politician in power to have uttered before. Then came a nearly heretical reference to the courage of the FLN guerillas. Their struggle, he said, "I personally recognize is courageous ... however cruel and fratricidal." Before the cheering stopped, some in the crowd must have wondered what exactly they were cheering for.

During his first year, de Gaulle set his generals to winning the war. France had by then completed the Morice Line, a complex of electrified fence and minefields that cut off the rebels from their sanctuaries in Tunisia and Morocco. Gen. Maurice Challe, the new commander of the French forces, developed tactics to keep the guerrillas on the run, and France had learned to induce more Algerians to fight alongside its own forces, the so-called *harkis*. By every statistical measure—insurgents killed, weapons captured, *harkis* recruited—the war was being won. All that was remained was for the guerrillas to seek surrender terms.

The army was not only winning, it was highly conscious that its honor was at stake. Soustelle explained it best, in a book published after he had broken with de Gaulle: the French army had made an oath to the Algerians and was bound by it. Every Algerian notable had asked the commanding officer of every village post "Are you leaving or staying?" If the notables refused to help the rebels, would the army protect them from reprisals? The army had always answered, "France remains and will remain," Soustelle wrote. He concluded, "So don't let anyone say that in committing themselves the officers committed only themselves. It was the whole army that made that oath, an oath that no one had the right or power to untie." This powerfully emotive argument was impossible for many French officers to ignore and explains how perilous de Gaulle's process of disentanglement would prove to be.

He began the task the following year. His cabinet was roughly evenly divided. His prime minister, longtime Gaullist Michel Debré, was an Algérie Française hawk. Even his closest ministers could only guess at de Gaulle's own thinking. In September 1959, he spoke of Algerian "self-determination"—a process whereby the Algerian people would choose, through universal suffrage ballot, between independence, which he depicted as "cruel and impoverished," a formal linking to France, or some less binding form of association. The FLN recognized that with these words, de Gaulle had acknowledged the legitimacy of their aim.

From that point forward, de Gaulle's main adversary was the French Right. General Massu, the hero of the Battle of Algiers, denounced de Gaulle as a "man of the Left" in January 1960, and in the next two years, de Gaulle faced down two coup attempts instigated by *pied noirs* allied with high-ranking dissident officers. He could not have squelched both without taking to the airwaves, appealing in a visceral and heartfelt language to the French people on television and to the army's enlisted men, who heard him on transistor radios. Their loyalty, he intoned, was to France, not to their commanders. Both coups were close-run things; both could have easily succeeded, giving France a Franco-style military dictatorship and a slow bleed in Algeria that might have endured for a decade or more.

De Gaulle fashioned a referendum to legitimize the path of negotiations he had embarked upon, and by 1961, the French people overwhelmingly backed "the bill concerning self-determination." He remained utterly, coldly realist: he did not want the Algerians to become part of France any more than the FLN wanted to. (In 1959, he privately remarked that under the full integration with France envisioned by some partisans of Algérie Française, his native village of Colombey-Les-Deux-Eglises would be turned into Colombey-Les-Deux-Mosquées.)

Rhetorically zigging and zagging, conscious always that he needed to maintain a certain baseline of military support to survive in power, de Gaulle moved toward negotiations with the FLN. After the collapse of the second coup attempt in 1961, the army and settler diehards of French Algeria formed their own terrorist organization, the Organisation Armée Secrète (OAS), and set out to assassinate de Gaulle while fomenting as much chaos as possible within Algeria to render the colony ungovernable. To what end? The best they could imagine was that some sort of apartheid solution could be created in Algeria. Some styled themselves a sort of *pied noir* Haganah. The broader strategy was never clear. But such was the rage against de Gaulle, and the number of officers who felt betrayed by him, that the OAS could carry out actions in both France and Algeria for over a year. They barely missed de Gaulle several times, and their terrorist "successes" in Algeria so poisoned the atmosphere that no settlers could remain there after independence. They brought terror to France as well. Jean Paul Sartre survived when a bomb meant for his apartment was placed on the wrong floor. André Malraux, the novelist who was de Gaulle's culture minister, was a target as well, but a plastique intended for him maimed a 4-year-old girl instead. By the end, OAS activities only increased the majority of Frenchmen who just wanted to be done with Algeria.

This Algeria fatigue was a sentiment de Gaulle nurtured, coaxing it along with his rhetoric. Asked at a press conference in 1961 whether the withdrawal of France from Algeria would open the colony to exploitation by the Soviet Union and the United States, he replied, with lofty formality, "I hope they both enjoy themselves there." Or again, at a 1961 press conference, "Algeria costs us, it's the least one can say, dearer than she brings in. ... In sum, decolonization is in our interest, and consequently, our policy."

At the final cabinet meeting, signing off on a negotiated settlement that essentially met all of the FLN demands (including the ceding of the disputed oil and gas rich Sahara), André Malraux declared that the end of the war marked a sort of liberation of France. Debré, overcome with emotion and still a fierce partisan of Algérie Française concurred, "It's a victory over ourselves." De Gaulle concluded, "It was vital to free France from a situation that had brought her so much misfortune." No one in authority had any illusions that the agreements would be airtight in their application or that the new Algeria would be any better than a revolutionary totalitarian regime.

Freed of its colony, France quickly began to modernize its own economy (which grew at an amazing 6.8 percent in 1962 after the armistice). Algeria remained full of French teachers, doctors, and technicians. The French constructed a flattering narrative for themselves: they had "given" Algeria its independence, because they wanted to, thus providing for the world a model for decolonization and modernization.

To the surprise of few, a darkness descended on Algeria. The first victims were the *harkis*, those who had served in the French army. Perhaps as many 100,000 were slaughtered, often with great sadism, being made to swallow their French medals before execution. Then the revolution turned on itself: Ben Bella, the country's first president, spent most of the 1960s in an Algerian prison, as he had spent much of the 1950s in a French one. But France was done with it.

So how could the Algerian war not speak to us? Its example has long resonated in Israel, and many even hoped that Ariel Sharon—a successful military man of the Right—could do what no liberal Israeli leader could accomplish and withdraw Israel from the West Bank.

But now its lessons are dear to America as well, as we search the horizon for a leader who can explain to the country—especially to the military and to the Republican Party—that its destiny doesn't lie in the long-term occupation of Arab lands. The rhetoric that justifies the Iraq War as part of colossal battle against "Islamofascism" could be lifted almost directly from the French colonial intellectual slogans of the 1950s—and is no less self-deluding. To leave Vietnam, America needed a man of the Right, Richard Nixon. Today, when we need our own de Gaulle to achieve a "victory over ourselves," we don't even have a Nixon.

The American Conservative
April 23, 2007

CARTER AT CAMP DAVID: TRIUMPH AND FAILURE

In the midst of the Egyptian revolution, a concerned Benjamin Netanyahu told his cabinet that the 1979 Egyptian–Israeli peace was "the cornerstone of peace and stability, not only between the two countries, but in the entire Middle East as well"—a pronouncement that soon made its way to the front page of *The New York Times*. While the people of Lebanon, Iraq, Gaza, and the West Bank might well wonder how much peace and stability they got from the deal, Camp David did indeed usher in a golden age for Israel, which was freed to pursue aggressive policies without having to worry about the Arab world's largest military.

How did this happen? A strategically-dominant Israel was not a goal of Jimmy Carter and the other Americans who negotiated the Camp David accords. Washington had been frightened by the 1973 war and hurt by the subsequent Arab oil embargo; strategists worried that continued turmoil in the region would allow the Soviet Union to make trouble with the West's energy supplies. In the previous decade, the Beltway consensus held that

Israel should give up the territory it had seized in the 1967 war in return for a comprehensive peace with its neighbors and security guarantees. The Palestinian leadership had been moving steadily toward acceptance of the two-state solution. Washington had sought a resolution of the Palestinian refugee problem, amplified by the Israeli occupation of the West Bank, since Eisenhower's time.

The Camp David Accords are thus a puzzle, because the results—which shaped the Middle East for a generation—were so different from what its American sponsors intended. Unraveling the puzzle reveals the constraints on an American president in dealing with Israel. Indeed, a principal lesson to be drawn from *Power and Principle: Memoirs of the National Security Adviser, 1977–1981*, Zbigniew Brzezinski's memoir of his tenure as Carter's national security adviser, and from his top Middle East aide William Quandt (in *Peace Process: American Diplomacy and the Arab–Israeli Conflict since 1967*) is that the Arabs should disabuse themselves of the idea that the United States will use its leverage over Israel to achieve a just peace.

The Camp David template governed the Mideast for 30 years. The Palestinians were stateless in 1979 and remain so. The Israel lobby displayed the muscle to define the limits of what an American president might plausibly achieve. This happened in an administration whose foreign policy principals believed that resolution of the Palestinian issue was an important strategic and moral interest, under a president who felt a warm personal connection to Anwar Sadat, which he did not feel toward Israel's leaders.

One can see why intelligent people believed that the situation was more fluid. In Brzezinski's account, central administration figures repeatedly broached the idea of breaking openly with Israel, and explaining to the American people their frustration with Israeli intransigence. And yet one senses this was never really a serious option. Israeli Prime Minister Menachem Begin seemed to know this, as Netanyahu and his team do today. In the end, Begin played the administration perfectly—exploiting its yearning for a diplomatic "success," maneuvering toward a separate peace that severed Egypt from the issue of Palestine, giving Israel a free hand to colonize the West Bank, annex the Golan Heights, and launch several wars against Lebanon.

No one can blame the consequences of Camp David on a lack of commitment on the part of Jimmy Carter and his foreign policy team. Secretary of State Cy Vance and Brzezinski differed over how to deal with the Soviet Union, but both believed a comprehensive Middle East settlement, which included a Palestinian homeland, was an American vital interest. Their staffs shared the conviction. The president was wholly on board. A devout Christian, Carter felt some emotional tie to Israel as "the land of the

Bible" and was put off by the disdain some world leaders, such as French President Valéry Giscard d'Estaing, felt towards the Jewish state. But he felt strongly that Palestinians were victims of injustice.

Early in his presidency, in a 1977 March town meeting, Carter said, "There has to be a homeland provided for the Palestinian refugees who have suffered for many, many years." Brzezinski recognized instantly that the comment would set off a political storm and records that, "Vance and I huddled on how best to handle this new development, but we received instructions directly from Air Force One that no elaborations or clarifications were to be issued on the matter." (Almost 30 years to the day after Carter's evocation of Palestinian suffering, Barack Obama, in an Iowa campaign appearance, used the same verb to depict the Palestinian plight. Like Carter, he came under strident attack from Israel's backers. While one could say that some things never change, there was one significant difference. Unlike Carter, Obama did subsequently "clarify" his remarks, claiming he meant that the Palestinians were suffering, because of the failings of their leadership.)

Coming into office, the Carter administration's plan was to prepare the ground for an international conference at Geneva, co-chaired by Washington and the Soviet Union. The administration knew that Israel would resist, but felt such objections could be overcome. Brzezinski records that he told Carter frequently that Israel would require "persuasion," adding "given the centrality of the U.S. pipeline to Israel's survival, most Israelis instinctively would shrink back from overt defiance of the United States, *provided* they were convinced the United States means business." (Italics in original).

But the window during which such persuasion could be attempted was narrow. In a succinct summary of the Israel lobby's strengths, Brzezinski observes, "The nature of American domestic politics was such that the President had the greatest leverage in his first year of office, less so in his second, and so forth. The more time he had for persuasion and for the subsequent progress toward peace to be manifest, the more opportunity he had to act. Friction with Israel made little sense in the third or fourth Presidential years, for such conflict would be adversely reflected in the mass media and in financial support for the Democratic Party."

The administration's chances of using the first year effectively grew slimmer when Israel's Labor Party lost the election to Menachem Begin's Likud-led coalition in May 1977. Washington sensed a looming showdown with the hawkish Begin. Brzezinski pressed for more administration voices speak out on the Middle East, and an initially reluctant Vice President Walter Mondale gave a speech calling for Israeli withdrawal to the lines and preparation of a Palestinian "entity." House Speaker Tip O'Neill told Brzezinski that "if the choice came down between the President and the pro-

Israel lobby, the country would clearly choose the President—but only if the choice was clearly posed." Senator Abraham Ribicoff, a Jewish liberal wary of Begin, passed word through Walter Mondale that Carter needed to stand firm. Cy Vance passed on gossip from veteran Washington insider Sol Linowitz that the Jewish community had reached the conclusion that "if they pressed hard enough, the President will yield." This apparently was the outcome of a meeting Carter had with Jewish leaders, in which he professed his commitment to Israel, while outlining his plans to push Tel Aviv towards a peace settlement.

By August, Carter, according to Brzezinski's diary notes, "indicated his increasing frustration with the Israeli position and his unwillingness to maintain a policy in which, in effect, we are financing their conquests and they simply deny us in an intransigent fashion and generally make a mockery of our advice and preferences. He was extremely tough-minded on this subject and he was echoed by Vance, who suggested that if the Israelis open up a single more settlement ... we should initiate talks with the PLO."

It is one thing to display tough-mindedness in a meeting with people who essentially agree with you. Carter might have survived a showdown with prominent American Jews over Israeli intransigence—we will never know. Certainly, many American Jews considered Begin's stance reckless. But it is hard to imagine any American president, especially a Democrat, with the stomach for such a showdown.

In November 1977, Egyptian president Anwar Sadat, in a dramatic gesture, sought to break the logjam by going to Jerusalem. In his speech to the Knesset, Sadat made it clear that in return for peace, Israel would need to make a full withdrawal, and allow the Palestinians to build a state on the West Bank and Gaza. Perhaps Sadat, whose primary concern was recovery of Egypt's own territory, had already decided he would settle for a separate peace, to settle for less. In the wake of Sadat's Jerusalem speech, Begin came to Washington and Carter pressed him on the Palestinian issue. Begin floated a concept of Palestinian "autonomy"—a vague formula that Brzezinski, sensing it might be pregnant with possibilities, sought to tease out. Autonomy, Brzezinski said, could mean anything from a "Basutoland under Israeli control" to a way station on the path to real statehood.

The spring of 1978 was taken up by a conflict over American arms sales to Jordan and Saudi Arabia, which Israel opposed. Brzezinski wrote, "During this period, all of us were under severe attack from the Jewish lobby, and much time was consumed in meetings and explanations. These were rarely pleasant, even though the top Jewish leaders were more understanding of our need to develop ties with the more moderate Arab states." Brzezinski complained sharply over dinner to Moshe Dayan about Israel's efforts to block the arms sales, offering that the president would win a confrontation, and threatening to go public on Israel's nuclear arsenal. In the end, the arms package, modified with more jets for Israel, did go through.

By the summer, whatever momentum had been generated by Sadat's gesture had evaporated. The Carter team hoped to unveil a proposal bridging previous Egyptian and Israel positions, one that confirmed U.N. Resolution 242 (which called for Israel to withdraw from the conquered territory and the Arabs to make peace with Israel—land for peace) got Israel out of the Sinai and advanced the Palestinians along a road to self-determination. "How are we prepared to deal with an Israeli rejection of our proposal?" Brzezinski asked Carter in a July memo. "Do we have the political strength to manage a prolonged strain in U.S.–Israeli relations? What kind of forces can we marshal and in what manner in order to prevail? These are the central questions, and they touch on both international and domestic sensitivities. Above all, you must decide whether at this stage you are prepared to see this matter through to the very end ... if we go public and then do not prevail, our Middle East policy will be in shambles. If we go 'public,' we must prevail."

Brzezinski's questions were simply too much for the Carter administration—to answer them would require a kind of war gaming about how to neutralize an important part of the American establishment and vital part of the Democratic coalition. In any case, there is no record that the administration ever explored them. Carter's response was to suggest a summit meeting with Begin and Sadat, an historic gathering where Carter himself could overcome the deadlock. Going in, Brzezinski urged the administration to be prepared for failure, to make clear that "refusal to accept our proposals would jeopardize the U.S.–Israeli relationship."

Invitations to Camp David were sent out in August 1978. The 13 days in September were unusual by any standard of diplomacy: three leaders and their national security entourages isolated in a compound in the Maryland hills with no press around. Carter worked like a man possessed, drafting original language for the document and engaging in nearly continuous meetings with Egyptian and Israeli officials in search of mutually acceptable formulations. For diversion, the Americans played a lot of tennis; Brzezinski played two games of chess with Menachem Begin.[1]

---

[1] The Brzezinski–Begin relationship touches on the historically complex relationship between Polish Jewry and Poland's Catholic elites. On Begin's first visit to the United States as prime minister, before a bank of TV cameras, he approached Brzezinski and presented him some documents, found in a Jerusalem archive, bearing on his father's activity as a Polish diplomat in Germany in the 1930s when he was engaged in saving Jewish lives. Brzezinski was "deeply touched by this gesture of human sensitivity, especially since it came in the wake of some of the personal attacks on me and on my role in seeking to promote a peace settlement in the Middle East."

Israel approached the summit with a single goal. Even before Sadat's peace gesture, Tel Aviv's foreign ministry had been working on removing Egypt from the conflict by working out a separate peace. Such a deal was overwhelmingly in Israel's interests—something Begin and the government recognized even as they quibbled over every hilltop and settlement and timetable for implementing the withdrawal. But the haggling served a larger purpose, as Brzezinski aide William Quandt points out in his analysis of Camp David:

> "Begin, more than any of the other negotiators, seemed to have a feel for the strategic use of time, taking the negotiations to the brink of collapse over secondary issues to avoid being pressed on key problems. Sadat, by contrast, simply refused to negotiate over those matters of deepest concern to him—Egyptian land and sovereignty—while leaving to his aides the unhappy task of trying to stand up to Begin on the Palestinian issue. Begin's position was also strengthened by his willingness to accept failure in the talks. Both Sadat and Carter were more committed to a positive outcome, and Begin could credibly use the threat of walking out, as he did, to extract concessions."

At one point late in the negotiations, Sadat, frustrated by Begin's refusal to give any ground on the West Bank, packed his bags and prepared to leave. Carter rushed to the Sadat cabin to explain that his departure would mean the end of the American–Egyptian relationship—that the failure of negotiations would be put on Sadat. It was a revealing moment: despite the fact that Sadat's positions were far closer to the White House's own than Israel's were, when push to came to shove, an American president could threaten Egypt, and did not hesitate to do so. The same was not true for Israel.

Negotiations on the West Bank and Gaza did not come to a head until near the end of the fortnight. Before then, the Israelis persisted in arguing that the war of 1967 gave Israel the right to change frontiers. Begin refused to accept the applicability of U.N. Resolution 242 to the West Bank. As the Israeli set out his vision of the West Bank, outlining all the controls, veto rights, and privileges he would retain for Israel, Carter exploded. "What you want to do is to make the West Bank part of Israel." Vance seconded the president. Brzezinski added, "This is profoundly sad—you really want to retain political control, vetoes, military governor, broad definition of public order. We thought you were willing to grant genuine self-government." Moshe Dayan, ever the diplomat, responded "Professor Brzezinski, we are not after political control. If it looks that way to you, we will look at it again." A breakdown was averted. Carter went back to redrafting, focusing on the idea that the Israeli proposal for home rule would be worked into a five-year transitional period. On the seventh day of the negotiations, the Israelis were still objecting to any drafting that highlighted the words "inadmissibility of acquisition of territory by war." Dayan told Vance that the summit would end in failure, and Carter's intransigence would be blamed.

But on September 16, the eleventh day at Camp David hills, the key compromise, actually an American concession, emerged. According to Bill Quandt's account, it was then that the American draft pertaining to Gaza and the West Bank was fundamentally changed. "The elements of 242, including withdrawal, which had previously been spelled out were deleted. The language was changed to make it clear that the negotiations, but not necessarily the results of the negotiations, would be based on the principles of 242. And the negotiations about the West Bank and Gaza were artfully obfuscated by creating two tracks, one involving peace treaty negotiations between Israel and Jordan and the other involving talks between Israel and representatives of the Palestinians." Quandt concluded, "It may take a lawyer to explain how, but Begin successfully protected his position that 242 did not apply to negotiations over the West Bank's future, the Americans accepted the ambiguity, and Sadat may well have wondered what all the verbal gymnastics were about."

To say the least, the ambiguity does not leap out from a simple reading of the Camp David Accords. The document does indeed make it seem that the West Bank negotiations are premised on 242, and set up a path toward Palestinian self-determination in some form. But unlike the more specific provisions over Israeli withdrawal from the Sinai, there is no explicit promise that the negotiations would actually lead anywhere. At least, Carter thought, he could help secure his preferred outcome by halting the West Bank settlement program that Begin had recently initiated. Carter, so he believed, elicited from Begin a promise to freeze the building of new settlements for the five-year duration of the Palestinian autonomy negotiations.

Carter promptly conveyed to Sadat the oral promise as he shuffled between the cabins of the two men. The Israelis promised him a letter the next day, affirming their promise. But the letter Israel delivered did no such thing. Instead, it linked the settlement freeze to the duration of the Sinai negotiations, which were to be wrapped up in three months. Carter refused to accept the letter, and asked for another one. Quandt writes, "Alarm bells should have gone off, but so many other issues were on the agenda that day, especially a diversionary argument over Jerusalem which erupted in the afternoon, that both Carter and Vance continued to act as if there had merely been a misunderstanding that would be cleared up as soon as Begin sent back a new draft."

The Americans never did receive a letter confirming what Carter believed Begin had promised. But for the wider world (except, significantly, the Arab world), Carter appeared to achieve what he wanted. As the summit ended, Brzezinski briefed the press. "There was an audible gasp when I announced the conditions of the Egyptian–Israeli agreement, particularly the point that the peace treaty would be signed in three months. The newspapermen could hardly believe it. The sense of excitement mounted steadily. As the briefing went on, I had trouble extricating myself.... At ten thirty, the President entered with Sadat and Begin, having landed a few minutes earlier by helicopter. There was thunderous applause as he announced the success."

Less than a week after this triumphant moment, Carter and Brzezinski were worrying openly about what they had wrought. Begin immediately went on a media tour in the U.S., claiming Israel's right to remain in the West Bank indefinitely and to continue building settlements. Brzezinski noted in his journal that Begin "is trying to create the impression that the only accord that really counts is the Israeli–Egyptian agreement. If he can get away with it, he will obtain a separate treaty and then the whole structure of peace in the Middle East will crumble." But get away with it he did. Of course, the peace did not crumble everywhere. Israel flourished. Begin and Ariel Sharon launched a bloody expedition into Lebanon in an effort to wipe out the PLO and Palestinian nationalism once and for all. Israel's occupation of the West Bank was reinforced by hundreds of thousands of colonizing settlers, and their accompanying road and checkpoint network. Muslim extremism, whose bitter fruit was tasted by America on 9/11, began to grow in the dank spaces of the Mubarak dictatorship, the only sort of Egyptian regime that could accept Camp David as guidepost of its regional strategy.

Less than two months after the Camp David framework was completed (but before the final treaty was signed), Carter and his foreign policy team were discussing the cable ambassador to Israel Samuel Lewis, which told of increasingly firm Israeli demands for money and of Israeli stubbornness on the West Bank. Brzezinski records that he raised the question "of whether we should in fact be pushing so hard for an Israeli–Egyptian treaty if it is our intention to resolve also the West Bank issue. Once such a treaty is signed, we will have less leverage." Carter interjected that the Israelis don't want to yield on the West Bank, and Dayan has seized the PR initiative in terms of interpreting the negotiations to the public. Brzezinski writes, "When I said that I thought the Israelis wanted essentially a separate peace, then U.S. payments, and finally a free hand in the West Bank, the President said that my remarks were brutally frank and perhaps oversimplistically stated. When I sarcastically responded 'Thank You,' he looked at me very soberly and said, 'Yes, but I agree with you.'"

But of course, once committed to Camp David, Carter had little choice but to push to see it through. Honesty about the U.S.–Israel relationship was kept behind closed doors. Once the accord was finally signed the following March, Israel did withdraw from the Sinai. Predictably enough, the Palestinian autonomy talks went nowhere. Begin appointed his interior minister Yosef Burg of the National Religious Party to conduct them. Burg believed Israel's right to the West Bank was embedded in scripture. The building of settlements accelerated. Moshe Dayan, who might have held a more forthcoming view of what autonomy for the Palestinians should mean, resigned from the government in protest. By then, the Israeli cabinet was in the settlers' hands. In the midst of the 1980 election campaign, Carter of course did nothing.

To recall this history is to recognize that so long as the Israel lobby is more powerful than the justice lobby, the United States is constitutionally incapable of being an honest broker in the Middle East. This unpalatable fact has asserted itself repeatedly, with Carter, Brzezinski and Vance, with George H.W. Bush and James Baker, and with Presidents Clinton and Obama. If a trend can be observed, it is that the United States has become even less able to stand up to Israel with each passing decade. And yet, looked at from a different perspective, the situation seems as fluid and subject to human agency as ever. If Israel's influence over the American state (witness Obama's repeated capitulations to Netanyahu) now seems decisive, its hold over the American societal imagination is far more tenuous than when Jimmy Carter entered the White House. Knowledge of the crime inflicted upon the people of Palestine may have grown fiftyfold in the past 30 years. At some point , there will have to be a recalibration, as American government begins to reflect these changing values. The tumult in the Arab world in the past month is a reminder, if one is needed, that no injustice need last forever.

Mondoweiss
March 6, 2011

Why I Owed Gore Vidal an Apology

For years now, I've felt a need to apologize to the late Gore Vidal. But a letter would not have sufficed, and I never ran into him, and now, of course, it is too late. I met Vidal once, when I was 25. We were at small cocktail party in Paris—at the apartment of my former stepmother and her beau, an American diplomat. I was trying to make points about the apparent alliance of the French communists and socialists, and Eurocommunism and related subjects—I was then early in the turn away from youthful leftism, a reader of *Dissent* and *The New Leader* and Raymond Aron's columns in *Le Figaro*. Vidal said something to the effect that it was nice that someone had invited "a young rightist" to entertain the party. I laughed while protesting that he was wrong. I was a liberal, my most recent job had been with Jimmy Carter's 1976 campaign. I didn't even know any "rightists." But Vidal had read the signs correctly. I was headed in that direction. Later that year, I would begin reading *Commentary*, and a few years after that, writing for it.

Nearly a decade later, I was married with children, a graduate degree, a job, an identity of sorts as a neoconservative writer, and a new circle of friends and associates, many of them unabashedly conservative. Into my mailbox one day came *Commentary*, my favorite magazine—with its featured essay, "The Hate That Dare Not Speak Its Name." In the elevator going up, I tried to guess who or what Norman Podhoretz was attacking. Within a few moments, the answer was clear: an article by Gore Vidal and left-wing tolerance of his anti-Zionism overflowing into anti-Semitism.

I'm trying to recall what I felt about *Commentary* pieces like this. I remember thinking generally that Israel was a burden, or perhaps a cross, which my Jewish neoconservative friends had to bear. While I often admired their ingenuity and tenacity in defending the Jewish state—rather the way one might admire a mother who gives effective care to a child with special needs—I was glad their burden was not mine. Beyond that, I didn't pay much attention; there were then many other subjects in *Commentary* and in the neoconservative universe to attend to. Perhaps too there was some sense that if I explored the Israel question too deeply, I would be forced to recognize I didn't really agree with the *Commentary* line. And since the *Commentary* line, broadly speaking, served as my connection into an entire sustaining professional and social network, it was an issue best left unexamined.

Anyway, I think I probably skimmed the Podhoretz article without paying it much attention. Stay in your lane is usually good advice, and this subject was outside of mine.

Five years later, I worked at the *New York Post*. I wrote unsigned editorials and a weekly column. I often tried to push at the subject I considered most important at the time—so many of my columns dealt with city politics and the race-and-crime nexus; I and others at the *Post* editorial page then believed that the future of New York's and perhaps American urban civilization hung in the balance.

But one couldn't do this all the time. One Monday evening with a column to write, I noticed a press mention that Gore Vidal was an advisor to Jerry Brown, who was then involved in very competitive primary contest with Bill Clinton. The New York primary was perhaps three weeks away. Clinton was favored, but Brown had won some New England states and had a little momentum. Suddenly, I recognized a subject for a column that could more or less write itself, and I could be home by 9:30 or 10, in time to see my kids and have dinner with my wife.

I'm grateful that 1992 *New York Post* columns are not on the internet, because what was produced is surely embarrassing. A copy of the Podhoretz *Commentary* piece was faxed to our office, and a column adducing that Vidal was the author of a vilely anti-Israel and anti-Semitic screed was duly produced, and questions of what does Jerry Brown think about this were raised. Of course, Vidal was soon summarily dumped from whatever advisory status he had with the Brown campaign. I proceeded on to a round of radio interviews, including a debate with Victor Navasky, who surely had better things to do than go through the Vidal-Podhoretz controversy once again.

My column was more or less solid. Vidal's *Nation* piece attacking the Podhoretz's was inflammatory, seasoned with anti-Semitic tropes. And I do think that it's important, for extremely well-founded moral reasons as well as practical ones, to avoid anti-Semitism in polemical discourse. But it now seems clear there are other factors to be weighed in assessing the Vidal piece. The target of Vidal's ire was plainly not Jews in any general sense, but the Podhoretzes and their loyalties to Israel and the problems such loyalties posed for America. It's not as if, in 1986, there were a whole slew of Tony Judts and M.J. Rosenbergs and Philip Weisses writing about this subject with verve and passion and judiciousness and sensitivity. No leading political scientists had excavated the workings and explored the consequences of *The Israel Lobby*. The subject of the U.S.–Israel relationship, if not taboo, was kept far off the national radar screen.

By writing something over the top, and easily perceived as anti-Semitic, Vidal had fired an illumination flare at a subject that richly deserved his readers' notice. How then to balance the torts in this case: accusing the Podhoretzes of not being real Americans because of their ties to Israel is reprehensible, but so too are Israel's policies of occupation and ethnic cleansing. The Podhoretzes use of their considerable talents and cultural influence to defend these policies—and, more, to render debate about them out of bounds—is reprehensible as well.

In any case, Jerry Brown lost the New York primary and was deprived of Gore Vidal's strategic advice. I had the lesson reinforced that it is seldom a bad career move for someone with an "Mc" in his surname to accuse someone of anti-Semitism, especially if there's any basis for the charge. If Vidal deserved no credit for the tone of his polemic, he clearly does for its foresight, especially the insight that Israel's belligerence, then seemingly a secondary or even tertiary factor in the determination of American foreign policy, would begin to weigh more heavily so long as we remained so closely tied to the country. Today, this seems almost beyond dispute. In any case, had I the chance, I would have told Vidal that my column was written out of conviction and at the time quite genuine affection for the Podhoretzes, but also some laziness and at least some subconscious sense that it would please those with a chance to favor my career. And for that I was sorry. I would tell him also that his piece, while still over the top, at least worked toward some important truths.

The American Conservative
August 6, 2012

Russia, Ukraine, and the New Cold War

One of the greatest failures of the Obama administration was its mismanagement of our relationship with Russia. Perhaps my greatest surprise in the past several years was how quickly the Washington establishment fell in line behind some variant of a new Cold War, hastening to ramp up belligerence toward Russia over the Ukraine crisis, a region where the United States had no real national interests at stake, and knew almost nothing about.

My own knowledge of Ukraine was slight as well, but I had learned quite recently one salient fact about the situation through a Ukrainian au pair who lived with us in Washington for a year—in 2010-2011—to help us care for our granddaughter. That is, that Ukraine was anything but a united country: our au pair, a nice and reasonable young woman in most respects, refused to socialize, or have anything to do with, those of her compatriots she regarded as "Russian"— that is, Russian-speaking (as a first language) Ukrainians from the eastern part of Ukraine. That was enough for me to conclude that the United States should risk very little, and certainly not a new Cold War, over the idea of a "unified" Ukraine, especially one under a fiercely anti-Russian government that came to power in a coup d'état.

It was a bit surprising that Obama would allow American policy to become so committed to fomenting an anti-Russian coup in Ukraine. Was there no one in the administration who perceived any downside to leaving an aggressive neoconservative, Victoria Nuland, in charge of the State Department's European policy? In any case, when the crisis erupted, I wrote several short pieces trying to remind Americans how the crisis might look from Russia's perspective, an exercise which ought always to be part of foreign policy considerations. I revisited the expansion of NATO debates of the 1990s, finding, not surprisingly, that the conservatives who skeptical about expanding NATO were often the same ones who thought invading Iraq was a crazy idea.

NATO's Wrong Turn

A rapidly congealing Beltway consensus seems to be forming around the idea of a new Cold War. The anti-Russia sentiment is partially rooted in the particulars of the Ukraine crisis, which flowed from the West-backed insurrection in Maidan that overthrew a democratically elected—if terminally corrupt—Ukrainian leader and replaced him with an unelected nationalist anti-Russian regime. These events sparked a predictable Russian countermove, Russia's taking back of (mostly ethnically Russian) Crimea with troops. In cascading fashion, this has descended upon an American political establishment that has responded as if it had been subconsciously yearning for a "bipartisan" and "unifying" mission of the sort the Cold War once provided. If initial poll numbers showed that few Americans had much of an interest in making a big fuss over Ukraine, or Crimea, the media and the politicians have been rapidly coalescing to change that. For the first time since 2004 or so, neoconservative commentators have the initiative in the opinion columns: they propose tough measures (NATO membership for Ukraine is now being bandied about, along with various military moves) as liberals emit me-too bleeps in a political pattern all too evocative of the fateful months preceding the Iraq War. Within several weeks, the new elite consensus will undoubtedly be able to point to poll numbers in favor of getting tough with Russia over an issue that few people had opinions about six months ago.

The Ukraine crisis is of course interesting and complicated in its own right (for instance, who commanded the snipers who fired on both police and demonstrators at Maidan, escalating the confrontation and upending the diplomatic arrangement reached days earlier?), but it is a subset of the larger question about Russia and NATO expansion at the end of the Cold War. This was debated in the mid 1990s in forums largely limited to foreign policy specialists. (I worked at the middlebrow *New York Post*'s editorial page during most of those years, and don't recall drafting a single editorial on NATO expansion from 1992 to 1996.) Yet the debate, which once was barely noticed beyond the specialist journals, now looms as critically important. And, if the current confrontation does lead to World War III, as one Ukrainian general has predicted, it will be clear that decisions taken quietly in the 1990s lit the fuse.

The collapse of the Soviet empire in 1989 to 1991 came so quickly that no one was prepared for it. The Soviet Union first lost its Eastern European empire, then collapsed into itself. Considering that the Cold War was the central fault line of world politics, and one with stakes such that a civilization-destroying nuclear war was at some level contemplated and planned for every day, this was a kind of political miracle. As Owen Harries put it in one of the most important essays of the 1990s:

> The Soviet regime, steeped in blood and obsessed with total control as it had been throughout most of its history, voluntarily gave up its Warsaw Pact empire, collapsed the Soviet system upon itself, and then acquiesced in its own demise—all with virtually no violence. This extraordinary sequence of events was by no means inevitable. Had it so chosen, the regime could have resisted the forces of change as it had on previous occasions, thus either extending its life, perhaps for decades more, or going down in a welter of blood and destruction. That, indeed, would have been more normal behavior, for as the English scholar Martin Wight once observed, "Great power status is lost, as it is won, by violence. A Great Power does not die in its bed." What occurred in the case of the Soviet Union was very much the exception.

Why did the Soviet Union choose to die peacefully? A large part of the answer was the understanding, explicit according to some but never formally codified, that the West would not take strategic advantage of Moscow's retreat. Had Moscow envisioned that the West would expand NATO to its doorstep, the Warsaw Pact and Soviet Union would probably not have expired peacefully. As Harries puts it, the bargain, whether implicit or explicit, made a great deal of sense for the United States:

> For, after all, its avowed objective was not the eastward extension of its own power and influence in Europe, but the restoration of the independence of the countries of the region. In effect, the bargain gave the United States everything it wanted (more, in fact, for the breakup of the Soviet Union had never been a Cold War objective), and in return required it only to refrain from doing what it had never expressed any intention of doing.

The critical complicating factor, at the time, was the fate of Germany, Europe's largest power and the source of most of its twentieth-century conflict: could Germany be reunited, as part of NATO? Evidently, yes. As Adam Garfinkle noted, in a valuable 1996 analysis of the NATO expansion debate:

> If it had been proposed to you in 1989 that the Warsaw Pact and the Soviet Union both would come peaceably to an end, that Germany would be reunited in NATO, and that all Russian military forces would withdraw behind their own frontier—and that all that was asked in return was that NATO not take advantage of this retreat by moving eastward—would you have accepted? Extraordinary as it would have sounded then, had it been put so succinctly and all in one breath, this is more or less what was in fact proposed in the "two-plus-

four" agreement for the reunification of Germany, and later accepted as the Warsaw Pact collapsed.

As the process proceeded, guided by the United States, Russia was told quite explicitly that the Western idea was not to move NATO up to its borders. Why did Russia not insist on a formal treaty to that effect? Obviously it was not in a position to do so—during the dynamics of the time, Russia was imploding and no more able to insist upon terms than the Bolsheviks were at Brest-Litovsk. But importantly, there also seemed to be no need as everyone, Russians and Americans and key NATO nations alike, were on the same page. As Sergei Karaganov, a leading Russian foreign affairs analyst who subsequently became an advisor to Putin, put it:

> In 1990, we were told quite clearly by the West that dissolution of the Warsaw Pact and German unification would not lead to NATO expansion. We did not demand written guarantees, because in the euphoric atmosphere of that time it would have seemed almost indecent, like two girlfriends giving written promises not to seduce each other's husbands.

Of course, the euphoria didn't last. Rapid liberalization proved deadly to the Russian economy and standard of living in the 1990s, and Putin came to power determined to put a stop to what was widely perceived as an anarchic period of Russian weakness. And the more versatile and powerful girlfriend did indeed seduce, first Poland, Hungary, and the Czech Republic, and has since pushed further into nations and regions that are perceived, by Russians, to be literally part of historic Russia. In his essay of 1997, Owen Harries described the NATO expansion decision as "ominous"—for the United States had decided to project American power into a highly sensitive region.

The expansionist victory came partly through the forces of bureaucratic inertia—NATO has many layers of vested constituencies, which needed new rationales to justify their salaries and continued existence. It was partially due to domestic American politics—Clinton in 1996 made his initial NATO-expansion speeches at campaign events crafted to appeal to Polish and East European voters. And it was partially due to a desire by traditional hawks, neoconservative and others, to continue a version of the Cold War, perhaps by sparking a "democratic crusade" in Eastern Europe. There was also a moral case—we would finally "do right" by those East Europeans twice abandoned—so the conventional narrative ran—first at Munich and then again at Yalta.

Another who perceived this choice to be woefully misguided was the 94-year-old George F. Kennan, the American strategist who had designed the doctrine of "containment" in the early Cold War. In a 1997 *New York Times* op-ed, Kennan suggested that expanding NATO would be "the most fateful error" of American foreign policy in the post-Cold War era, which could be expected to "inflame the nationalistic, anti-Western and militaristic tendencies in Russian opinion; to have an adverse effect on the development of Russian democracy ... and to impel Russian foreign policy in directions decidedly not to our liking." Kennan was perhaps overly prescient, for Russia's negative reaction did not emerge immediately. Moscow, faced with a more immediate and deadly Chechen insurgency, seemed too distracted to focus on NATO; it would take half a generation before NATO expansion became an obviously sensitive issue. In 1998, the Senate would go on to vote for NATO enlargement by a margin of eighty-nineteen. One of the nineteen, Daniel Patrick Moynihan, inserted Kennan's op-ed into the Congressional record, along with a laudatory letter Kennan had sent to Owen Harries and Harries' own piece.

Another participant in the 1990s debate was Rodric Braithwaite, Britain's former ambassador to Moscow. His *Prospect* essay from 1997 asked which path is better for victors after a war: the models of 1815, when a defeated France was brought into the "concert of Europe," and 1945, when Germany, or much of it, was integrated into the Western system; or Versailles, where after World War I a defeated Germany was humiliated and made to pay. It is clear that the first George Bush, in the early 1990s, was thinking along 1815 and 1945 lines. But incrementally his policy was reversed by his successors, first by the Clinton-Albright duo, and then by his son, and now by Obama, the latter prodded by his belligerent Assistant Secretary of State Victoria Nuland.

Of course, it is not really possible that Russia will respond to its Versailles the way Germany did, remilitarizing and for a time dominating its adversaries. It is almost certainly too weak for that. But it can begin to act irresponsibly in global affairs, perhaps most menacingly on nuclear proliferation. It is a state with many weapons and many nuclear scientists. Russia can also re-forge its strategic links to China. Of course, unlike during the 1950s, an anti-Western Moscow would be the junior partner in a Beijing-Moscow alliance. But it's still a combination the United States should not be working to bring about.

The American Conservative
March 28, 2014

WASHINGTON PUZZLED AS PUTIN DOESN'T BACK DOWN

Consider an analogy to get a sense of how Russia might perceive America's Ukraine policy. It is imperfect of course, because unlike Russia,

America has no history of being invaded, unless you count the War of 1812. But a comparison might be instructive nonetheless:

By 2034, China's power position has risen relative to America's. America has evacuated its East Asian bases, under peaceful but pressured circumstances. The governments of Korea and Japan and eventually the Philippines had, by 2026, concluded it was better off with a "less provocative" more neutral arrangement. The huge naval base at Subic Bay became home to a multilateral U.N. contingent. China's economy had been larger than America's for a while, though American per capita income is still somewhat higher. American technological innovation edge has largely disappeared, America still has a lot of soft power—people over the world prefer Hollywood movies to Chinese and America's nuclear arsenal exceeds the Chinese. But the countries are far more equal than today, and throughout much of the world it is assumed that China will be tomorrow's dominant "hyperpower."

A political crisis erupts in Mexico. Mexico has a freely elected but typically corrupt government, whose leading figures are linked to Wall Street and Miami Beach by ties of marriage and money. But many in Mexico—where anti-gringo nationalism remains a potent force—want to become the first "North American partner" in the China led Greater East Asian Co-Prosperity Sphere. Young Mexicans proclaim defiantly they are "people of color" and laud the fact non-white China is rising while America, country of aging white people, is in decline. Their sentiments, materialistic and infused with personal ambitions are so permeated with anti-American, anti-imperialist Third Worldist rhetoric that it is difficult for outsiders to sort out the true motivations. When the Mexican government, under American pressure, rejects a Chinese invitation for candidate membership in China's East Asian Co-Prosperity Sphere, long prepared protests erupt in Mexico City.

The core group of protest leaders and organizers have been on the Chinese payroll for some time, as the heads of various civic action and popular democracy initiatives, many with an obvious anti-gringo flavor. Soon Chinese politicians and movie stars begin flocking to Mexico City to be photographed with the protesters. Thus encouraged, protester demands escalate, including not only the resignation of the government, Mexico's adhesion to the Chinese economic bloc, but a military alliance with China. The NSA captures a cell phone conversation of the Chinese ambassador discussing who will hold what posts in the next Mexican cabinet. Three days later, sniper fire of undetermined origin riddles the protestors and police, and any semblance of order breaks down. Mexico's president flees to Miami.

The above scenario parallels pretty directly the run-up to the Ukraine crisis, before Russia began to respond forcefully. One can of course see the ambiguities of right and wrong. Why should America have anything to say about whether Mexico has a revolution and joins an anti-American military alliance, some would ask. Mexico is sovereign, and should be able to join any international grouping it wants.

What is most striking about the Ukraine crisis is how much the Washington debate lacks any sense of how the issue might look to other interested parties, particularly Russia. Putin is analyzed of course—is he, as Hillary Clinton suggested, following Hitler's playbook? Or is he merely an aggressive autocrat? Or perhaps he is "in his own world" and not quite sane? But in open Washington conversation at least, and perhaps even at the more reflective levels of government, all talk begins with the premise that Russia's leader is somewhere on the continuum between aggressive and the irrational. That he might be acting reactively and defensively, as any leader of a large power would be in response to threatening events on its doorstep, is not even part of the American conversation. Thus in the waning days of American unipolarism, America diplomacy sinks into a mode of semi-autism, able to perceive and express its own interests, perceptions, and desires, while oblivious to the concerns of others.

A rare and welcome exception to blindness was the publication in Foreign Affairs of John Mearsheimer's cogent essay on the Ukraine crisis, which with characteristic directness argues that Western efforts to move Ukraine in the NATO/EE orbit were the "taproot" of the present crisis. Prior to Mearsheimer, one could find analyses tracing how various neoliberal and neoconservative foundations had, with their spending and sponsorship of various "pro-Western" groups, fomented a revolution in Ukraine, but they were generally sequestered in left-liberal venues habitually critical of American and Western policies. In the Beltway power loop, such voices were never heard. The policy of pushing NATO eastward, first incorporating Poland and Bulgaria and then going right up to Russia's borders moved forward as if on mysterious autopilot. That such a policy was wise and necessary was considered a given when it was discussed at all, which was seldom. Was Obama even aware that a leading neoconservative, a figure from Dick Cheney's staff, was in charge formulating American policy towards Ukraine—with designs on igniting revolutionary regional transformation? One has to assume not; confrontation with Russia had not been part of Obama's presidential campaign or style, and since the crisis began his comments have always been more measured than the actions of the government he purportedly leads.

As Mearsheimer points out, there remains still a fairly obvious and quite attractive off-ramp: a negotiation with Russia that settles formally Ukraine's non-aligned status. There are useful precedents for this: Eisenhower's negotiation with Khrushchev that brought about the withdrawal of foreign troops from Austria in 1955 is one, and so of course is Finland. No one who contemplates where the Ukraine crisis might lead otherwise—with a war that devastates the country or perhaps brings in outside powers to devastate all of Europe, or even explodes the entire northern hemisphere—could sanely consider Austria or Finland—prosperous and free countries—to be bad outcomes. Nevertheless, the entire conversation in Washington revolves around measures to make Putin back down, and accept the integration of Ukraine into the EU and eventually NATO. People act baffled that he won't.

There is a mystery to the way Washington works—how an entire political class came to see as American policy that that Russia be humiliated at its own doorstep as logical without ever reflecting upon whether this was a good idea in the larger scheme of global politics nor whether the West had the means and will to see it through. Because to see it through likely means war with Russia over Ukraine. (The West-leaning Ukrainians, of course, be they democratic or fascist, want nothing more than to have American troops fighting beside them as they become NATO partners, a tail wagging the dog). America's policy makes sense only if it is taken for granted that Russia is an eternal enemy, an evil power that must be surrounded weakened and ultimately brought down. But very few in Washington believe that either, and virtually no one in the American corporate establishment does. So it's a mystery—a seemingly iron-clad Washington consensus formed behind a policy, the integration of Ukraine in the West, to whose implications no one seems to have given any serious thought.

Russia's leaders and diplomats have been telling America to butt out of Ukraine in unambiguous terms for a decade or more. Did American diplomats and CIA agents push for an anti-Russian coup d'état in Kiev knowing that and pursue it anyway? The sheer recklessness of such an action would border on criminal—but oddly enough, no one who truly counts in Washington, Republican or Democrat, seems even to consider it even slightly misguided.

The American Conservative
September 4, 2014

The American Dilemma

In the 1980s and 1990s, at the New York Post and occasionally for Commentary, I wrote quite a bit about "urban" issues, the ever controversial nexus of politics, race, and crime. When the crime rate keeps going up, few issues seem more important. But when the crime rate recedes, as it began to do noticeably in the mid-1990s, those issues recede. Unfortunately, we may now be witnessing one of those turnabouts in the national conversation: the Black Lives Matter movement, which spotlights, and greatly exaggerates, police brutality, and shocking spikes in the crime rate in many cities. I've written little about this for TAC or elsewhere, and hate the idea that race and crime are going to become critical subjects again. But all the signs are there. Below are a few commentaries addressing what seem to be prodomal signals of a new era: a warning to some allies who care about Palestine's freedom that aligning themselves with Michael Brown and the more outlandish claims of Black Lives Matter would alienate many Americans; a piece noting the visceral hostility toward average white males expressed by many vanguard figures of the cultural left; an appreciation of Heather Mac Donald's intrepid work calling attention to the apparent upsurge in crime. Are new battles about race and identity politics on the horizon for the United States? Alas, it would seem so.

Ferguson Is Not Palestine

In the morning e-mail came something from the activist group CODEPINK, headlined "From Ferguson to Palestine, Come Out to Join Us." Listed were various events: a vigil for Michael Brown at the Justice Department, a meeting of "fighters for social justice" at a popular Washington cafe the following evening, similar events in that vein. Also on the list was a talk by professor Richard Falk, formerly U.N. special rapporteur on Palestine, to discuss Israel's latest land grab around Jerusalem.

CODEPINK is not alone in seeking to connect Ferguson to Palestine: pro-footballer Reggie Bush tweeted something about it over the weekend, and Annie Robbins of the important *Mondoweiss* website publicized the Bush tweet. Then there's this: a post by a board member of the right-wing Zionist group StandWithUs, connecting anti-Palestinian Israelis with the Ferguson police, both holding the line of civilization against peoples full of rage and an unjustified sense of their own victimhood. There was some Twitter pushback against the StandWithUs post, and *The Times of Israel* eventually removed it. The pro-Palestinian website Electronic Intifada portrayed this as some sort a victory, rather as if the Palestinians had won the right to possess Ferguson as "their" symbol. Rania Khalek writes that, "Zionist organizations are rattled by the growing displays of solidarity between people in Ferguson, Missouri, and Palestine." While it's true that such displays are growing, I doubt seriously that any Zionist organizations are rattled by them. If they have any political savvy, and they surely do, they would instead welcome it—as did the StandWithUs board member.

Why? Well, for starters, Palestine really is occupied, and Palestinians in the West Bank and Gaza have no political and civil rights, and those who reside in Israel proper are now being told that Israel can take away their citizenship at any time.

Ferguson, by contrast, is a complicated situation. The one simple thing about it is the fact that if Michael Brown hadn't leaned into a police cruiser in order to assault a police officer and to try to seize his gun, he would be alive today. As always, there is a broader social and historical context: a considerable amount of police brutality directed at blacks, exemplified by episodes like this, on top of many layers of American history in which blacks were enslaved, and after emancipation, subject to fierce legal and customary discrimination. I largely agree with John McWhorter, who asserts that throughout America there are large segments of the black community who consider the police morally bankrupt, and that this is a huge national problem. It is certainly a problem with no easy answer. There wasn't one in the 1960s when finding a decent, family-sustaining job was achievable for most people willing to work regular hours, and it is no easier now in an economy far, far more geared to rewarding the very rich, highly skilled, or very talented, while the working class has lost ground steadily for forty years.

The thing about Palestine, however, is that it is actually not that complicated. Resolving the issue in a fair and practical way is of course difficult. But it has long been an article of faith among pro-Palestinian activists that if Americans could see the land-grabbing, see the checkpoints Palestinians are subjected to, see the difficulty of trying as a student to commute through roadblocks and checkpoints to Bethlehem University from Ramallah, they would understand that Palestinians are subject to a blatantly unjust and racist regime, facing conditions no American would put up with for a moment without resisting. And they would see that this Israeli regime—heavily subsidized by American tax dollars—is animated by ideologies sharply at odds with American values, at least with how those values have evolved over the past fifty to a hundred years. Perhaps Israel's treatment of the Palestinians resembles South Africa under apartheid, perhaps it resembles the American South of the pre-civil rights era; perhaps it is worse than both. It does not, in any way, shape, or form, resemble Ferguson, Missouri, where all American-born blacks possess the same constitutional and civil rights as white Americans.

To the extent that the American Left succeeds in creating an impression of some sort of rhetorical and moral equivalence between Ferguson and Palestine, describing both venues as places where a virtuous, oppressed people confronts brutal and murderous white racism, they will harm the prospects of Palestinian struggles ever being considered sympathetically by a critical majority of Americans. For the fact is, the more Americans learn about Ferguson, the less sympathy Michael Brown and his cause receives. The young man surely should not have been shot to death—Officer Darren Wilson probably blundered in a dangerous and chaotic situation. But to hold Brown blameless is something that most Americans won't do.

Before the grand jury decision was announced, a Huffington Post/ YouGov poll indicated that only 22 percent of whites thought that Officer Wilson was culpable, versus 64 percent of blacks. After the release of the grand jury report, after Ferguson residents showed their displeasure by widespread looting and burning, after mainstream news showed the Brown family lawyer getting decimated in on-air debates about the facts in the case, after Michael Brown's stepfather mounted a podium to tell Ferguson residents to "burn the bitch down," the poll numbers are not going to shift more in favor of the racist whites versus innocent blacks narrative. That the United States is so divided racially, on this issue and others, is, of course a national problem. But it is surely not one that Palestinian activists should seek to exploit by linking their cause to the losing side.

In all of this, of course, are echoes of the American 1960s. The activism of that decade began with a movement of civil rights activists, white and black, risking their lives to secure for blacks in the South their fundamental constitutional rights. It expanded with opposition to the Vietnam war. It reached a crisis point when liberalism, the dominant ideology of the age, had to confront the reality of black rioting in northern cities, demonstrating how complex the racial issue was, how difficult it would be resolve it. Part of the Left soon embraced the idea that any black demand, any black behavior, was justified. Some New Left theorists advanced the notion that ghetto blacks were a revolutionary vanguard in the mother country. "Off the Pigs, Power to the People" did, really, become a New Left slogan. ("Pigs" was the common epithet for police officers. "Off" meant kill.) Black Panther chic advanced to the salons of the Upper East Side. It wasn't especially obvious to everyone at the time, but these were sign posts that the movement had imploded, had driven itself mad, and was so committed to hating "whitey" that it was on the road to becoming essentially irrelevant to any serious politics in America.

There are more than a few whiffs of that era in the current Michael Brown madness. Most Palestinian activists realize that if they could win for their people in historic Palestine the rights possessed by each and every black citizen of Ferguson they would have gained a victory of world-historic proportions. Nevertheless, one can understand the temptation of connecting to a movement in America that does at this moment seem energetic and hip, which seems to be treated with enormous deference and respect in the dominant media, and which must seem for all the world like an unstoppable emergent groundswell. Added to this is the important if seldom-noted fact that black members of Congress have, on average, been far more ready than their white colleagues to see the need for justice in Palestine, and have been more willing to question and challenge the self-righteousness behind America's blind and often murderous policies in the Mideast. The connections emerging from those sentiments should, of course, be welcomed and nurtured.

Ferguson, however, is a bridge too far. Nothing could please the Likud coalition more than to see the Palestinian cause linked, in the minds of the average, mainstream American, to that of the Ferguson rioters. For the pro-Palestinian Left to work to reinforce exactly that linkage will be seen as dreadful mistake, for which Palestinians will surely pay a higher price than American Leftists will.

The American Conservative
December 3, 2014

Abandoned by the Left

One reason for the continued vital role for *TAC* is that the left makes itself so difficult to identify with. Here is a personal example: white male, late middle age, Christian background, Obama supporter (volunteered in both campaigns) believes that major problems facing this country and the world are global warming, accelerating inequality, the outsourcing and general drying up of middle class jobs. Opposed the Iraq War from the moment the neocons began to push for it (September 12, 2001?); opposes the militarized war-as-first-or-second-resort mindset so dominant within the Beltway;

supports Obama's effort to explore detente with Iran. Supports a reduction in defense expenditures—the savings could be spent on infrastructure, debt reduction, education, health care subsidies. Pretty much a portrait of a 100 percent liberal Democrat, no?

Yet a person like this encounters at every step prominent purveyors of the dominant liberal narratives who spare no effort to repel him. If our would-be liberal is, as mentioned, white, Christian by background, male, he may know that he, or his male children, are intended as the indirect targets of public shaming by Lena Dunham, the newly anointed "voice of her [millennial] generation." Dunham writes in her highly praised best-selling memoir that she was sexually assaulted by a conservative Republican named "Barry" at her private college.

The account of the assault isn't, I don't believe, central to the book; it seems to be thrown in like a ketchup pack with the burger takeout. Of course she was sexually assaulted. Aren't most coeds? Isn't that what conservative Republicans do? As it happened, there was a guy at her college named Barry who fit Dunham's description, and he and his lawyer have gotten together, to, I hope, sue the author and her publisher for libel. But the very casualness of Dunham's lie is telling—the rape accusation is put forth unthinkingly, as if it is simply expected by her intended readership. She couldn't bother to take the time to invent some details to avoid a potential lawsuit. One begins to get the idea that for the liberal cultural elite, it is natural to lie about campus Republican rapists. Haven't Obama and Biden both said that 20 percent of women on campus are raped by white Republicans? Or by white somebodies? Well, there is an actual statistic of one-half of 1 percent of women raped or sexually assaulted annually, or roughly one-tenth the rate claimed by Biden and the president. Far too many of course. But why bother with accuracy when the point is to defame an entire group, and no one will challenge the defamation?

Dunham's book was only an amuse-bouche for the season's hammer blow against white male "rape culture." Sabrina Rubin Erdely's eviscerating (but as it turns out, largely fanciful) indictment of the University of Virginia, centered on the brutal gang rape of a coed named Jackie. Rolling Stone, which published the mis-reported piece, has acknowledged its error, though there is underway a widespread effort to turn the fiasco into a journalism school how-to tale about how many voicemails a prudent reporter must leave in an effort to contact the accused. If you read the piece, you may not have noticed the details that didn't make sense or hang together, but cannot fail to recognize who the bad people are. Erdely had earlier considered basing her "rape culture" narrative on events at other colleges, but chose instead to do her "reporting" at a place where the perpetrators could be unambiguously presented as white Christian males—a group which would likely be underrepresented at any other prestige college. So amidst the misreporting, there were many hate-signifiers—"the toned, tanned, overwhelmingly blonde" members of the UVA student body, the "genteel" aura of the college, which reeks of "old money" and "privilege," a place where "social status is paramount." The students, Erdely claims, all admire Thomas Jefferson, even to the degree of calling him by the familiar "TJ": where else but in the epicenter of gang-rape culture would an American founding father be so revered?

The centerpiece of the piece was, it turns out, a lie—there was a Jackie, but she never was raped. But there is a truth that can be extracted: Sarah Rubin Erdely, who took the trouble to misreport the piece, really really despises the type of people whom she feels predominate at the University of Virginia, and *Rolling Stone* was very happy to give her its not-unimportant platform. And squadrons of Democratic bloggers—I'm waiting for someone to compile a list—were eager to publicize and amplify the group libel.

Of course, the enemy is not only white male "rape culture." It's also the police, with their unrelenting murderous targeting of innocent black men. It seemed as if an unconscious wave swept through the major media in August, reporting on the major international event going on at the time was no longer enjoyable. There was a minor police blotter item, a young black man committed a robbery, got in a fight with a cop, and got shot. But Jake Tapper & Co. arrive on the scene with camera crews, and all the world is presented with Ferguson, Missouri, as Selma, Alabama. The story eventually becomes twinned with another, in New York, when an ostensibly amiable black man with asthma is told by the cops to stop selling loose cigarettes, refuses to do so and is taken down, stops breathing and dies. Nobody who saw that Eric Garner video thinks this guy should be dead, including most emphatically the cops who tried to arrest him. There are two main prisms through which to view the tragedy: a) the difficulty of making arrests of suspects who are noncompliant and have serious health problems, or b) racist white cops intent on murdering innocent black men. Which version comes closest to the truth? Which version is the one embraced by the Democratic media, and hammered at us twenty-four hours a day?

And make no mistake, the target is white police officers. In the '60s, the loony left called them pigs, and advocated their murder. I once believed those days would never return, but in the day of outrage that took place over the weekend, one could see photos of demonstrators recreating the pig meme with masks and other accessories. The left's dehumanization of the white police officer has a broader cultural significance; the police of course are men and women with jobs to do, but more broadly represent law and order: when they are repeatedly vilified by dishonest claims that they are waging "war" on black males, it means something far more serious than a desire for precisely calibrated policing is intended.

In recent days, two important essays have been published analyzing the disconnect between the Democrats and the white working class—a disconnect which may have fatal consequences for the Democrats in the coming years. In the *Times*, Thomas Edsall systematically goes through the sources of the erosion of white working class life in America: the collapse of the industrial job market is the main thing, but was surely exacerbated by the simultaneous Democratic party effort to aid and empower other previously disenfranchised and impoverished groups—except white working class males. The fact remains that no group in America is on a steeper downward trajectory economically—not blacks, not Hispanics, not women. Edsall cites a slew of comparative polls of whites and blacks demonstrating both greater improvement of black income from generation to generation and greater optimism about the future. There is, literally, no program put forth by any major party to do anything about the collapse in white working class incomes.

A more pointed statement comes from the international affairs blogger John Schindler, a former Naval War College professor whose views about Russia I mostly disagree with. But Schindler describes powerfully his sense of political homelessness, with which I can very much identify. About the Democrats, he writes:

> I worry deeply about rising inequality in America, which has been growing my whole life and shows no signs of abating, rather the contrary. It is making the country something very different from what it was for several happy generations. Accepting that mass prosperity, which peaked in the middle of the last century, making us the envy of the world, is gone for good will change American politics in ways that we can only yet see in outline. We cannot stop globalization and technological changes that promise to up-end the economy, nor should we try to, but wise and compassionate politicians will seek to soften their impacts on fellow citizens.

> The obvious home for socio-economic reform, the Democrats, once the proud party of working people like many of my forebears, has lost its way. Its emphasis on identity politics at the expense of basic socioeconomic fairness has driven away countless average people who are struggling and want justice, yet don't like being lectured endlessly about how racist, sexist, and cisnormative they are.

Schindler gives good *TAC*-ish reasons for skepticism about the Republicans: free-market absolutism and the neoconservative foreign policy adventurism are now deeply embedded in the GOP. But the essay closes with a pointed warning about complacency—we tend to think the continued, unrelenting immiseration of the working class, combined with exploitation of every identity politics issue to shame and humiliate a selected target group can't possibly have bad consequences. He continues:

> Moreover, having spent quite a bit of time in the Balkans, I have an acute sense of how fragile civilization really is. Beneath the pleasant surface there lurk monsters, and those monsters are us. In a few short years, Yugoslavia went from being a success story, a benign socialist regime with a high standard of living and apparent amity among its photogenically diverse peoples, to a charnel house of terror. Economic decline and ethnic resentments, combined in evil fashion, led to war and genocide. It's nice to pretend this can't happen, but history shows plainly that it can. After all, American optimists in the 1850s, the TV talking heads of the day, considered the Civil War that was looming ominously to be impossible—right until cannons roared at Fort Sumter.

Schindler is on to something here, something few have acknowledged. The current trends in America, Wall Street getting richer, everyone else getting poorer, politicians of both parties feeding brazenly at Wall Street's trough, the party of the Left in full blown attack gear not on inequality, which it has done nothing to address, but picking at and rubbing raw the scabs of identity politics—this can't keep going on indefinitely without something really bad happening.

The American Conservative
December 17, 2014

THE AMERICAN CENTURY IS OVER

Someday American politicians will recognize that the world isn't asking for their leadership. The image of America as benevolent superpower may endure in parts of Eastern Europe and in the former Soviet Republics, where some imagine American jets are going to abolish geography and clear out the Russians. But nowhere else.

At the time of this writing, an Orioles–White Sox game in Baltimore has been cancelled because of rioting in the city while on Saturday 37,000 fans were confined inside the stadium for hours after a game ended because of mayhem outside. The state, which cannot protect crowds of dating couples and parents with children outside of Camden Yards, is not going to make eastern Ukraine safe for neoliberalism.

In the run-up to the Baltimore riots, Congress debated ways to tell Europeans what their Mideast policies should be. Working with an AIPAC-drafted playbook, Maryland Senator Ben Cardin and Illinois Representative Peter Roskam attached language to a large trade bill intended to squelch the growing movement in Europe to label as such Israeli products that originate in the occupied territories. The AIPAC amendments defined as primary American goals in trade talks the discouragement of European economic sanctions against Israel. Mike Coogan's account of the behind-the-scenes maneuvers highlighted some glimpses of House legislators stunned at the brazenness of AIPAC in action. First hearings on the bill were moved to a smaller room to keep out the public. Then, at the last moment, pro-Israel anti-boycott amendments were tacked on with language treating Israel and "Israeli-controlled territories" as identical. One congressman asked Chairman Paul Ryan why members of the Ways and Means Committee were unable to consider public health, or labor standards, or food safety in debating the trade legislation, but were able on short notice to rubberstamp an AIPAC-sponsored amendment. He didn't receive an answer.

The larger point made by the U.S. Congress is that it is wrong for Palestinians to fight for their freedom by terrorism or any form of armed struggle, but it is also wrong to seek their rights by peaceful political means such as boycott. If you are a Palestinian, you have no legitimate way to seek political and civil rights, no avenue is open to you—and Congress is going to intervene in American trade policy to try to enforce that. Congress will make it a priority to instruct U.S. trade policymakers to protect Israeli settlements, considered illegal by virtually every country in the world. About measures (labor practices, health, and safety standards) that might protect U.S. workers and U.S. consumers, Congress doesn't have time for. By the way, Cardin, who introduced the senate version, represents Baltimore.

One connection between U.S. trade policy and the Baltimore riots was made explicit by John Angelos, the Oriole's chief operating officer and son of the Oriole's owner. Wrote Angelos:

> That said, my greater source of personal concern, outrage, and sympathy beyond this particular case is focused neither upon one night's property damage nor upon the acts, but is focused rather upon the past four-decade period during which an American political elite have shipped middle class and working class jobs away from Baltimore and cities and towns around the U.S. to third-world dictatorships like China and others, plunged tens of millions of good, hard-working Americans into economic devastation, and then followed that action around the nation by diminishing every American's civil rights protections in order to control an unfairly impoverished population living under an ever-declining standard of living and suffering at the butt end of an ever-more militarized and aggressive surveillance state.

The innocent working families of all backgrounds whose lives and dreams have been cut short by excessive violence, surveillance, and other abuses of the Bill of Rights by government pay the true price, and ultimate price, and one that far exceeds the importance of any kids' game played tonight, or ever, at Camden Yards. We need to keep in mind people are suffering and dying around the U.S., and while we are thankful no one was injured at Camden Yards, there is a far bigger picture for poor Americans in Baltimore and everywhere who don't have jobs and are losing economic, civil, and legal rights, and this makes inconvenience at a ballgame irrelevant in light of the needless suffering government is inflicting upon ordinary Americans.

You need not hold the rioters as blameless as Angelos does to recognize there is truth in his argument. For two generations, while politicians have been celebrating "free trade," America has been hemorrhaging good working class jobs. The economic devastation has probably hit the white working class harder than blacks, but as William Julius Wilson and others have argued, de-industrialization, which followed on the heels of the civil rights revolution, ensured that the black community would remain largely impoverished despite its political gains. In any case, we live in a far less equal and economically secure country than we did in the 1950s and 1960s.

As images of hoodlums rampaging in Baltimore traverse the globe, the Solons of Capitol Hill still imagine the world is eager to follow American leadership. The tacking on of "pro-Israel" provisions to a trade bill without debate is but a prequel: the big enchilada for Republicans in Congress is the derailment of the Iran negotiations. In the Capitol Hill bubble, it is assumed that the countries of Western Europe and Russia and China would follow the American lead and intensify sanctions against Iran on America's say-so, a belief with no basis in reality. Obama and John Kerry have recognized correctly that the sanctions regime has gained as much from Iran as it is going to get; Europe or China (and, of course, Russia) will not sign up for more.

Already, Washington has found to its consternation that its Western partners can't be dissuaded from joining a China-sponsored international banking arrangement. If the Republicans in Congress succeed in collapsing the Iran negotiations—altogether possible—they will discover that Washington is in a coalition with Israel and Saudi Arabia and no one else. Any future president, Republican or Democrat, will find his ability to negotiate terminally compromised, as world leaders will conclude that an American chief executive cannot keep his or her word.

The American century ended some time ago; perhaps the curtain was finally drawn when Secretary of State Colin Powell laid out the case for war before the U.N. and said things about Iraq that turned out simply not to be true. Those in Congress don't yet realize it, but they will.

The American Conservative
April 30, 2015

Heather Mac Donald's Inconvenient Facts

It's hard to recall the last time a relatively short op-ed received the sort of instant vituperation rained upon Manhattan Institute fellow Heather Mac Donald's recent piece in *The Wall Street Journal*. What explains it?

In her piece, Mac Donald parsed recent statistics showing an uptick in urban crime, which are not yet comprehensive but certainly suggest that the 20-year trend of reduced crime is being reversed. Sharp spikes in the homicide rates in Milwaukee and St. Louis, Atlanta and Chicago. The terrifying surge in Baltimore shootings since the riots last April mostly came too late for her overview.

Then she suggested a reason for the rise in crime: "The most plausible explanation of the current surge in lawlessness is the intense agitation against American police departments over the past nine months."

The stats Mac Donald cites are what baseball fans would call a "small sample size," and it might take several years of data to know conclusively that a crime upsurge is happening. But that can't quite explain the strong language Mac Donald's opponents deployed. "More sophistry than science," opined Yale Law professor Tracey Meares. Bernard Harcourt, a Columbia professor, slammed Mac Donald for producing "fiction" designed to "undermine the recent gains of the country's newest civil rights movement." Liberal websites linked to these so-called rebuttals again and again, as if terrified that, if left unrefuted, Mac Donald's arguments would gain irresistible momentum.

Why charges of "sophistry" and "fiction"—rather strong language from academics? The figures Mac Donald gathered were, everyone acknowledged, correct. Perhaps what was troubling was her quotations. One New York City had cop told her, "Any cop who uses his gun now has to worry about being indicted and losing his job and family." A Milwaukee police chief is quoted as saying he has "never seen anything like" the current hostility toward police.

Or perhaps it was her suggestion that longstanding laws and due process procedures are in danger of being circumvented to accommodate the new anti-police sensibility. In New York state, for instance, efforts are now underway to create a special prosecutor to put cops on trial when a grand jury doesn't come forth with an indictment.

The overall result is what the St. Louis police chief called "the Ferguson effect"—cops are essentially retreating to a reactive mode, answering 911 calls and investigating crimes, but not going out of their way to proactively police crime-prone neighborhoods. Police officers simply don't know how to deal with a dominant media narrative intent on portraying them as a violent blue gang.

But I suspect there is more to it than that. At a more emotive level, Mac Donald is being faulted for addressing honestly a difficult subject that most would prefer to avoid. The charge of pervasive police "racism" is, after all, driven in great part by the fact that police arrest, or stop and frisk, blacks at rates higher than they do whites or other ethnicities. But is racism the reason for this differential? In a *Slate* interview, Mac Donald notes that per capita rates of gun violence are eighty-one times higher in Brooklyn's Brownsville, a predominantly black neighborhood, than in nearby Bay Ridge, which is predominantly white and Asian. Under such circumstances, should Bay Ridge be policed in exactly the same way as Brownsville? If you answer yes, you may establish your "non-racist" bona fides, but also that you couldn't care less about the optimal allocation of scarce police resources in Brooklyn.

The difficult subject that Mac Donald gets to (more so in the *Slate* interview than in *The Wall Street Journal* piece) is that the underlying issue is not policing, but crime. People may not like the fact that blacks are arrested in disproportionate numbers, but this is due far more to disproportionate rates of criminal behavior than to racist police officers. It's a fact that most people probably know and yet prefer not to state, which results in a stilted and not particularly honest national debate about policing.

Awareness of differential crime rates may be largely excluded from the debate, but so long as America is a democracy, it can't be entirely squelched. Here we come to another reason for the strong reaction against Mac Donald: recent American political history. Rising crime helped the Republican Party nationally in the Nixon and Reagan eras, helping to fuel several landslide victories. Republicans were not above subtle efforts to insinuate that Democrats were properly "the African-American party"—in some instances trying to spur demands that a black be placed on the Democratic national ticket.

Would such tactics work in today's more multiethnic America? It can't be ruled out. While there is little research on the subject, my impression from recent political battles in New York City is that Asian neighborhoods can be every bit as brittle in response to perceptions of black crime as the stereotypical white ethnic neighborhood of yore. Leading Hispanic politicians have spoken out against alleged police racism, but it may be more surprising how small a role Hispanic activists have played in the overall movement to depict cops as racist. Much of white America in the late 1960s approached racial issues imbued with an acute sense of America's history of slavery and de jure segregation and more than a little bit of guilt—sentiments that new immigrants are likely to share little or not at all.

Concerns that broadening the discussion of "racist" cops to include rising crime rates threatens the national political fortunes of the Democrats are probably well-grounded. Writing as someone who supported Obama over McCain and Romney, and has no regrets over it, I think it is unlikely Obama could have been elected in a political atmosphere colored by urban rioting.

If their response to Heather Mac Donald is an indication, progressives feel the way to prevent Republicans from reaping any "backlash" gains is to place very tight boundaries around all discussion of cops, crime, and racism. It's a strategy that is unlikely to work for very long in a genuinely free society.

The American Conservative
June 10, 2015

Bring Us Your Poor

In the late 1980s, Fortune asked me to do an immigration piece. I traveled to Texas, spent some time with the Border Patrol, interviewed the major players in the Washington debate, and managed to figure out the main contours of the American legal immigration system, which is based mainly on family reunification.

What I learned prepared me to become sympathetic to the restrictionists when the issue became politically more salient in the early to mid-1990s with the victory of California's Proposition 187, and Peter Brimelow's important essay in National Review. *I became quite friendly with Brimelow and NR editor John O'Sullivan, and wrote a fair amount for the magazine then. I was asked to join the board of the Center for Immigration Studies, led by Mark Krikorian, and think—and still do—that it's an extremely smart organization.*

But there's something about immigration as an issue that becomes wearying for a writer— the nature of the debate never really changes. (It's quite different in Europe, even more so after the massive migrant surge encouraged by German prime minister Angela Merkel). I drafted an immigration speech for Pat Buchanan's campaign in 2000, and if a politician today called on me for an immigration speech, I'd come up with pretty much the same thing. If one has journalistic or writerly ambitions, making variations of the same argument over and over is not very satisfying.

In the mid 2000s, Mark Krikorian published a book on immigration, making arguments for lower immigration rates with which I entirely agreed. Yet in reading it, I couldn't help but realize that poor Mexicans, legal or illegal, had absolutely nothing to do with creating the biggest problem then facing the United States, which was an out of control, neoconservative directed, foreign policy, which had ignited an invasion of Iraq and was threatening to start more wars. In any case, by then I found I cared about foreign policy—read about it, thought about it, argued about it, far more than I did about immigration. And in caring about foreign policy, I realized that many of my new allies were on a different side of the immigration debate, or, in some cases, actually new immigrants themselves.

That realization fueled this essay, written for World Affairs Journal, *a somewhat neoconservative journal whose editor, Lawrence Kaplan, was in the midst of reconsidering many of his long held views in the wake of the Iraq War failure. It attempts to explain why I think ultimately the neoconservatives may have scored a sort of "own goal" by so decisively routing the immigration restrictionists from the Republican Party or at least from the major organs of the conservative media.*

This conclusion was confirmed in the recent battle over Obama's Iran deal when young American-born or recently immigrated Iranian-Americans played a critical role in lobbying for the deal, and in pushing for an eventual possible détente with Iran. And though I was formerly and still am an advocate in lower rates of immigration, I delighted beyond measure that these young people are in America and at the vanguard of efforts to restore a bit of realism and sanity to American foreign policy.

My review of Krikorian's book (not included here) foreshadowed some of these points, prompted some critics, including, I think, Krikorian himself, to make comparisons to Bertold Brecht's infamous crack about the German lack of enthusiasm for Soviet-style communism: the East Berlin government should dissolve the people and elect another one. It's a fair point: changing American demography does change American political culture. I remain conscious of the negative impacts, but, have to acknowledge, somewhat to my surprise, that some of the changes have been pretty positive.

In any case, there are few immigration restriction arguments here, for the simple reason that I haven't written many in the last decade, though I remain sympathetic to most of them. The issue is obviously far more critical in Europe, which has less history of assimilating massive waves of immigrants, and where the issue has Islamist overtones that are relatively absent in America. And, of course, America is blessed by being bordered on two sides by large oceans. Nonetheless, whites in Europe and the United States are both experiencing a version of what some French have begun to call "Le Grand Remplacement"—the great replacement of the founding ethnic group by others. I do believe, as Ronald Reagan does, and Angela Merkel evidently does not, that a country that doesn't control its borders isn't really a country.

Not So Huddled Masses: Multiculturalism and Foreign Policy

The modest contemporary literature on the connection between America's immigration and foreign policies contains this assertion by Nathan Glazer and Daniel Patrick Moynihan, from the introduction to their 1974 volume, *Ethnicity: Theory and Experience*: "The immigration process is the single most important determinant of American foreign policy ... This process regulates the ethnic composition of the American electorate. Foreign policy responds to that ethnic composition. It responds to other things as well, but probably first of all to the primary fact of ethnicity."

Yet the authors noted a nearly complete absence of discussion of the issue, and they pursued it little themselves. Rather, they tossed it in as a supplement to their general argument: ethnicity was not going to wither away, leaving only colorful residues for annoyance or celebration. It would remain a primary form of social life in the United States.

Nonetheless, ethnicity played little role in the foreign policy battles of the 1960s and 1970s. One could discuss the cultural divide between hippies and hardhats, between war protesters and the "Silent Majority" without reference to race, creed, or national origin. Some scholars would note a dominant ethnic component in the New Left, as well as in the less visible New Right, but such considerations were hardly part of the national conversation.

They certainly had been in the past, in the battles over American entry into World Wars I and II. Glazer and Moynihan implied they would be in the future as well. For the two were writing in the wake of the historic 1965 Immigration Act, which had overturned the restrictionist regime of the 1920s. That post–World War I legislation, which brought to a halt the Great Wave of immigration that had begun forty years earlier, was designed explicitly to freeze the American ethnic balance. By the 1960s, in the warm glow of the civil rights revolution, this was no longer plausible.

In any case, the backers of the 1965 act did not imagine huge demographic changes: there would be, they claimed, some modest increase in the number of Greek and Italian immigrants, but not much else. The sheer inaccuracy of this prediction was already apparent by the early 1970s. The 1965 act allowed entry of immigrants from any country, so long as they possessed certain job skills or family members living here or had been granted refugee status themselves.

The family reunification provision soon became the vital engine of immigrant selection. By the 1980s, it had greatly increased numbers of Asians and of Hispanics—the latter mostly from Mexico. The European population of the country was now in relative decline—from 87 percent in 1970 to 66 percent in 2008. If immigration continues at present rates (and barring a long-term economic collapse, it is likely to), by 2040, Hispanics will make up a quarter of the American population. If that does not guarantee a somewhat different foreign policy, there is also the prospect of a substantial expansion of America's once miniscule Muslim and Arab populations.

To those attuned to the historic battles over twentieth-century American foreign policy, ethnicity was an obvious subject. It played a major role in the debate over American entry into World War I, which was vigorously opposed by most German-Americans, anti-tsarist Scandinavians, and many Irish-Americans. Leading pro-war politicians railed against "hyphenated-Americans" with a ferocity nearly unimaginable today. And while opposition to America's entry into the war cut across all regions and groups, the noninterventionist position always maintained a strong core of support in the upper Midwest, where Americans of German descent dominated. In the 1950s, the widely read political analyst Samuel Lubell concluded that isolationism was always more ethnic than geographical, and owed its durability to the exploitation of pro-German and anti-British ethnic prejudices by the Republican Party. Lubell claimed that isolationists, far from being indifferent to Europe's wars, were in fact oversensitive to them.

This is surely too reductionist an argument. But the volatile ethnic mix at home did inhibit Woodrow Wilson from taking sides in Europe. "We definitely have to be neutral since otherwise our mixed populations would wage war on each other," Wilson was reported to say in 1914. The "hyphenates," bullied into silence by 1917, had their day after the Armistice when their opposition helped to lay low Woodrow Wilson's dreams for the League of Nations. Walter Lippmann interpreted post-war isolation through this ethnic prism: any policy that put America in alliance with some European countries against others risked exacerbating America's own ethnic divisions. Near the end of his career, Arthur Schlesinger Jr. described the arguments that took place between the outbreak of war in 1939 and Pearl Harbor as "the most savage national debate" of his lifetime, one that "unleashed an inner fury that tore apart families, friends, churches, universities, and political parties."

In any event, America's intra-European divisions began to melt away quickly after Pearl Harbor, as military service became the defining generational event for American men born between 1914 and 1924. The mixed army squad of WASP, Italian, German, Jew, and Irish became a standard plot device for the popular World War II novel and film. The Cold War generated a further compatibility between ethnicity and foreign policy. East European immigrants and refugees emerged to speak for the silenced populations of a newly Stalinized Eastern Europe. Suddenly, all the major European-American groups were in sync. Italian-Americans mobilized for mass letter-writing campaigns to their parents and grandparents warning of the dangers of voting Communist. Greek-Americans naturally supported the Marshall Plan.

Bipartisanship now meant that both parties had to woo ethnic Americans. (And not always so tactfully: the 1948, GOP platform promised to work for the restoration of Italy's African colonies). Eastern Europeans lobbied for the rollback of Soviet rule, enshrining it as a GOP platform plank if not a practical commitment. Americans of East European background remained staunchly anti-Communist long after anti-communism surrendered its luster in the aftermath of Vietnam, allying with neoconservative Jews and hamstringing

Nixon and Kissinger's détente policy. As anti-communism became an engine of Americanization, the Cold War showcased the hyphenated American.

Twenty years after the fall of the Berlin Wall, America has entered a new era of ethnicity and foreign policy, whose contours are only just now emerging. During the 1990s, when multiculturalism was in vogue, leaders of old and new minority groups steered American foreign policy toward the cause of their ancestral homelands. African American and Hispanic leaders touted the success of American Jews in lobbying for Israel as an example to be emulated. At one major Latino conference, participants nominated themselves the vanguard of a "bridge community" between the United States and Latin America.

Ethnic lobbies, the old as much as the new, quickly filled the empty space left behind by the Cold War. Traditional realists like former defense secretary James Schlesinger and Harvard political scientist Samuel Huntington bemoaned the diminished sense of national cohesion and purpose. Ethnic lobbies, they feared, would inhibit the United States from exercising global leadership. Indeed, if one were to examine some of the major policy milestones of the Clinton era—active participation in the Northern Ireland peace process, the military occupation of Haiti, expanded trade embargoes on Cuba and Iran, the revelation of the Swiss banking scandals—it could be argued that ethnic lobbies were, as much as any coherent grand strategy, the era's prime movers.

After a brief spasm of patriotic and military display following the attacks of 9/11, we have picked up where we left off the day before. Which is to say that the preliminary indications point toward a future that will bear some semblance to the politics of the 1990s and the World War I era when ethnic constituencies operated as a brake on executive power and military intervention. There is no evidence that the rallying cries put forth by America's neoconservatives and liberal hawks—democratization of tyrannies, the global war on terror, the fight against radical Islam—have gained significant traction among first- and second-generation immigrant communities. Certainly they do not resonate with anything like the intensity that anti-communism did after World War II. On the basis of what is visible thus far, today's and tomorrow's Mexican-, Asian-, and Arab-Americans will more resemble the Swedes, Germans, and Irish of a century ago than the Poles, Balts, and Cubans of the Cold War era.

The plainest indicator is voting behavior. The obvious point to make is that most of the new immigrant groups tend to vote Democratic—a trend that has intensified since the Republican Party twinned itself with the war in Iraq and, more generally, with the "war on terror," even as the

Democratic Party has reverted to a traditional skepticism regarding foreign entanglements.

Consider first Hispanics, a group that has always leaned Democratic. George W. Bush received 35 percent of the Latino vote in 2000 and 40 percent in 2004. John McCain's share dropped to 30 percent. The GOP's harsher tone on immigration surely played a role in this. But it bears noting that in one recent survey of Hispanic voter attitudes, the same percentage cited Iraq as an important issue as cited immigration.

Though Latinos constitute the largest new immigrant group (and Mexican Americans count as the only national group whose relative size rivals that of German Americans in the early twentieth century), their foreign affairs activism remains modest. Apart from highly-mobilized Cubans, it is not clear Latinos have either the resources or will to influence foreign policy in a singular way. By virtue of history and geography, they are as much the unwilling subjects of American expansion as they are immigrants—a circumstance captured by Jorge Dominguez's pithy remark that "the boundary migrated, not the Latinos."

There is little evidence that Mexicans have much loyalty to the Mexican state, which most, with good reason, view as corrupt. In fact, before immigration became a harshly contested issue in the 1990s, a majority of Mexican Americans tended to think there was too much of it. Moreover, it seems unlikely that this increasingly Democratic constituency will become a pillar of support for globalism of any sort, much less military interventionism. Obviously, one can't draw broad conclusions from a single political figure. But Colorado's former senator Ken Salazar, named by President Obama to head the Interior Department, gave an address at last summer's Democratic convention that, for all its rooted-in-the-soil rhetoric, might, with slight shifts of emphasis, have been delivered by an editor of the paleoconservative journal *Chronicles*.

The Asian-American shift from aggressive red to pacifistic blue has been far more dramatic. This group, once heavily weighted with refugees from Chinese and Vietnamese communism, voted Republican in 1992 and 1996. But by 2004, the Asian vote began to trend heavily Democratic, an estimated 60 percent for Kerry over Bush, and 63 percent for Obama over McCain. Like most voters, Asians ranked the economy first, but according to one recent survey, the war in Iraq rated second. Seventy percent wanted the U.S. to leave as soon as possible.

Beyond their turn to the Democrats, there is little hard evidence upon which to gauge the future influence of Asian immigrants on U.S. foreign policy. While there are surely Chinese Americans who yearn for greater freedom in Beijing, they evince little of the refugee-from-Communism zeal displayed by East Europeans or Cubans of the Cold War period. Generally, Chinese Americans seem proud of China's progress and emergence as a great power. It follows that, as their political participation grows, it may become a constituency that encourages American accommodation to a powerful China, or at least one that does not weigh in on the side of confronting it.

The Iraq War is likely to be seen a great clarifier in the partisan identification of the expanding Latino and Asian electorates. In the Gender and Multicultural Leadership Project's 2006–2007 survey of minority state and local elected officials, only 24 percent of Latino respondents and 19 percent of Asians believed the United States had made the correct decision to invade Iraq.

And what of America's Arab and Muslim populations, hailing from regions where the United States is presently engaged in two wars? Their numbers tend to be smaller, and hard to tally precisely. But according to Daniel Pipes, the most prominent of those alarmed about the prospect of "Islamism" gaining a foothold in America, there were three million Muslims in the United States in 2002. The U.S. census estimates a current population of 1.25 million Arab Americans, the majority Christian. (The Arab American Institute estimates that over three million U.S. citizens have some Arab ancestry.) But this population, comparably tiny, grows steadily through immigration. According to statistics compiled by the Arab American Institute, the Arab American population doubled in size between 1980 and 2000, with about twenty-six thousand new Arab immigrants entering the United States every year.

Once a swing group, which split evenly in the 2000 election between Bush and Gore, Arab Americans have essentially abandoned the GOP. Republican identification had dropped to 20 percent according to one 2008 estimate. Not surprisingly, the Israel-Palestine conflict is the main area of contention, where Arab American views part most dramatically from those now predominant in Congress. Past generations of Arab Americans have assimilated seamlessly enough, usually by declining to call attention to their background. Those who rose into the public eye typically adopted a low profile on anything related to the Middle East. But that is changing. One can see early harbingers: Congressman Michael McMahon, recently elected to represent Staten Island and parts of Brooklyn, promised some of his Arab constituents that they could chaperone him on a tour of the occupied West Bank. Of course, members of Congress who have toured Israel with Israeli guides number in the hundreds at least. But this kind of politicized sightseeing may soon become a competitive enterprise.

Indeed, political competition over the Middle East now riles most elite American colleges, where it did not twenty years ago: almost every campus boasts an active Arab American student organization, often cooperating with left-liberal Jewish students—and presenting a narrative of the Israel-Palestine issue far more critical than what was recently a commonplace. The parents of these students were immigrants, unsteady in their English, uncertain of their place in America. Their children have no similar restraints.

It may be decades before we talk seriously about a revived and very different kind of "China lobby" or a new "Palestine lobby." But the demographic landscape has changed already, and the political coloration of the change does not seem in dispute. Those sections of the country—the South, lower Midwest, and the regions touching the Appalachian mountains—that have received the fewest immigrants from the waves of immigration of the past one hundred and thirty years not only count as the most Republican; they are the regions least likely to send white antiwar politicians to Congress. They provide a disproportionate share of the nation's soldiers. (If one were to subtract the very poor and very white state of Maine, one would need to go through a list of twenty states ranked in order of per capita Army recruitment to reach a state that John Kerry carried in 2004.) One political conclusion is obvious: current rates of immigration will not only diminish the "white" proportion of the American population; they will also diminish the political weight of those regions with the most hawkish and pro-military political cultures.

These observations about immigration and foreign policy complicate present debates among Republicans and conservatives. Consider first the more influential neoconservatives, whose viewpoints were neatly summarized during the campaign by Rudy Giuliani and GOP nominee John McCain. Both boasted hawkish views on Iraq and other war on terror-related issues; both sought out neoconservative foreign policy advisers.

Both men were entirely out of sync with the Republican base on immigration. As mayor, Giuliani liked to tout New York as a "Capital of the World." During the presidential campaign he was accused by rivals, with some justification, of running New York as a "sanctuary city" for illegal immigrants. Similarly, John McCain's campaign was nearly derailed by grassroots hostility to his proposal for normalizing the status of illegal immigrants (derided as "amnesty").

The Giuliani and McCain positions corresponded to the neoconservative perspective on immigration. True, the 9/11 attacks made neoconservatives, and everyone else, more conscious of border security, and nudged some neoconservatives in the direction of restrictionist positions. But at bottom neoconservatism is a movement that originated among urban Jewish intellectuals, often the children or grandchildren of immigrants themselves, and it retains a good deal of that sensibility. Yet the demographic and political base for a neoconservative foreign policy may be found, to an overwhelming extent, in Protestant red state America, the areas least settled by new immigrants.

And what of the immigration restrictionists? They have contradictions of their own to sort out. They include Democratic environmentalists and liberals worried about immigration's impact on wages. But most of the restrictionist momentum comes from the traditionalist or paleoconservative camp. Paleoconservatives tout their attachment to old communities, to "the permanent things." They tend to be more opposed to change, more skeptical about the universal appeal, or relevance, of American ideals to the wider world. In some notable cases, they view themselves as the heirs of the Old Right isolationism that opposed American entry into World Wars I and II.

Paleoconservatives compose too small a faction to have much of a say in the Republican Party. (Pat Buchanan, the most prominent paleo, has been effectively banished from GOP policy debates since 1996.) But there remains a broader category of Republicans, including some prominent intellectuals, with considerable paleo tendencies, sentiments shared by a substantial portion of the American public. Consider two men with long and highly influential careers, the late George F. Kennan and Samuel Huntington.

As a State Department official in the 1940s, Kennan was the primary architect of the Cold War containment strategy. But he spent much of his career arguing that the United States had placed too much emphasis on the military aspects of containment. He was frustrated by what he perceived as an uninformed and moralistic streak running through American foreign policy. In particular, he despaired over the power of ethnic lobbies to influence American policy. These lobbies, he once wrote, "seem more often than not to be on the militaristic or chauvinistic side." He urged the United States to exhibit more humility and less hubris in its approach to the international scene.

As much as Kennan the diplomat had immersed himself in foreign cultures, he was an ardent immigration restrictionist. In *Around the Cragged Hill*, published when he was nearly ninety, Kennan lamented the cultural changes brought about by poor immigrants. If they came to America in sufficient numbers, they would create "conditions in this country no better than those of the places the immigrants have left ... turning America into part of the Third World ... [and] thus depriving the planet of one of the few great regions" able to maintain a "relatively high standard of civilization." Kennan also touted the virtues of small republics, and proposed that the United States might better manage its own civilizational problems if it divided itself into smaller self-governing segments, some of which would become culturally part of Latin America.

Harvard political scientist Samuel Huntington was the other leading WASP intellectual to take on the immigration question. Writing in *Foreign Affairs* in 1997, Huntington worried that the end of the Cold War had left the country without a defining mission. He cited John Updike: "Without the cold war, what's the point of being an American?" During the mid-1990s, he noted grimly, the void of national purpose was being filled by the special pleading of ethnic subgroups, with little trouble finding receptive ears in Congress. In his final book, *Who Are We?*, published in 2004, Huntington probed deeper. What would become of America's national identity in an age of mass and especially Hispanic immigration?

> "National interests," he wrote, "derive from national identity. We need to know who we are before we can know what our interests are." Throughout much of the past century, that identity was clear enough. America was a Western democracy, and both terms were significant. But a changing country would assume new identities and frame its vital interests differently. If American identity were to be defined by commitment to the universal principles of liberty and democracy, then "promotion of those principles in other countries" would guide our foreign policy. Yet if the country was a "collection" of various ethnic and cultural identities, it would promote the interests of those entities, via a "multicultural foreign policy." If we were to become more Hispanic, we would reorient ourselves accordingly toward Latin America. What we do abroad depends on who we are at home.

To Huntington, America, the historical nation that had existed from the Jamestown and Plymouth Rock settlements until well into the last century, was Anglo-Protestant to the core, as Protestant as Israel is Jewish or Pakistan is Muslim. Huntington was referring to an Anglo-Protestantism of culture, not race or religion—but his ideal culture was definitely the product of the early settlers. The English Puritan Revolution was "the single most important formative event in American political history." Out of the culture of dissenting Protestantism emerged a secular "American Creed" open to all. The Creed placed emphasis on individual conscience, on work over idleness, and on personal responsibility to overcome obstacles to achieve success. It forged a populace ready to engage in moral reform movements at home and abroad. Americans became accustomed to an image of their nation as one with a divine mission.

Previously, the nation's elite had been able to "stamp" Protestant values on waves of immigrants. But because of Mexico's geographic proximity and the sheer number of immigrants, the old assimilation methods would no longer suffice. The major political battles of the 1990s over bilingualism and multiculturalism foreshadowed a larger renegotiation concerning whether the new immigrants would subscribe to the American Creed at all.

Huntington favored lower immigration rates and hoped for a reinvigoration of America's Protestant culture and a renewed commitment to assimilation. But he was not optimistic, and other national possibilities presented themselves. One was a bilingual, bicultural America, half Latin-Americanized; another a racially intolerant, highly conflicted country; still another was a multicultural country subscribing loosely to a common American Creed, but without the glue of a common culture to bind it. Huntington considered the American Creed without its cultural underpinning no more durable than Marxist-Leninism eventually proved in Russia and Eastern Europe.

Protective of the uniqueness of America's Anglo-Protestant culture, Huntington was a nationalist who hoped to maintain the American "difference" from the rest of the world. But he was acutely aware that one of the distinguishing aspects of Anglo-Protestantism was its messianism, the sense of America as a chosen nation—and one not inclined to leave a corrupt world to its own devices. Anglo-Protestantism had transformed the United States, in Walter McDougall's words, from "promised land to crusader state."

Thus, while many have laid the blame for the war in Iraq with the Bush administration or the neoconservatives, that may cast the net too narrowly. Andrew Bacevich is one author who describes a much longer fuse to the impulse that led America to miscalculate how receptive the world would be toward a military campaign to end tyranny. In *The New American Militarism*, Bacevich noted that evangelical Protestantism, which had evolved from political quietism in the first half of the century to respectful deference to the Cold War establishment during the Billy Graham era, had, by the 1980s, evolved into a passionate embrace of military culture. The American officer corps made a transition from being mostly Episcopalian to heavily evangelical. And evangelicals embraced not just the soldiers and their values, but militarism as a chosen foreign policy. As Bacevich starkly put it: "In the developed world's most devoutly Christian country, Christian witness against war and the danger of militarism became less effective than in countries thoroughly and probably irreversibly secularized." Conservative Christians have fostered among the faithful "a predisposition to see U.S. military power as inherently good, perhaps even a necessary adjunct to the accomplishment of Christ's saving mission."

Bacevich's analysis illuminated a principal weakness of Huntington's prescription. For if solidifying the American nation required a re-invigorated Anglo-Protestant culture, the initiative would have to come to a considerable degree from Anglo-Protestants themselves. Reading Huntington (and Kennan as well), one cannot but sense that what they really seek is a revival of something resembling the American national elite of the 1940s and 1950s, exemplified by the foreign policy "wise men" of the Truman era (of whom

Kennan was one). But that particular Protestant elite, whose cousins held the commanding positions of America's industries and universities, was more or less banished from the national stage in the 1960s. Not only is its return impossible; it barely exists. What has replaced it as the dynamic core of American Protestantism is the evangelical culture Bacevich describes, rooted in the South and West, whose attitudes were epitomized by the Bush-Cheney administration.

If the emergence of an American elite able to cement a strong national identity and coherent national interest is unlikely, what options remain for a country now irreversibly multicultural? Huntington saw the choice as either imperialism or liberal cosmopolitanism, both of which would erode what is unique about America. Imperialism seems an unlikely choice since the Iraq War, an experience few Americans in or out of the military will want to repeat anytime soon.

What seems more likely is the entrenchment and expansion of a worldly, cosmopolitan elite, increasingly multicultural and transnational, that bears little connection to the WASP establishments of the twentieth century, the cold warriors, or even the Bush administration. American foreign policy will necessarily become less ambitious, more a product of horse-trading between ethnic groups. Messianism, in either its Protestant or neoconservative variants, will be part of America's past, not its future. Americans will not conceive of themselves as orchestrators of a benevolent global hegemony, or as agents of an indispensable nation. Schlesinger, for one, exaggerated the extent of the fall when he averred that a foreign policy based on "careful balancing of ethnic constituencies" was suitable only for secondary powers, like the late Austrian-Hungarian Empire. But he exaggerated only slightly.

As I have noted, George F. Kennan, patron saint of both foreign policy realists and many paleoconservatives, spent the long second half of his career urging a greater sense of humility abroad. The rethinking of global commitments, the readiness to modify the go-go economy that seems to require them—these have become a refrain of some of Kennan's heirs. So here is a second paradox, which parallels the irony that neoconservatives support an immigration policy that undermines their own political base. The realists and America-Firsters will find their foreign policy aspirations at least partially satisfied via the unlikely avenues of immigration and multiculturalism. The paleoconservatives, losers in the immigration wars, will end up winners of an important consolation prize: the foreign policy of what remains of their cherished republic.

World Affairs Journal
Spring 2009

OBAMA'S AMNESTY-INEQUALITY TRAP

Such inconvenient things, elections. So much the better if the elites of both parties could quietly meet in a plush and smokeless private room to decide what's best. That, anyway, is what the "immigration reform" establishment must feel after the President Obama announced he was backing off his announced intention to push amnesty by executive order prior to the November election. As *The New York Times* reported:

> What had once looked like a clear political imperative for both parties—action to grant legal status to millions of undocumented immigrants—had morphed instead into what appeared to be a risky move that could cost Democrats their majority in the November midterm congressional elections.

The *Times* went on to explain how years of the highest level of elites lobbying the Republican Party to understand that amnesty was in their interest were undone by a few weeks of the southern border seeming out of control. Polls showed that voters somehow perceived what the Washington consensus refused to admit—that the prospect of an imminent amnesty made illegal border crossing more attractive, both to the coyote smugglers and to would-be illegal migrants themselves.

It's been more than a decade since immigration was a major concern of mine. I can think of numerous reasons why diverse multicultural immigration has been or might eventually be quite OK, even on balance beneficial. Most importantly, it could raise some political roadblocks to unwise military interventions, as the war-as-first-resort coalition is generally white and Protestant, and the diminution of that bloc's influence is perhaps a blessing. I would wager also that immigrants from all regions are somewhat closer to the global consensus, more resistant to the "Israel right or wrong" ideology now regnant in Congress. But this is supposition, based on present voting patterns and cultural assumptions, not yet tested by events.

Still, it's hard not to be struck by the failure of the immigration debate, on every side, to touch on the heart of the matter. The heart of it isn't the end of white cultural and political dominance (the end of America, as some would have it) though that is surely an element behind some immigration restriction sentiment. It's that mass immigration is a frontal assault on America as a country with a fair degree of social equality; a characteristic that nearly defined the country of the '50s, '60s, and '70s, the decades of the baby-boomers' youth. The writer and speaker who now carries forth this argument best, indeed practically the only one, is Mickey Kaus, author, one of the America's first important bloggers, quixotic one-time California Senate candidate.

Last year, Kaus spoke at the Center for Immigration Studies, where he analyzed the broader effect of mass immigration on the economy. Some excerpts:

> And it's not because I think immigration overall will be a drag on the economy as, as some argue, the third generation of immigrants sinks into single parenthood and dependence. That might happen, but I assume for the purposes of this argument that, overall, immigrants bring a drive and a work ethic that will boost overall gross national product, dynamic scoring. Unfortunately, gross national product isn't everything. It also matters how it's distributed, at least and certainly at the bottom of the income distribution.

> And this is the beginning of the problem, the first big problem with amnesty, because it's very hard to believe that uncontrolled unskilled immigration won't hurt the very people who have been screwed the most over the past three decades. That is unskilled workers, especially young people, especially high school dropouts, and especially men. They are the people who have been hurt the most by the outsourcing trend as unskilled jobs have moved abroad. Now we're saying those unskilled jobs that have to be performed here, you don't get those either because we're importing people from abroad to do them.

He continues:

> I spent a lot of time—I drove up from Florida these past few days. I spent a lot of time listening to country music, both good and bad, and the theme of about half the songs, I'd say, the ones that aren't about true love or cheating on your true love, the theme is something like this: I may not be very sophisticated, I may drive a truck, but I go to work every day and I feed my family, and it's not easy, and there's a dignity in that and that makes me a hero just as much as you, buddy.

> That's basically a lot of what—the sentiment that those songs appeal to, and it's a good sentiment. The idea is that a full-time job enables a life of dignity even if it's not an affluent life. And that assurance is what uncontrolled immigration would erode. Even if some people make the most it—even if a lot of people make the most of it—even if some waiters can make more money in tips because they have busboys filling the water glasses, they can serve more tables; even if some drywall installers open up a drywall-installing shop and employ people making $9 an hour, lots of people won't do better.

Kaus went on to argue that mass immigration undermines the key premises of welfare reform, the important and quite conservative Clinton legislation of the 1990s. Welfare reform essentially encouraged (or compelled) recipients to get jobs, and most of them did, and did better. It was part of a moral argument that it is better in almost every way to hold a steady job than to hustle in the illegal economy, or commit serious crime. Welfare reform aimed to combat the pervasive notion that minimum wage jobs were "chump change" and not worth the bother. But obviously if you tilt the labor market against the poor by bringing in more and more unskilled workers, the low salaries will remain low. That is what has happened in the past two decades, which have seen almost all national income gains go to the most successful.

When I was a kid (and spending nearly half the time in a very well-off family) one could often hear grownups complaining almost continually about how hard it was to get good help—for gardening, or pool cleaning, or whatever. It must have been tough, but somehow the rich survived it. One virtually never hears such complaints now. Instead we have an economy where tens of millions of people at the bottom are continuously teetering on the edge of bankruptcy, loss of health care, etc. But upper middle class teenage girls can get their toenails tended at a spa without great expense.

I would submit that a country where the rich have to complain about their difficulty getting good help is morally superior to one where the working class is under constant threat of falling into dire poverty. This is a kind of philosophical prejudice, difficult to argue conclusively. One can of course point to ways in which the lives of upper middle class and above Americans are enriched by the existence a large class of poorer immigrants. The freedom of American women, indeed of almost all "first world" women, was surely enhanced with child care options made possible by an influx of poorer immigrant women. Nonetheless, there are probably better ways to solve child care problems than eliminating the border.

It may be a stretch to say that some unarticulated upsurge of the general will, a sentimental nostalgia for a more socially equal America, forced Obama to scale back his amnesty promise. Most analysts point to White House fears of the amnesty issue's effect on Senate races in the Midwest and upper South, where Obama's intention threatened to brand forever the Democrats as the amnesty party among its white voters. No matter how much sympathy the stories of individual illegal immigrants might evoke, the amnesty issue gives the indelible impression that the "immigration reform" crowd wants simply to erase the southern border. For what does having an amnesty every twenty years mean, except that you find borders inconvenient as a measure of controlling the movements of people?

If Mickey Kaus is the most prominent figure to make the explicit linkage between growing inequality and mass immigration, it won't be enough. And so far, there are few prominent Democrats ready to make the case. One wonders why, for if ever an issue called for a "Third Way" pro-middle and working-class Democrat to make some waves, it is this one. Immigration remains singular as the issue where there is a large discrepancy between the popular sentiment and the elites of both parties. In the parliamentary systems of Europe, slow-down-immigration sentiment can at least express itself politically. In the U.S., when John McCain is allied with "liberal" Chuck Schumer, and Bill Gates and Sheldon Adelson have spoken with one voice, what chance to do proponents of a more socially equal America really have?

The American Conservative
September 10, 2014

Ten Years After

It is difficult to draw up a balance sheet of the battles fought in TAC and elsewhere over a dozen years. The New Republic *which so smugly mocked* The American Conservative *as doomed at its founding exists no longer, and it has become a different publication under different ownership. It is fair to say that a conservative magazine skeptical about promiscuous American interventionism is not as shocking as it was in 2002. One the other hand, neither TAC nor anyone else has succeeded in dislodging the neoconservatives from their hegemonic positions within the Republican Party: remarkably, the 2016 election campaign has indicated that GOP is by and large as reflexively hawkish, and as ready to adapt neoconservative talking points, as it was in the past three election cycles. And it seems likely that the Democrats will nominate, with Hillary Clinton, a figure far closer to neoconservatism than Obama.*

Obama's legacy in foreign affairs will turn largely on the Iran negotiation, a subject I addressed several times in TAC and elsewhere. Of course, the consequences of the nuclear deal remain unclear, and Iran is still run by a nasty dictatorship—albeit one ruling uneasily over a large well-educated and somewhat pro-American civil society. Time will tell when that civil society will prevail, but bombing Iran—the main neoconservative alternative to the deal— would have been catastrophic. Even now, before there is a glimmer of real détente, Obama's effort can be fairly compared to Nixon's opening to China—without which I doubt the United States could have won the Cold War.

David Brooks's Dilemma (and Ours)

Consider one of David Brooks's dilemmas. In last Friday's *Times*, he wrote a pretty good column about the contemporary American power elite. As he described it, sixty and more years ago, blue blood WASPs ran America's financial institutions and foreign policy (something of a simplification, but let it pass), ethnic bosses ran the cities, and engaging working class drunks filed the newspaper stories. Now those critical sectors are run and staffed by the meritocracy, people who did well on the bubble tests and went on to succeed at elite universities. We have, Brooks explains, "opened up opportunities for women, African-Americans, Jews, Italians, Poles, Hispanics, and members of every other group."

Then he acknowledges the new regime isn't working out as well as expected. None of these major institutions is now doing its job adequately, and the country knows it. We need, Brooks concludes, to reevaluate our definitions of merit, and leadership because "very smart people make mistakes, because they didn't understand the context in which they were operating." This is true, and for a newspaper column, a profound observation.

But there is a salient body of fact that Brooks elides, and therein lies a tale. While opportunities have opened up for women and all the non-WASP groups Brooks mentioned, all groups have not rushed with equal force into the breach. If one takes, for example, the issue of Mideast diplomacy, it has been noted recently that most of the country's important Mideast diplomats are Jews, most of writers covering the Israel-Palestine conflict for *The New York Times* are Jewish, as are two of three of the president's top political advisers. Dig in a different direction, and one finds a similar kind of thing, as observed on this site, of the financial players engaged in selecting the next senator from New York.

There is no need to exaggerate the phenomenon, and indeed a need not to—outside of New York, there are plenty of rich Protestant power brokers, the South is important politically and Jews are seldom influential there, etc. But to say the least, the collapse of the WASP ascendancy has not been equally rewarding to all of the groups Brooks cites at the top of his column. Indeed for some of them, like Catholics, that collapse has probably coincided with a net reduction in cultural and political influence.

Brooks avoids mentioning this, as do virtually all writers. The reason is obvious: nearly any analysis, indeed any mention, of Jewish power is overburdened with sensitive historical associations. Unspecified but ominous reference to this history is the main polemical weapon Leon Wieseltier uses in his effort to take down Andrew Sullivan for his writing on Israel and Palestine. Some of Sullivan's arguments, Wieseltier asserts "have a sordid history"; Sullivan is one of those who proclaim "without in any way being haunted by the history of such an idea that Jews control Washington"; Sullivan adopts an explanation which "has a provenance that should disgust all thinking people." No need then to examine the truth or the untruth of Sullivan's argument, a vague allusion to history suffices. Criticism of Israel is tied to the modern history of European anti-Semitism, and to an extensive bibliography of generally tendentious books about Jewish power, from Alphonse de Toussenel's *Les Juifs, Rois de L'Epoch* (published in 1845) forward. Of course, this discourse was an auxiliary to the Holocaust. About this Wieseltier (and the countless others who polemicize in this manner) are correct: discussions of Jewish power have sometimes had terrible consequences.

But where does that leave twenty-first century Americans? One example is the case of David Brooks, who clearly knows what he is leaving out of his column about the American power elite. Brooks is Jewish, and a Zionist, and in no danger of being labeled an anti-Semite by Leon Wieseltier or anyone else. But still he is hesitant; presumably because he doesn't want to write something that either might encourage anti-Semitism, or (more likely considering his readership) enhance public understanding of the Israel lobby. At least the first of these motives is commendable. But the reticence has a consequence: when Brooks writes a column about the American power elite and its weaknesses, he needs to avoid one of the essential aspects of his subject. That can't really be satisfactory to him, or to his readers. It's a dilemma with no obvious solution to it.

Mondoweiss
February 21, 2010

Ten Years in the Right

Ten years ago, *The New Republic* greeted news of *The American Conservative*'s pending arrival with a mocking piece titled "Buchanan's Surefire Flop." Franklin Foer's article now seems an almost museum-quality exhibit of neoconservative and liberal hawk hubris—the beating heart of an elite consensus that suppressed meaningful discussion about the wisdom of invading Iraq.

Pat Buchanan and his partners "couldn't have chosen a worse time to start a journal of the isolationist right," wrote Foer. When President Clinton waged war on Serbia, some conservatives opposed foreign military interventionism. But "no one on the Right is listening anymore" to anti-interventionist arguments. The 9/11 attacks had "produced a war on terrorism that has virtually ended conservative qualms about expending blood and treasure abroad."

Foer cited polls: 94 percent of Republicans supported Bush's foreign policy. A triumphant Norman Podhoretz was quoted: there really was no conservatism distinct from neoconservatism anymore. A magazine whose thrust would be to attack neoconservative foreign policy prescriptions was doomed to fail.

A decade later, how can *TAC*'s impact be assessed? Clearly, the magazine did not flop—it has steadily expanded its readership and survived an economy extremely inhospitable to print media. But if the Iraq War was a "clarifier," it was unfortunately not a terribly strong one. If success is to be measured by influence on the conservative movement or the Republican Party, *TAC* still has a great deal of work to do: astonishingly, the neoconservatives—the group who sold the idea of the Iraq War to the last Republican president—are now if anything more entrenched in the GOP foreign policy brain trust than in 2002.

Who might have predicted, seven years after it was clear that the Iraq War was one of greatest strategic disasters in American history, that Paul Ryan would be receiving foreign policy tutoring from Elliott Abrams and two Kagans? To be a neocon in twenty-first century America is truly never to be held accountable for one's errors.

There is, to be sure, a much wider understanding among the attentive American public of *TAC*'s central message: of America's need for a conservatism distinct from the neocon version, more Burkean, more prudent, less remote from the concerns of average Americans, less tied to the Israeli right.

Foer's piece distilled the conventional wisdom of 2002: even conservatives who disliked the neoconservatives on other grounds—for their support of high levels of immigration, for example—shied away from frontal assaults on their foreign policy. Two months before the magazine's launch, I dined with a young economics writer who would soon write brilliantly for *TAC*. On the war, he advised a symposium—out-and-out opposition would only marginalize the magazine. Needless to say, his advice was not taken.

What Foer and the conventional wisdom missed was that the foreign policy debate had already become three-sided by 2002. It had evolved considerably since 1991 when Buchanan was one of a handful of conservatives to oppose the first Gulf War. Opposition to that war was primarily "isolationist" in spirit with Buchanan and a small cadre of others pitted not only against the neocons but a wide array of foreign policy realists. The point is not to debate whether that war was necessary or strategically justified (though afterwards, the hawkish realist Robert W. Tucker wrote in *The National Interest* that bombing a more or less defenseless Iraqi army in the open desert violated just war precepts). Desert Storm was not in the main a neoconservative enterprise; it was planned and executed by an internationalist establishment, sanctified by U.N. resolutions, and backed by a broad allied coalition. George H.W. Bush had essentially followed the script that had governed American foreign policy since the early Cold War.

Several months after Desert Storm's conclusion, a memorandum produced under the guidance of undersecretary of defense Paul Wolfowitz was leaked to *The New York Times*. It laid out a post-Cold War strategy for maintaining American global hegemony: Russia was still to be treated as an enemy; the U.S. needed to sustain a military powerful enough to suppress the emergence of any new regional power; America ought to be ready to go to war over the Baltic countries. As the leakers anticipated, the Wolfowitz plan was greeted with derision and mockery, and the Bush administration quickly made it clear that the memorandum was merely a "draft"—the kind of outside-the-box exercise an official might try in his spare time. More sober grownups were in charge.

But by 2002, Wolfowitz was number two at the Pentagon, and the building was filled with supportive neoconservatives. The grownups had largely lost access to the neophyte president's ear. Brent Scowcroft, the first Bush's national security advisor at the time of Desert Storm, was reduced to writing op-eds lamenting that attacking Iraq would jeopardize the broader aims of the war on terrorism. More or less unnoticed, the foreign policy pecking order within the GOP had been overturned during the 1990s. The neoconservatives had risen from being a significant but minority faction to a position of dominance.

Realists, including those with Republican leanings, remained influential outside Washington, in the major universities: in the fall of 2002, several dozen prominent international relations scholars published an advertisement decrying the rush toward war. But they lacked Beltway power. Unlike their neocon rivals, they had no network of think tanks and echo-chamber outfits, no Fox News or talk radio to disseminate their views, no columnists to advance their ideas or undermine their opponents'. Rather like the vanished WASP establishment to which many of them were culturally and temperamentally linked, realists seemed ill-suited to the contemporary rules of political conflict. But if the realist retreat was bad for the country, it would help secure *TAC*'s philosophical foundation.

Thus critics like Foer were wrong when they predicted that *TAC*'s only real audience would be the anti-globalist Left. Foer had concluded his piece by gibing that "Workers of the world unite" would soon be Taki Theodoracopulos's rallying cry. In fact, neoconservative war-mongering was viewed skeptically throughout the democratic West, including in Europe's major center-right parties; in every country save Israel, the Iraq War was unpopular. *TAC*'s potential audience included all those who feared a neocon-led United States would be igniting wars throughout the Middle East and isolating itself.

But if Franklin Foer was wrong, why did *TAC* not make more headway with the conservative establishment? True, our writers never really experienced the shunning David Frum had urged in "Unpatriotic Conservatives," his 2003 *National Review* attack on the outspoken antiwar right. Robert Novak and Pat Buchanan remained popular among the Republican rank and file. Five years after Frum wrote, most Republicans wanted to forget all about the Iraq War—and many were ready to acknowledge that *TAC* had been right to warn against it.

At the same time, they were unable to draw any conclusions from the observation. George W. Bush might have been treated as a non-person and his eight-year presidency an afterthought at the 2012 Republican convention. But prominent Republicans opposed to an aggressive foreign policy remain a minority. Ron Paul's ceiling in the primaries seemed to be in the 20 percent range, and while a more establishment figure might have done better, there may be good reason why someone like Chuck Hagel never ran.

I think the answer is that the aging conservative movement needed, and acquired, a glue to substitute for the anti-communism that held its disparate factions together from the 1950s to the 1980s. Fear and hatred of Islam now serves that function. Many grassroots conservatives justifiably perceive an America besieged by demographic changes, globalization, and the collapse of job security, while Republicans have few answers to offer. As a substitute, talk radio and the activist right—the organs that link the GOP to the grassroots base—supply a belligerent attitude toward the Islamic world.

What can make allies of a lower-middle-class evangelical from Tennessee and a hedge-fund operator in New York passionately interested in Israel? The sense that America's survival is somehow threatened by Islam, whether in the form of a mosque in Murfreesboro, a Palestinian trying to travel from one town to another in his homeland, a nuclear program in Tehran, or a genuinely hostile terrorist group.

A more measured view—that Islam is a historic civilization now in the throes of a tumultuous coming-to-terms with modernity, a process America is fortunately situated to observe from some distance, treat with judiciousness, and perhaps assist—has surprisingly little traction. Instead the right adopted the full "clash of civilizations" narrative. And eventually, as America became an occupier of Muslim countries, taking casualties and inflicting them, the clash acquired its own bloody momentum. It mattered not whether Islam is Sunni or Shia, democratic or monarchic, reactionary or modernizing. The "Islam-is-the-enemy" spirit may have been as alien to Dwight Eisenhower, Richard Nixon, and George H.W. Bush as it is to Pat Buchanan. But it is now perhaps the most critical element holding together the conservative coalition.

If *TAC*'s successes in changing GOP politics have thus far been modest, the magazine's central arguments continue to resonate with an ever wider public. In 2012, perhaps ten times as many Americans have a good sense of the problems caused by neoconservative ideologists as when we began. In the last decade, there have been perhaps a dozen good books on the subject—not enough to dethrone the neocons, but enough to illuminate their ideology.

The same can also be said of the Israel lobby. In 1990, when Buchanan made an off-the-cuff remark on "The McLaughlin Group" that Capitol Hill was "Israeli-occupied territory," it was seized upon by his foes as evidence of anti-Semitism. To speak in such a way was to break the most serious of taboos. Since then, two of America's leading political scientists, John Mearsheimer and Stephen Walt, have published *The Israel Lobby and U.S. Foreign Policy*, which systematically explored the phenomenon Buchanan alluded to—and became a national and international bestseller. Tom Friedman, the bellwether centrist *New York Times* columnist, has written that Benjamin Netanyahu's ovations in Congress are bought and paid for by the Israel lobby, and while some people complained, there was wider acknowledgment that he was simply stating a fact. That neoconservatism and the Israel lobby are now openly and widely discussed inside and outside the beltway is a major victory.

Moreover, if the current crystallization within the GOP looks dispiriting, there are several signs that point to better days ahead. In early contests where he had the resources to campaign competitively, Ron Paul—whose foreign policy stands had much in common with *TAC*—won the under-30 vote by wide margins while drawing more donations from active-duty military personnel than any other candidate, Republican or Democrat. Even GOP insiders seem to understand that neoconservative foreign policy has little national backing at the grassroots, a fact indirectly acknowledged by the treatment of George W. Bush at the GOP convention.

The path Ron Paul forged in two campaigns will be followed and surely widened by others. One can look to his son Rand, casting iconoclastic votes in the Senate, or to congressmen like young Justin Amash, a Paul supporter from Michigan. Moreover, while younger neoconservatives have seldom served in the armed forces, it seems inevitable that the ranks of both parties will increasingly include many more veterans of Iraq and Afghanistan. The Republicans among them are likely to scoff, not too quietly, at marching orders issued by *The Weekly Standard*. They will want a different kind of conservative magazine instead—one that takes a realistic and sober view of America's challenges at home and abroad.

The American Conservative
November 14, 2012

The Coming Love Affair with Iran

Things are moving so rapidly on the Iran diplomacy front that it's difficult to keep track. But the last week, the U.N. speeches, Iranian President Rouhani's generally well-received "charm offensive," the anticipation of a lunchtime handshake, the hawks' relief when it didn't happen, and then the phone call heard around the world makes one think the glaciers of Mideast diplomacy could break up with surprising rapidity.

Structures seemingly solid and impervious to change can collapse quickly when the time is right: the Maginot Line, the Berlin Wall. Who believed in 1987 that Eastern Europe would be more or less free of Soviet dominance within three years, or that the Soviet Union itself would collapse? Not, to my memory, a single high-ranking diplomat, businessman, or university professor.

So imagine: the nuclear diplomacy track gets going, and Iran makes it clear that it will trade transparency and inspections to ensure non-weaponization. Obama does what he can to strip away the sanctions, encouraged by Europe, which is eager to trade and invest in Iran. And suddenly Americans realize there is this large, sophisticated Muslim country, with a large middle class and a huge appetite for American culture and business. It is not a U.S.-style democracy, far from it—but no country in the Middle East is. At worst, it is in third place. Compared to the state of political freedom in China in 1971, contemporary Iran is a New England town meeting.

Recall: in 1971, American elites fell in love with China. The "China Lobby"—that large complex of anti-communist Chinese and Americans with personal and professional ties to China who felt jilted by the Revolution and that had prevented any rapprochement until then—proved to be a proverbial "paper tiger" once President Nixon decided to reach beyond it. American elites were suddenly enthralled by ping pong and pandas. *New York Times* columnist James Reston had an appendectomy with no anesthetic beyond acupuncture, and it worked out wonderfully—and became the source of hundreds of respectful news stories about Chinese medicine. For years, China was the new flavor on the block. Growing ties with China were the backdrop to everything: America could be humiliated in Vietnam and the world hardly noticed.

Iran, of course, is a smaller deal—smaller in its size, cultural and military weight, and aspirations. But it is a Muslim country that is highly educated (which seems to be the nexus of the problem for Washington's hawks) and is moving seriously toward democracy. It is not Saudi Arabia, whose ruling princes have all the corruptions and weaknesses associated with vast unearned wealth. Iran has all the traits of a modernizing state—mass literacy, mobilized working classes. It has managed to hold its head high throughout almost thirty years of confrontation with Washington. It promises a vast market for American businesses to help rebuild its infrastructure. My guess is that many Americans will fall in love with the place—or at least with the combination of exoticism and profits that détente with Iran promises. Yes, there will be blind and naive aspects to the love—when is there not?—but it will unleash powerful forces that governments cannot control.

So who loses? Obviously we aren't talking about a reversal of alliances. Israel will remain one of the cornerstones of American Middle East policy. But note: "one of." Israel has grown accustomed to a weirdly disproportionate role in Washington, as the one country to which America looks for interpretation and guidelines to action in the Mideast. Normalcy with Iran would almost certainly muddle that. As Israeli analyst Daniel Levy[1] spells out, Israel simply does not want an Iran that is relatively independent or powerful. It has grown accustomed to a tremendous amount of regional hegemony, in great part because every other state in the region is either an American client state or considered beyond the pale. An Iran brought into the fold would fit into neither category.

An Iran with its own ties to America and the West would be a self-reliant and independent power, not a military threat but certainly a state wielding considerable cultural and economic "soft power." A procession of American tourists into Teheran, followed shortly by students and businessmen, would change American perspectives on the region. Israel's ability to act as America's ears and eyes and ultimate interpreter of regional events would almost certainly be diminished, perhaps radically.

I expect Netanyahu and the Israel lobby to use every diplomatic trick they can muster to thwart an American–Iranian rapprochement before it happens. They may succeed; that would be the cynics' view. As the chattering classes are saying in Teheran right now, the Israel lobby will "not allow it." But Israel, even with its well-entrenched lobby, doesn't hold all the cards, and we may find out it holds fewer than we think.

The American Conservative
September 30, 2013

Israel and the Saudis, United in Jealousy

It may be hard to pity John Kerry, but in the last couple of days, I've felt for the guy. America has competitors and rivals, and enemies, too. But the problems posed by so-called friends are more vexing. On Wednesday, Kerry was in Rome for a scheduled seven-hour meeting with Israeli Prime Minister Benjamin Netanyahu. Seven hours, that's right. Three weeks ago, Netanyahu

---

[1] See Levy's elaboration on this point on page TKTK.

got a lengthy meeting with Obama while the U.S. government was on verge of shutting down. Max Blumenthal quipped that one of Obama's main jobs is to be the "Bibi-sitter"—for his efforts to make sure that Netanyahu doesn't start a war in the Mideast or call up his minions in Congress to thwart U.S. diplomacy.

Then there are the Saudis, the other "pillar" of the U.S. Mideast alliance system. Unlike the case of Israel, no one even pretends there are "shared values" in play. It's a pretty pure protection racket: we provide protection to the Saudi monarchy, and they use their oil wealth to aid the U.S. in other objectives, most importantly keeping the price of oil stable. This arrangement made a fair amount of sense post-1945 when keeping Arabia in the Western camp and the Soviets away from Mideast oilfields seemed of paramount importance, as it was throughout the Cold War. But the inherent problems of a close relationship dealing with a medieval theocracy with piles of money are now becoming more obvious.

One problem is that they basically don't like us, at all; another is they seemingly prefer their women to be covered in shapeless black sacks; a third, that U.S. troops cannot be stationed there, lest Saudis feel compelled to blow up U.S. buildings in retaliation. (Most of the 9/11 hijackers were Saudis.) The Saudis use their vast wealth to spread their brand of Islam throughout the Muslim world, a brand which happens to be more anti-modern and anti-Western than any other kind. They are upset when Obama balked at intervening in Syria on behalf of the Saudi-backed jihadi rebels, and of course ignore the fact that the Palestinians still have no state sixty-five years after the Zionists got one. My guess is that the Saudis care far more about the jihadi forces they support in Syria than the Palestinians, who are, by regional standards, a basically secular and forward-looking group. They have shown their anger by refusing to take the seat in the U.N. Security Council that they spent years lobbying for.

And of course Iran. Here is where the Saudis, the other little rich gulf states, and Bibi Netanyahu are on the same page. You can see why Iran frightens them. It is governed by Shiite Muslims, and there are restive Shia minorities in most of the Gulf states, pressuring and sometimes demonstrating for civil and political rights. And of course Iran has a genuine middle class and a scientific infrastructure, which is why both Israel (which behaves as if it has a right in perpetuity to a regional nuclear weapons monopoly) and the Saudis, who are perhaps embarrassed by their own relative backwardness, feel threatened.

So here comes John Kerry, needing to mollify Netanyahu and the Saudi monarchy, while trying to oversee negotiations with Iran without being completely hamstrung by an AIPAC- and Tea Party-dominated Congress.

Oh, and don't forget European pique at the fact that the NSA has been reading their email and monitoring their phone conversations—news of which has been splayed over the front pages in the very European capitals where Kerry is attempting to mend fences.

So of course Kerry is having a difficult time. But this is to be expected. The stakes in the current Iran negotiation are enormous: if they succeed in blocking Iran's quest for a nuclear bomb-making capacity while ending the diplomatic and economic blockade of the country, the impact will resonate throughout the region. Iran has modernized despite obstacles both self-imposed (by its own Islamic revolution) and imposed from without. It is entirely natural that Israel and Saudi Arabia should be jealous of American interest in country, natural that they would think that American attentions to Iran (and tourism and business investment) long bottled up, would burst out and soon come to rival or exceed the attentions we bestow on them. And natural that they will pull out all the stops to prevent a successful negotiation.

I would wager nonetheless that the forces in favor of a rapprochement of Iran with the West will prevail. It is to some extent simply bizarre that the United States—which does, to a very considerable degree, believe in and support democracy and science and progress—finds itself permanently estranged from one of the Islamic countries that is most modern and most democratic. Not to fault Israel and Saudi Arabia, but Iran as well as Turkey should be on friendly terms with the United States.

Israeli spokesmen like to pretend that the current emotion for a rapprochement is based solely on a "charm offensive" waged by the new Iranian president and his American-educated foreign minister. I would argue it goes deeper. Perhaps some variant of a maxim formulated (if memory serves) by Robert Nisbet is at play: don't underestimate the importance of boredom as a force for political change. To be bound so tightly to Israel and Saudi Arabia—one the sort of ethnostate dreamed up by East Europeans in the last century, the other an exemplar of medieval backwardness—this is our destiny, forever?

The American Conservative
October 25, 2013

THE U.S.–ISRAEL POLITICS GAP

Last Friday, Israeli settlers attacked the vehicles of American diplomats on the West Bank with stones, clubs, and axes. American security personnel accompanying the two cars reportedly drew their weapons but did not use them. The American consular officials were trying to investigate the destruction by Israeli settlers of Palestinian olive trees—on land owned by a Palestinian-American. (In an amusing sidebar to this not especially funny incident, the Israeli Defense Forces apparently took down from its website a video link describing rock-throwing at cars as "terrorism"—it had been put up to justify harsh Israeli military response to Palestinian boys who throw rocks at Israeli settler cars.)

The Obama administration's response to the incident thus far has been timid, almost apologetic in tone; it released a statement by a minor State Department spokesman saying it was "deeply concerned" by the attack and was "working with Israeli authorities" in their investigation of the incident. One might think that a non-lethal assault on American diplomats in the Mideast would attract some American media attention, especially one carried out citizens of "America's greatest ally." But there has been little coverage: a short paragraph in the *Times*, some minor additional mentions, that's all.

The incident serves as sort of coda for the holiday season: over the break, American diplomats worked feverishly to beat back a Palestinian-sponsored U.N. resolution calling for immediate negotiations to establish a Palestinian state within a one-year deadline, and for Israel to end its occupation. Their efforts succeeded: Nigeria unexpectedly abstained at the last moment, depriving the measure of the nine votes it would have needed to pass the U.N. security council. The U.S. might then have vetoed it anyway, but a veto would have embarrassed an administration that claims to favor a two-state solution.

Meanwhile, as Congress recessed, AIPAC bragged how it had shepherded through Capitol Hill three resolutions increasing, if such a thing was possible, American support for Israel. One designated Israel as a "major strategic partner"—a designation, AIPAC reminded everyone, not given to any other country on the planet.

Israel's relationship to the American Congress is truly something to behold. Visiting Israel over the break, Sen. Lindsey Graham came up with an interesting formulation to describe it. In an interview with Sheldon Adelson's Israeli paper, Graham assured Israelis that the much-described chilliness of President Obama's relationship with Prime Minister Netanyahu was actually of little consequence: "Presidents come and go. Bush 41's administration had problems with Israel's policies. In business terms, the anchor tenant is the Congress." It's a revealing metaphor, suggesting Israeli ownership of the American–Israeli relationship. Americans pay rent, which Congress is always willing to do.

At a joint press conference with Netanyahu, Graham assured him that Congress will "follow your lead" regarding American negotiations with Iran. What a remarkable statement from a critical American legislator—

essentially conferring leadership on a vital national security issue to a foreign country! This too was barely noted by the American media, which is a bit of a surprise as it is widely understood that Netanyahu wants American negotiations with Iran to fail, so better as to draw the United States into a war with the Persian state.

The ability of Netanyahu to supervise the American Congress is all the more remarkable in view of how generally ambivalent the American public has become about Israel. This is not to say of course that most Americans are hostile to Israel; most are supportive. But recent polls indicate that most Americans generally want Washington to be even-handed between Israel and the Palestinians; one surprising recent finding was the surging number of Americans who favor a "one-state solution" in which both Israeli Jews and Palestinian Arabs have civil and voting rights in historic Palestine. It's less shocking than it seems: Americans are making a go of multiculturalism at home, though its a route few of them would have chosen fifty years ago. According to a poll recently presented at the Brookings Institution by the University of Maryland's Shibley Telhami, 73 percent of Americans favor either a two-state solution or one-state solution with equal rights for both people—a figure roughly three time the combined number of those who favor either Israeli annexation of the West Bank or a perpetuation of the status quo of Israeli occupation, occasionally punctuated by bouts of let's-pretend peace talks.

Generally, younger people and Democrats are more favorable to the Palestinians than the Republican and the elderly. And pro-Israel voices are more passionate (and donate far more campaign money) than other Americans.

The point, however, is not that the American public is divided—though it is, or that public sentiment is shifting inexorably away from strong support for Israel to a more neutral stance, though that is true as well. It is that the actual sentiments of Americans are almost completely unrepresented in the American Congress, which has recently vowed—by almost unanimous votes—to back Israel's right-wing government whatever it does. Perhaps it is too much to now expect a Congressional resolution apologizing to the Israeli settlers for the efforts of American diplomats to investigate their destruction of Palestinian olive groves, but would such a resolution really be surprising?

The American Conservative
January 7, 2015

How Obama Can Stop Netanyahu's Iran War

Some interesting polls form a background to the collision of major historical forces unleashed by Israeli Prime Minister Netanyahu's decision to solicit an invitation to address the U.S. Congress in March.

First, released several days ago, is a Bloomberg global poll of investors, traders, and financial analysts. One can make one's own assumptions about how representative this group is, or of what: I would take it to be part of the international capitalist business class, but not necessarily its top echelon. The group ranks geopolitical threats to world markets as follows: global terrorism, 26 percent; Russia-Ukraine, 26 percent; cybercrime, 13 percent; not sure, 10 percent; Islamic State, 9 percent; South China Sea, 6 percent; climate change, 6 percent; Iran 2 percent ... equaled by Israel-Palestine 2 percent and exceeding Ebola at 1 percent. In other words, Iran is barely on the radar as a threat to peace and economic stability.

Several months ago, the Brookings Institution released a major poll of American attitudes toward Israel supervised by University of Maryland professor Shibley Telhami. One question asked what outcome respondents wished for the Israel-Palestine conflict. A plurality of Americans supported the Obama administration's efforts to push Israel and the Palestinians toward a two-state solution. A nearly equal number favored a one-state solution in which everybody, Israeli and Palestinian, had equal rights and could vote in all of historic Palestine. Only 22 percent supported options favored by Netanyahu's present ruling coalition, either annexation of the West Bank without giving citizenship the Palestinians or the continued status quo of Israeli occupation.

The poll showed that 16 percent of those who rated Israel/Palestine as one of their three top issues were somewhat more "pro-Israel" than the overall group, but not overwhelmingly so. Of this group, 55 percent wanted the U.S. to favor Israel, 39 percent wanted the U.S. to be evenhanded, and 6 percent favored the Palestinians.

No one could look at these poll numbers and fail to conclude that the current stance of Congress, which skews toward unconditional backing of the Israeli right, does not come close to representing the sentiments of the American people. Indeed, it is one of those situations that call for a market correction: everything seems like it never is going to change, until one day, to everyone's surprise, something happens and it suddenly does. Then everyone Crack house and Obama Crack house and Obama back and point out how obvious it was that the previous status quo was unsustainable and correction inevitable.

John Boehner and the Republican leadership in Congress, in close consultation with the Israeli ambassador Ron Dermer (formerly a Republican operative from Miami Beach), arranged an invitation to Netanyahu to address the body. The subject of the Israeli's speech will not be Israel's relations with the Palestinians, which Netanyahu dearly wishes that the world ignore. It is the so-called Iranian threat, and indirectly America's and the P5 + 1 countries negotiation with Iran, which he hopes to derail.

The invitation, solicited and accepted without consultation with the White House, has had the interesting effect of causing discord all around, outside the Israel lobby and within it as well. The Obama administration was predictably livid, seeing the speech as a blatant move by Israel's government to subvert the administration's diplomacy by giving a boost to various bills in Congress designed to thwart negotiations. The administration announced that neither Kerry nor Obama would meet Netanyahu while he was here. Quotes from an unnamed American "senior official" who spoke to *Haaretz* revealed a degree of anger at the Israeli leader's maneuver: "We thought we'd seen everything. But Bibi managed to surprise even us. There are things you simply don't do. He spat in our face publicly and that's no way to behave."

Even a number of Netanyahu's most reliable backers wonder whether the Israeli has overreached. Michael Oren, a right-winger who served four years as Netanyahu's ambassador to Washington, said the invitation smelled of a "cynical political move" that could "hurt our attempts to act against Iran." *Commentary* worried that Israel's blatant disregard of normal protocol could give some Democrats cover for supporting the negotiations and that the whole episode seemed to muddle as much as buttress Israel's case against the Iran negotiations. Ron Radosh—not before accusing Obama of "verging on" anti-Semitism for using that well-known code word "donors" when asking his fellow Democrats to refrain from backing diplomacy-busting bills—came down on Oren's side. On the other side, Norman Podhoretz's son-in-law Elliott Abrams backed Netanyahu, quoting in his favor this four-year-old passage from historian Walter Russell Mead:

> Israel matters in American politics like almost no other country on earth. Well beyond the American Jewish and the Protestant fundamentalist communities, the people and the story of Israel stir some of the deepest and most mysterious reaches of the American soul. The idea of Jewish and Israeli exceptionalism is profoundly tied to the idea of American exceptionalism. The belief that God favors and protects Israel is connected to the idea that God favors and protects America.

Stirring words, surely, if you are a right-wing Zionist. But I don't think anyone can look at the recent polls, such as Telhami's cited above, or others that correspond to it, and think they describe contemporary American reality. There are surely some Americans who love Israel in this sense, but the far larger sentiment, nourished out of long frustration with Israel's stonewalling of the peace process and the brutality of its military campaigns against Palestinian civilians, is a good deal more complicated. What remains is the power of the Israel lobby, exercised in great part through Congress by the leverage exerted by major donors.

The stakes are greater than a test of one's affection towards Israel, the Zionist project, or the belief (or lack of it) that the Palestinians should have any rights at all in their native land. They are greater than whether Congress should be meddling in American diplomacy by passing sanctions legislation in the middle of negotiations, or whether those sanctions would actually "throw a grenade" into the talks, as Mossad chief Tamir Pardo described it. They are really over whether the United States should go to war against Iran at Israel's behest. War is off the table for now—though it was less than eight years ago that leading neoconservatives were pushing loudly and openly for George W. Bush to attack Iran. But there is every possibility that the next president, a non-Rand Paul Republican or Hillary Clinton, would be far more amenable than Obama to Israel's war entreaties.

The bills now working their way through Congress are an intermediate step, a threshold before war, after which the following steps would likely ensue: a blow up in the negotiations—hawkish Arkansas Senator Tom Cotton said this was "very much the intended consequence" of the legislation—the reintroduction of more severe sanctions, which may hurt the Iranian people but will likely convince Iranian leaders that negotiation with the United States is futile; an end to the intrusive inspections mandated by the existing provisional agreements between the P5+1 and Iran, further advances in the Iran's ambiguous nuclear program, leaving the next president with the option of containing a nuclear capable Iran or going to war. Netanyahu and the neocons believe that under such circumstances, the choice would be war.

If that juncture is reached, we can expect the neoconservatives to claim the war will be a cakewalk. They've had practice with their lines. Charles Krauthammer, their best polemicist, has been sounding the tocsins lately about "Emerging Iranian Empire." Here's some of what he had to say about invading Iraq in 2003:

> Hence Iraq. This is about more than the terrible weapons. It is about reconstituting a terrorized society. A de-Saddamized Iraq with a decent government could revolutionize the region. It would provide friendly basing not just for the outward projection of American power but also for the outward projection of democratic and modernizing ideas, which is why the Administration plans an 18-month occupation for a civil and political reconstruction unlike any since postwar Germany and Japan. If we succeed, the effect on the region would be enormous, encouraging democrats and modernizers—and threatening

despots and troglodytes—in neighboring Iran, Saudi Arabia, Syria, and beyond. To do this, however, America must give up patrolling from over the horizon. It must come ashore.

Americans don't like that. They do not hunger for exotic lands. America is perhaps the only hegemonic power in history in constant search of "exit strategies." But Sept. 11 taught that what the U.S. needs in the Arab world is not an exit strategy but an entry strategy. Iraq is the beckoning door.

The Arabs fully understand this historic shift from containment to construction. They see that pan-Arab reformation is the deepest meaning of an American entry into Iraq. That is why the Arab League so strenuously opposes the intervention. The rulers of the 22 Arab states—not a single one freely elected — understand that Iraq is only the beginning and that reformation ultimately spells their end. Not a happy prospect for them, but a real hope for their long-repressed people—and for those threatened by the chaos and fanaticism bred in that cauldron of repression.

Obviously the invasion, which has smashed Iraq, killed hundreds of thousands, and created perhaps a million refugees, cleared the stage for ISIS, and left Iraq vulnerable to an al-Qaeda-style takeover, did not work out quite as Krauthammer forecast. Nor was there any prospect that it would.

So now the neoconservatives are laying the ground for their next war. Bombing Iran won't do the job, say defense analysts like Kenneth Pollack (a somewhat chastened Iraq hawk). We will need to occupy the country—four times as large as Iraq, with two and a half times the population. If you liked the occupation of Iraq, you'll love war against Iran.

The weird thing is that such a war is totally unnecessary. Iran is actually our ally against the fundamentalist jihadis of ISIS and actually the only Middle East country using any real muscle to combat ISIS. It's a country with a fashionable, culturally pro-Western middle class that lives in uneasy coexistence with a fundamentalist regime that is about as well-respected as the Brezhnev-era Communist Party was in the Soviet Union. The revolution, the hostage crisis, were more than 35 years ago. Anti-Americanism in Iran is more or less dead as a mobilizing force. Yet this is the country that Netanyahu and the neocons want us to bomb and invade.

I believe Obama can win his showdown with Netanyahu, win it decisively, and in so doing forever transform the relationship between the United States and Israel. But he can't do it without laying his cards out very clearly, in a major speech, probably a televised speech. The points made would resemble those suggested in a seminal article by Robert Merry in *The National Interest* two and a half years ago. He would have to explain that the United States' national interests on Iran have diverged from those of Israel, and why, and iterate that his constitutional duty is the protection of America's national interest. He could explain that a war against Iran would quadruple the chaos in the Middle East, abort the economic recovery, and sever the United States both from its allies in Europe and its more ambivalent strategic rivals/partners, Russia and China. The only countries that would be pleased would be Israel and the Saudi princes. The American military, exhausted from 15 years of war, would face another 15 years of occupation duty. The jihadist Sunnis, ISIS, and all the rest, Iran's fiercest enemies, would of course be delighted at the destruction of the Shi'ite regime they view as apostate. But who else would be?

Above all, Obama could stress that as president he will no longer stand for American policies being subject to manipulation by a foreign power. In speaking in terms of American national interest, he will find reservoirs of support Democrats haven't touched in many years. As Merry makes clear, the pushback would be fierce. But a president who explained his decisions in terms of refusing to concede the country's sovereign command over decisions of war and peace to a minor foreign power would be victorious.

The American Conservative
January 28, 2015

How the Iran Deal Serves America

If Iran's nuclear program were the primary concern of those lamenting the deal that John Kerry and representatives of five major countries concluded with Iran last Tuesday, they would be relatively pleased. Under the agreement, Iran will be stripped of 98 percent of its enriched uranium, all of its plutonium producing capacity, and two-thirds of its centrifuges, and will be placed under the most rigorous inspection regime in the history of nuclear proliferation negotiations.

The cartoon image of Iran racing toward the bomb—presented last year by Prime Minister Netanyahu at the United Nations—may not have been reality-based, but if that's what Israel is worried about, it can relax. Iran will not be racing toward the bomb.

But of course Israel is not pleased at all, and many of its volunteer spokesmen and politicians in the United States are railing against the deal as virtually the worst thing to happen in history. Netanyahu has let no one outdo him in hysteria. Iran is seeking to "take over the world," he told an Israeli audience last week. (As the leaders of Russia, China, France, Germany, and Britain signed onto the agreement, one wonders how they all managed to miss the world takeover threat Netanyahu sees so clearly.)

Netanyahu's followers in the United States, AIPAC, the Republicans in Congress, and the Iraq War neocons will dutifully suit up and mount a serious effort to scuttle the deal. (AIPAC has ordered staffers to cancel their summer vacations.) But something far different from Iranian centrifuges is at stake. It has never been clear to the U.S. intelligence community (or for that matter to the Israeli one) that Iran wanted a nuclear weapon to begin with, and it is far from obvious what advantages, if any, Iran would accrue if it managed to cobble together one or two nuclear weapons. There really isn't any evidence that Iran's leaders want the destruction of their 5,000 year-old Persian civilization, which would be the inevitable consequence of using the supposed bombs that Iran's leaders have always denied any interest in seeking.

But the deal means something far more than outside supervision of Iran's reactors. President Obama and his foreign-policy establishment want, I believe, at least to explore the possibility that Iran can fit into the roster of American diplomatic options in the region, where reliance on our traditional allies has run into a dead end. The obvious comparison is to Nixon's trip to China, which turned out to be an effective way of mitigating the disaster of the Vietnam War and actually ensured that the aftermath of that war was far from unfortunate for the United States. The chaos that has been ignited in the Sunni world in great part by George W. Bush's invasion of Iraq and the after-effects of a losing war in Afghanistan might be partially offset in Iran.

The turn to Iran was foreshadowed in the immediate aftermath of 9/11—when Tehran was the only city in the Muslim world in which there were public and spontaneous displays of sympathy for the United States, and shortly thereafter there was some considerable on-the-ground cooperation in Afghanistan with Iranian intelligence on the overthrow of the Taliban. Of course this cooperation was short-circuited by the neoconservatives in the Bush administration, who persuaded the president to include Iran in the "axis of evil."

One doesn't want to overestimate the possibilities for such cooperation, which may turn up empty. But it is obvious that Iran is much more than the "world's number one sponsor of terrorism," the agitprop phrase that Israel has sought to wrap it in. Iran is—in distinct contrast to every other Muslim country in the region—a large state with a partially democratic political system (no one at this point would deny that Iranian popular elections really matter), a very young and well-educated population, a middle class, a film industry, a fashion industry, a real cuisine, and a large number of young people who want to at least partially identify with the West. To compare and contrast the cultural compatibility of Iran and Saudi Arabia with the United States is a kind of joke.

Saudi Arabia has never been more an ally than an oil spigot: most of the 9/11 hijackers were Saudis, and the U.S. government is still coy about the extent of Saudi government financing of the 9/11 attacks. Most recently, Saudi Arabia has been cooperating with al-Qaeda of the Arabian Peninsula, which would seem to make it a "state sponsor of terror" if one is counting. It is sufficient, one would think, to take with a grain of salt the argument that the Iran negotiation is a betrayal of our "traditional allies" in the region.

Of course, the other main opponent of the Iran deal is Israel, and Israel's American spokespeople make frequent references to Saudi Arabia's hurt feelings only as a way to portray their opposition as being grounded in something broader than Israel's wishes alone. And it may turn out that a United States with more normal relations with Iran would be slightly less deferential to our "only democratic ally" in the Mideast. Sophisticated observers figured this out early on, long before there were any details about centrifuges and inspections to speak about. Daniel Levy, the Israeli analyst and former peace negotiator, wrote about this in *Foreign Policy* in September 2013 when John Kerry and Javad Zarif had done little more than pass notes in the U.N. corridor:

> If Iran is willing to cut a deal that effectively provides a guarantee against a weaponization of its nuclear program, and that deal is acceptable to the president of the United States of America, why would Netanyahu not take yes for an answer?

> The reason lies in Netanyahu's broader view of Israel's place in the region: the Israeli premier simply does not want an Islamic Republic of Iran that is a relatively independent and powerful actor. Israel has gotten used to a degree of regional hegemony and freedom of action—notably military action—that is almost unparalleled globally, especially for what is, after all, a rather small power. Israelis are understandably reluctant to give up any of that.

> Israel's leadership seeks to maintain the convenient reality of a neighboring region populated by only two types of regimes. The first type is regimes with a degree of dependence on the United States, which necessitates severe limitations on challenging Israel (including diplomatically). The second type is regimes that are considered beyond the pale by the United States and as many other global actors as possible, and therefore unable to do serious damage to Israeli interests.

> Israel's leadership would consider the emergence of a third type of regional actor—one that is not overly deferential to Washington but also is not boycotted, and that even boasts a degree of economic, political, and military weight—a deeply undesirable development.

The fact is that Israel has used this regional military hegemony, and the political inability of any American president to oppose it, in ways that cannot help but generate hostility to the United States on the part of virtually all Muslims in the region, no matter where they fall on the Sunni-Shiite divide. When Israel assaults a more-or-less defenseless Gazan population and kills 500 Palestinian children, using a high-tech military provided entirely by the United States, Americans pay a price, though those ignorant of the region do not recognize this.

The United States of course will always be allied with Israel, and this alliance would go more easily if Israel made peace with the Palestinians. But it's hard to imagine any American president would not welcome more diplomatic options in the region than those provided by Israel and Saudi Arabia. Perhaps this explains why Jeb Bush seemed over the weekend to cast a glance toward the exit door of the Republican crazy train, proclaiming that he would not necessarily abrogate an Iran agreement on day one of his presidency.

The American Conservative
July 20, 2015

Netanyahu's Lobby vs. the World

The Iran deal debate is huge and historic: a committed and eloquent president in his prime, able to mobilize scientists and diplomats and most of Washington's foreign affairs establishment on one hand; opposing him, groups funded by a few billionaires, able to saturate selected congressional districts with television advertising and frighten many office holders. It's a subject that will draw historians for decades to come. If the government of Israel and its friends are able to block the Joint Comprehensive Plan of Action (Israeli security professionals are not enthusiastic about the deal but, unlike Netanyahu, generally favor it as the best thing possible), it will be perceived to be just as pivotal as Woodrow Wilson's failure to secure the United States' adherence to the League of Nations, effectively dooming that organization.

On the face of it, the international coalition in favor of the deal should seem overwhelming. That diplomats from France, Germany, and Britain spent last week in Congress warning that all hell would break loose if the deal were scuttled was barely reported in the American press, but it did happen. The U.N. Security Council voted 15-0 in favor of the deal. If, against such odds, Netanyahu, AIPAC, and the perennially well-funded let's-start-a-war-against-Iraq crowd—*The Weekly Standard*, Foundation for the Defense of Democracies, *Commentary*, *The New York Sun*, etc.—can overcome the combined foreign policy establishments of the United States, Russia, China,

Britain, France, and Germany, it will be truly an event for the ages. If the result of scuttling the deal is war, which Obama believes, and which the more honest of the deal's opponents publicly hope, they will fully own the war. If the result is an Iranian rush to the bomb and no war, they will own that result as well.

If one is to look clearly at American politics, and indeed much of the world's, it is apparent that the old concept of dual loyalty (often used as a smear) is no longer relevant in a day that celebrates competing identities. Dual loyalty was a charge leveled at European Jews in the heyday of European nationalism, which insinuated that Jews remained more loyal to their own group than to their country of citizenship, and of course this charge was often inextricably tied up with the most extreme anti-Semitism. During the same historical period, leading American politicians railed at hyphenated Americans—Germans and Swedes and other opponents of intervention in the First World War, for example—and afterwards, often repressive pro-assimilation legislation was turned against immigrants of almost every stripe.

It is now obvious that many in the West have complicated and potentially competing loyalties. European nationalism of the nation-state variety is a subdued and increasingly less pronounced sentiment, and a high proportion of college-educated European baby boomers consider the European Union a noble and idealistic endeavor that competes with or even overrides their sense of Frenchness or Italianness. In America, too, not only are we "all multiculturalists now" but our patriotism comes in different layers. Many young Americans feel themselves part of a new transnational, tech-savvy, entrepreneurial bourgeoisie, which imagines itself as borderless; many more are married to persons of another nationality or faith. Personal experiences, even a stint in the Peace Corps, can produce some ties of allegiance. Who at some moment has not contemplated where they might try to emigrate— France? Ireland? Canada? Australia?—if politics here took a truly bad turn? Or even if they didn't.

So let's stipulate that the loyalty questions now spilling out over the Iran debate are muddy. Is it over the top when *The Huffington Post* headlines an (excellent) article by David Bromwich "Netanyahu and his Marionettes"? Some think so. But truth also has its claims—and much of Capitol Hill's embrace of the Netanyahu position would simply not exist were it not for campaign funds from Israel-linked organizations. If something of this importance is true, should it not be written?

Last week the *Times* ran an AIPAC-inspired story in which various unnamed AIPAC officials accused the White House of using "dog whistles" in its efforts to combat the campaign against the deal. This was a subtle sign, shortly followed by much tougher accusations of anti-Semitism in the *Tablet*,

The Weekly Standard (by Elliott Abrams, no less), *The Wall Street Journal*, and the *New York Post*. Obama is notoriously cautious and lawyerly in his language, and not a phrase in his American University speech could be fairly construed as a "dog whistle"—unless you are AIPAC and so thoroughly accustomed to politicians' obsequiousness that any opposition can cause a temper tantrum. But to be sure, in left-wing websites and other venues dual-loyalty accusations have been made. Chuck Schumer likes to tell Jewish audiences that his name means "guardian" in Hebrew while promising them that he will conduct himself as Israel's guardian. Is it an anti-Semitic dog whistle to point out that fact? Does it mean his assessment of the deal is based on what he deems best for Israel, rather than his own constituents? Is it politically effective to point that fact out? I would probably answer no, yes, no—but clearly we're in uncertain waters here.

New factors are coming into play as well. The National Iranian American Council filled an important role in briefing journalists and lobbying legislators throughout the negotiation process; in the *Times*, there recently appeared an ad signed by hundreds of prominent Iranian Americans in support of the deal. The Iranian-American community has been apolitical for years—probably most of its most prominent professional members are refugees or the children of refugees from Iran's Islamic revolution. Still, given the choice between a deal that may open up Iran to the world and the bombing of their country that America's neoconservatives yearn for, they overwhelmingly prefer the former. Are they too under the spell of a kind of dual loyalty? Yes, of course: what kind of person would want to see their parents' country bombed and destroyed?

The Iranian-American community now ranks, I believe, as the single best-educated ethnic group in the United States, and is, generally speaking, professionally quite successful. It is relatively small, but knowing quite a few of its members, I hope its political influence will only grow. Even 10 years ago, few prominent Iranian Americans would have signed such a letter. But the American polity concerned with foreign policy is evolving every day. Obama is in many ways a result of that. And deference to Israel is slowly but steadily becoming less mandatory.

Some predictions: the effort to stomp out criticism of the JCPOA's opponents by charging anti-Semitism, unwarranted in virtually every case, will not succeed. Basically, this is not a matter of defending a groundbreaking book by two prominent scholars, or the record of a intelligently reactionary presidential candidate. The Iran deal is a broad establishment project, a world establishment project—and charging anti-Semitism isn't going to cut it. But that said, individual members of Congress do live in dread of getting on AIPAC's bad side. And a massive fear-mongering media campaign has moved and will continue to move the polls against the deal. Crude TV ads are really effective, as any student of American politics knows.

How will it end? I would predict the Democrats will sustain Obama's veto of the Netanyahu-inspired legislation. The political landscape will be transformed. But it will be transformed whatever happens. Whoever said that the Israel lobby is a night flower, which flourishes in the dark and withers in the sunlight, is likely to be vindicated.

The American Conservative
August 12, 2015

The Great Replacement

Like millions all over the globe, I consider France my second country. I speak French poorly but passably, have visited Paris many times for short and long stays, and long ago did a year of research in French government archives for a history doctoral dissertation. (The subject was the perennial and still very much alive issue of how France could inculcate young people from the territories of its colonial empire with French loyalties.)

These following pieces were written before the horrific November 13 attacks in Paris, part of an ISIS terrorist offensive that included mass casualty assaults in Baghdad and Beirut. But these recent events confirm one assumption underlying the two pieces: the Euro-American globalist establishment belief that France and the rest of Europe can and should accommodate rapidly growing populations of Muslim immigrants is almost certainly deluded and utopian. One need not endorse every attitude and program of the populist parties of the so-called extreme Right to conclude that on this question, they are basically correct. Marine Le Pen's National Front is the most successful of these parties, and under her leadership has emerged as a genuine contender to lead France. Readers of the pieces below will see that I consider the widespread efforts to denigrate her party as somehow beyond the pale to be shortsighted and elitist. It is worth recalling that de Gaulle was once seen as a dangerous quasi-fascist in most Anglo-Saxon establishment opinion.

It seems inevitable that the Paris attacks will open a new chapter in the conflict between the West and radical Islam. The United States faces many complex choices, and would do well to try to see the situation with fresh eyes, rather than continue to view the region through the lenses of its "allies," Israel and Saudi Arabia. My view is that ISIS cannot be contained, and that eventually its key bases so near to Europe must be eradicated. One must hope, in any event, that Western statesmen choose their battles with more wisdom and foresight than did Americans after 9/11.

CHRISTOPHER CALDWELL'S 'REFLECTIONS'

Somewhat against my expectations, I found Christopher Caldwell's *Reflections on the Revolution in Europe* extremely impressive—complex, multifaceted, nuanced. One of its virtues is its sense of openness and uncertainty about questions that are genuinely difficult. How many baby boomers, raised in an era when campus bookstores were stuffed with titles about Marxism, would have anticipated that discernment of the trends and qualities within Islam would have become one of the more necessary sociological skills of our time? And yet it is so—in an era when multicultural questions are difficult, those regarding Islam tend to be the hardest of all. There have been glimpses of this on *Mondoweiss*: Phil Weiss's candid post about his unease at the advance of the headscarf in Gaza and the correlated limitations on women's liberty—and the thoughtful responses his post generated.

The revolution to which Caldwell is referring is not indigenous to Europe, but likely as significant as 1789 in France (the subject of Edmund Burke's "Reflections" from which Caldwell ambitiously derives his title). But it is taking place on European territory. It is driven by the rise of Islam within Europe through immigration, a subject until recently as sedulously avoided by European elites as the discussion of the Israel lobby has been within the United States. But after fatwas against famous novelists (and their editors and translators), murders and riots over cartoons, riots of a more mundane nature, shocking assassinations of a provocateur filmmaker and the murder of a leading anti-immigration politician, it is avoided no longer.

Had I to weigh the extent to which the Islamic world is more victim or victimizer of America and the West, the scales would tilt decisively toward America as the more guilty party. The Iraq War, whose rationale was constructed on a web of lies and propaganda generated by a small group of neoconservatives, has killed hundreds of thousands, and made refugees of millions of Iraqis, without (not that it should matter) any real benefit to the United States. Add to the crime of Iraq Washington's multibillion dollar annual subsidy of Israel's conquest and settlement of the Arab sections of Jerusalem and the West Bank—a policy patently illegal under international law that has proceeded without interruption for two generations—and it easy to see how any Muslim-Palestinian, Iraqi, or otherwise could feel justified in opposing America and the West.

But long before I read Caldwell's book, I would have placed Muslim immigration into Europe on the other side of the ledger. Granted that much of this immigration has been legal—even if it takes advantages of loopholes (for marriage and "family unification") never intended by those who drafted Europe's laws. Much of Islamist political activity within Europe is legal too—

not of course the bombings of train stations, or the "honor killings" of Muslim women who seek access to same menu or sexual and romantic choices that Western women have. But yes, completely lawful has been exploitation of Europe's welfare system and the protections of its "hate-speech" laws, which—with an assist from Europe's own multiculti inhibitions—have long rendered Europe's political establishment mute on an issue with the potential to transform completely its civilization.

There is no great need to rehearse the demographic data underlying this transformation, which are, easily accessible. Europe's Muslim population is now relatively small over all, considerably larger in major cities, larger still in the elementary school systems. If trends continue at anything near their current rate, Christianity won't be Europe's first religion by the end of this century.

But what is one to make of this transformation? Here Caldwell's digressions are the most thought-provoking. For instance, he contrasts the attitudes of the late Pope John Paul II and the current Pope Benedict on Islam. John Paul II was (besides being a Polish patriot and key figure in the peaceful unraveling of the communism) an opponent of unbridled global capitalism and secularism in general. In many realms he saw Islam as an ally. Devout Christians, Muslims, and Buddhists, he believed, have more in common with one another than with atheists. He apologized for the Crusades, promoted dialogue with other faiths.

Benedict apparently doesn't agree. That is the backstory to the speech he made in Regensburg in 2006—one he had to spend a lot of time "explaining" or apologizing for afterward. He believes that secular Westerners have a lot in common with their religious peers, that it is no accident that democratic socialism and human rights have flourished primarily in the Christian West. They are the offshoots of Christian culture. Secular intellectuals therefore should sympathize with the Church, even if they are not believers or church-goers. While trying to convince the secular to join the flock he is "trying to convince them that they are, in a way, in it already." Unlike his predecessor he has made more effort to dialogue with atheist intellectuals like Jürgen Habermas than with Muslim clerics.

Who is right? As a staffer for Pat Buchanan's regrettably ignored 2000 presidential campaign, I was privileged to witness a variant of the John Paul II strategy: PJB was the luncheon speaker at a large conference of American Muslims, and his memorable lines were jokey ones that went something like, "American Muslims are sometimes described as patriarchal—authoritarian believers in large families. It sounds to me very much like my own father." This went over very well.

The European civilization threatened by Islamic immigration is not traditional (i.e., somewhat Buchananite) Europe, but postmodern liberal Europe—a regime that has existed for a generation or two and may well have been slated to die out from demographic causes alone, with no assist needed from Pakistani or Turkish immigrants. Caldwell's discussion of Muslim values is more dispassionate, not hostile or polemical. Some newly alarmed European liberals have charged that Islamism opposes core European principles "that developed from Galileo to gay marriages." Wait a second, says Caldwell, observing that while gay marriage may become a core European principle sometime, right now it is an innovation, "sheltered from parliamentary accountability by human rights laws." Further: "What secular Europeans call 'Islam' is a set of values that Dante and Erasmus would recognize as theirs; the collection of three-year-old rights they call 'core European principles' is a set of values that would leave Dante and Erasmus bewildered."

So Europe may now have a moderately big problem with Islam, with a larger one in store. The question Caldwell raises indirectly without answering is whether a people that has more or less chosen to have, on average, scarcely more than one child per family, has effectively forfeited its right to care about its collective future.

Caldwell is an editor at *The Weekly Standard*, and nothing in his book challenges that magazine's lack of wisdom about the Iraq War or the Israeli dispossession of the Palestinians. Occasionally, he seems to treat those topics as kind of made up excuses, more fodder for a radical Muslim grievance industry than real issues. He is obviously quite wrong about this, but this shouldn't overshadow his book's strengths. I came away persuaded that the rise of Islam within Europe will eventually become as large an issue of contention in the American relationship with the Muslim world as Iraq and Palestine are now.

What is also clear is that I would mourn the loss of Europe's social liberalism, in spite its excesses. (Which is more troublesome, Amsterdam's window displays of naked prostitutes or the burka?) Much of what any sane conservative should want to conserve is the Enlightenment's legacy of free inquiry and speech. Yet this is the accomplishment whose survival is put into question by this ongoing revolution in Europe.

Mondoweiss
August 30, 2009

NOT YOUR FATHER'S NATIONAL FRONT

In an early chapter of Michel Houellebecq's best-selling novel *Soumission*, the laconic, alienated but professionally successful narrator (François, an expert on the nineteenth-century Catholic writer Huysmans) explains his lack of interest in French contemporary politics. "A center-left candidate is elected and governs for one or two terms depending on his degree of charisma; for obscure reasons, he is never elected to a third term. The populace tires of the candidate and more generally of the center-left, and one observes the phenomenon of *alternance démocratique*, and the electors bring the center-right to power, for one or two terms depending on the individual candidate. Oddly enough, the Western countries were extremely proud of this system which was in effect nothing more than the sharing of power between two rival gangs, and occasionally started wars to impose it on countries which didn't share their enthusiasm."

As readers of the novel or its reviews are aware, this system was soon to be upended in France—yielding an election in which the much-reviled nationalist-populist, right-wing National Front presidential candidate faced off against a politically agile and globally ambitious Muslim, the son of an immigrant grocer and a graduate of the top French administrative and political school, who had bested his center-left rival in the French version of the primary election. Such a disruption was inevitable, as Houellebecq's narrator points out in one of his sociological asides, as the demographic and social system that served as the foundation of *alternance démocratique* was gradually rotting away at its foundations. The patriarchy of previous generations, for all its constraints on individual autonomy, had at least the benefit of being able to reproduce itself, yielding families, which reproduced children and created new families, which reproduced families, for century after century. Post-1968 France, not so much.

France is probably still an election cycle or two away from the political scenarios sketched out in *Soumission*. But one element of the Houellebecq scenario has already come to pass, at least in part. The Front National has become the largest and most interesting element in the political conversation. A visitor to Paris is struck almost immediately by the fact that virtually all the political commentary seems to be about Marine Le Pen and the party she inherited from her father and is trying to transform. Both because the National Front has a past as an extremist party, and because it threatens the *alternance démocratique* as sketched out by Houellebecq, nine-tenths of the commentary falls on a continuum between the mildly hostile and the rabidly negative. Nonetheless, the party—a marginal political group 40 years ago—has grown. In the first round of last week's departmental elections—local elections for positions about which very few people understand the actual responsibilities—the National Front produced a very respectable 25 percent score, exceeded by the center-right coalition party of former president Nicolas Sarkozy but comfortably ahead of the ruling socialists. The vote total equaled the FN's score in the European legislative elections last year, which was considered a major breakthrough. Four years ago, the FN scored 15 percent in the local elections, so the FN can point to a clear and seemingly unambiguous rise toward major party status.

This is the legacy of Marine Le Pen, since 2011 the FN's president. She is in her mid-40s, twice divorced, three kids, attractive and charismatic with a straightforward manner. She has the look of a woman who may have partied more than studied in her youth, with the husky voice of someone who has smoked her share of cigarettes. She possesses some odd political talents. A regular and quite justified complaint made by the FN is that the center-right only talks about immigration as an issue during the run-up to elections; in power (and Sarkozy or his predecessors have been in power a lot in the past 30 years) the center-right does absolutely nothing to address an issue which, in the opinion of some, has the potential to bring to an end France as an historic and cultural entity. The most recent campaign was no exception: suddenly, days before the election, French TV screens filled with Sarkozy-aligned candidates demanding, in a transparently anti-Muslim gesture, the end to the serving of pork-free meals in school cafeterias. Several years ago, when Marine Le Pen was in the process of emerging as the major public figure of the FN, a TV interviewer asked her about a similar rise in Sarkozyite anti-immigrant rhetoric. She paused, smiled into the camera, and broke into an effective rendition the song "It's Only Words" by the late and much-beloved Franco-Egyptian torch singer Dalida.

Unlike Sarkozy's, Marine Le Pen's party has never had the power to change the immigration system, but she is able to address the subject with insight and tact. A few days before the departmental vote, she went on the TV program "Toutes Les France," hosted by Ahmed El Keiy. She arrived in a large studio set up as a living room, where about 20 college-age students awaited her. The students, presumably chosen as representative of a multicultural French future that Marine Le Pen rejects, were by my estimation about three quarters of color. Madame Le Pen had walked into the lion's den. One fully expected the session to disintegrate—as it would with any American politician—into a mouthing of defensive and politically correct platitudes. A young black woman, an engineering student, asked her what kind of place did her version of France have for her. Marine replied, first of all, by asking "Are you French?"—and when the reply was affirmative, said that was wonderful and it was great she was becoming an engineer, and she wanted to protect French jobs and French culture. All right, but then came the follow-up. Marine's party opposes birthright citizenship, whereby children born in France automatically receive French citizenship. And the host raised the fact that the FN has historically opposed immigration, and if

Marine's father, Jean-Marie Le Pen, had any say over the matter in the 1990s, the parents of this young engineer of Senegalese background wouldn't have been permitted to immigrate to France. That rhetorical game is now a near-constant in French politics—how do Marine's views differ from her father's? Can she be cornered into repudiating her father? Scholars at top universities have written book-length semiotic analyses exploring whether the language of Marine's FN is really different or only appears to be. (The conclusion is a bit of both, but Marine has avoided any actual repudiation of her father.) In any case, for the candidate, it seemed a potentially tricky moment.

Marine repeated that she was delighted that this young woman was French, was planning to have here a career as engineer. And then—offered the chance to separate herself from her father's views—she refused. It would not be terrible, she continued, addressing the young woman, if you were an engineer in the country of your parents, Senegal, which also needs engineers. Indeed, that might be a good thing. And in fact, she opposes the policy of Sarkozy and others to skim off the intelligentsia of the various former French colonies and bring it to France—it probably does more harm than good to world economic development. That process is part of the *mondialisation sauvage*—savage globalization; it sounds better in French—which she and her party strongly oppose.

Of course, regardless of whether it would be better for more people if engineers of Senegalese background made their careers in Senegal, smart young people of color graduating from good French schools and working in France is not what makes immigration a major French concern. The worry is the far larger number of second- and third-generation immigrants who are not well integrated into middle class careers. One can point to any number of dramatic indicators: the weeks of rioting and car burning which erupted in the suburbs surrounding Paris 10 years ago; the population of the French prison system; the murders of Jewish students in Toulouse last year; the *Charlie Hebdo* assassinations; and the killings at the kosher supermarket. These all have combined aspects of a religious conflict with militant Islam and elements of a growing underclass problem—the fact that it can be both at the same time expands it exponentially, making it far more challenging than anything Americans now face.

One can take the subway from Paris to the Basilica of Saint Denis, a magnificent and vast cathedral constructed in the Middle Ages, an awe-inspiring monument to peak Christendom, a place where dozens of French kings, princes, and princesses are buried. A quarter mile from the church, you are in the streets of Saint-Denis, once part of the Red Belt and a communist stronghold, now an impoverished Third Worldish urban zone. I walked the length of the main market street at three in the afternoon, and it felt not threatening, though I probably was the only white person. Two hours later, a considerably greater number of idle and tough looking young men were hanging around. Much is made of the contrast between Texas and Mexico, the much storied border between the developed and undeveloped world, but Texas and Mexico and New Mexico and Arizona are essentially part of the same civilization. Walk the three football fields from the Saint Denis Basilica to the streets of the town, and, quite simply, you cross from a monument of one civilization to a new world that is completely different.

The National Front has made immigration a key issue since the birth of the party. It has long been a question whether the origins of the National Front disqualify it, or should disqualify it, from a role in French political life. The FN was created from a coalition of various right-wing currents in French life in the '60s, all which had been on the losing side of major conflicts. At the FN's birth one can find neofascists, political descendants of the proponents of Pétainism (a sensibility that comprised, in 1942 or thereabouts, a rather large percentage of Frenchmen) and of collaboration. One could also find those who rebelled, sometimes violently, against De Gaulle's negotiation of independence for Algeria—whose sense of betrayal by the general was intensified in many cases because of their previous reverence for him. You could find many hardline anti-communists, opponents of détente and frank admirers of Pinochet and Franco. Jean-Marie Le Pen, a rakish, charismatic, former Poujadist deputy, operated comfortably in these milieus and was able forge them into a semi-serious political party and make it into a vehicle for his own political career. The senior Le Pen's discourse was populist and often racialist; his anti-Semitic remarks, sporadic, probably calculated, and usually ambiguous, have been well documented. Jean-Marie Le Pen was able to run several moderately successful presidential campaigns, achieving a status as France's principal right-wing tribune, but he could never, ever be president of France or part of a governing coalition.

Marine Le Pen's ambition is to overcome that. The rhetoric of the party has changed: gone are any racially tinged or anti-Semitic remarks. About a dozen of the 7,000 candidates the FN ran for the departmentals were compelled by the party to withdraw—often for expressions of the kind of juvenile racism or homophobia that crops up with relative frequency in the Facebook postings of low-level Republican officials in the U.S. The French liberal press did a major investigative sweep of all the FN candidates' social media presence, and they of course found some crude banana jokes or remarks conflating homosexuality with bestiality—but overall it seemed somewhat surprising how little of it there was. This is now a much bigger party than Jean-Marie Le Pen's, one that runs candidates for every elective office in France and is extremely reliant on people who have not been professional politicians. But its overall extremism level seems, at least impressionistically, a good deal lower than the Tea Party's.

So if the FN no longer promotes a racially tinged nationalist populism, what does it stand for? Essentially, the FN has become the party that questions French integration into Europe and opposes an Anglo-Saxon dominated global marketplace in which France has lost control of its own economic destiny. Marine Le Pen's most important speeches have targeted what she calls *mondialisation sauvage*, or sometimes *totalitarianism mondialiste*. The bête noir of the FN is ultra-liberalism (in the European sense), an unrestrained capitalism that destroys everything in its path—families, communities, nations. She denounces the G8, the G20, the IMF; she opposes the "ultra-liberal diktats of the high priests of the EU." She calls for economic patriotism, adding if economic patriotism doesn't please the EU, we will do without the EU. She has promised to put France's adhesion to the European currency to a referendum. More generally, though, the FN has been muted on foreign policy questions, her party has opposed foreign intervention in Afghanistan and Syria, and is far less anti-Russian than the other major parties.

In other words, under Marine Le Pen, the FN has embraced opposition to economic globalization as its major theme, relegating everything else to secondary or tertiary positions. While the FN of her father was fully in favor of free enterprise, she is not. It is perhaps not surprising that many of the FN's new pockets of support comes from depressed industrial regions that once voted communist. The voters of the National Front may have more in common with the voters of the various Left socialist parties than they yet realize.

This emphasis on the global economy has coincided with the thoroughgoing de-racialization of the FN's political agitation. The shift was foreshadowed several years ago, when Marine Le Pen served as the director of strategy of her father's last presidential campaign, in 2007: one Marine-inspired poster showed a young French/North African woman, dressed in tight jeans, a little exposed skin of an outthrust hip, flashing a thumbs down sign: "Nationality, Assimilation, Upward Mobility, Laicism: the (establishments of the) Left/Right have BROKEN THEM ALL." The thoroughly assimilated *beurette* becomes for Marine Le Pen's National Front a stand-in for Marianne, the feminine symbol of *La République*, which the left-right globalist establishment is in the process of destroying.

Another French political tradition the new FN has partially succeeded in appropriating is Gaullism. The irony in this is beyond obvious: Jean-Marie Le Pen's Front National had connections both to Pétainists and to the

French right-wing elements that considered de Gaulle a traitor over Algeria and tried to have him killed.

But nearly 45 years after de Gaulle's death, what party in France does approximate a modern version of what the general might have stood for? The nominal heritors of Gaullism, the center-right parties of UMP, represent essentially France's winners, its businessmen and those who are comfortable enough with globalism, with an increasingly European rather than a French identity, the Davos men and women who make up the ruling class in much of the capitalist West. And they do have a certain claim to de Gaulle. But there was much to de Gaulle that was also reactionary, extremely prickly about Anglo-Saxon power, fiercely protective of French sovereignty. Would de Gaulle, who called for a "Europe of nation-states," have embraced the euro? Would de Gaulle be lining up under Washington's leadership to impose sanctions on Russia? On Iran? It is far from obvious that he would. Marine Le Pen's claim that the FN has become France's Gaullist party is not absurd on its face.

The new, nearly mainstream Front National remains a very young party still trying very hard to attract capable, highly educated people to its ranks. Marine Le Pen can go head-to-head in debate with anyone in France and hold her own; so can any of a dozen or so new National Front figures she has recruited or attracted to the party within the past five years. But one senses this is still an organization with a weak bench: on TV on election night, the FN seemed sometimes to be represented by very young people, somewhat fearful of saying the wrong thing, who were overshadowed by more experienced and telegenic personalities of the center-right and center-left.

That said, the FN's upside potential is truly vast. Marine Le Pen's National Front is far and away the largest party in a major country to challenge the Washington-dominated, neoliberal, globalist consensus. It is easily the largest anti-immigration party to emerge in the West, and one that is clearly striving, with not inconsiderable success, to navigate the narrow shoal between national self-preservation and racism. For the first time in many years, political events in France merit close observation, for Marine Le Pen's success, hardly foreordained, but hardly impossible, could rewrite the history of a decadent West.

The American Conservative
March 26, 2015

Sources

The essays in this book are reprinted with permission from the original sources below.

Why Many Arabs Hate America
www.antiwar.com/orig/mcconnell8.html

An Open Letter to David Horowitz on the Israeli–Palestinian Conflict
www.antiwar.com/mcconnell/mc011502.html

Untested Savior
www.theamericanconservative.com/articles/untested-savior

Obama over McCain
www.theamericanconservative.com/articles/the-right-choice-2/#mcconnell
Golfer in Chief

www.theamericanconservative.com/articles/golfer-in-chief

On the Trail in Virginia
lobelog.com/on-the-trail-in-virginia

Among the Neocons
www.theamericanconservative.com/articles/among-the-neocons

The *Weekly Standard*'s War
www.theamericanconservative.com/articles/the-weekly-standards-war

Let Me Shine Your Shoes, Sir
www.theamericanconservative.com/articles/let-me-shine-your-shoes-sir

They Only Look Dead
www.theamericanconservative.com/articles/they-only-look-dead

In Search of Forever War
www.theamericanconservative.com/articles/in-search-of-forever-war

Chosen People
www.theamericanconservative.com/articles/chosen-people

Thought Leader
www.theamericanconservative.com/articles/thought-leader

The Neocons Overreach on Hagel
www.theamericanconservative.com/2013/01/15/the-neocons-overreach-on-hagel

A Friend's Lament
www.theamericanconservative.com/articles/a-friends-lament

Divided & Conquered
www.theamericanconservative.com/articles/divided-conquered

The Lobby Strikes Back
www.theamericanconservative.com/articles/the-lobby-strikes-back

The Special Relationship with Israel: Is It Worth the Costs?
www.mepc.org/journal/middle-east-policy-archives/special-relationship-israel?print

Five Years Ago Today, Walt and Mearsheimer Gave Americans the Vocabulary to Discuss a Central Issue
mondoweiss.net/2011/03/five-years-ago-today-walt-and-mearsheimer-gave-americans-the-vocabulary-to-discuss-a-central-issue

Normalizing Relations
www.theamericanconservative.com/articles/normalizing-relations

Netanyahu's Machine
www.theamericanconservative.com/articles/netanyahus-machine

I Like and Respect Israel, But It's Not America
www.theamericanconservative.com/2012/09/26/i-like-and-respect-israel-but-its-not-america

Why Americans Don't Understand Palestine
nationalinterest.org/commentary/the-official-line-palestine-7769

Will Israel Go Fascist?
www.theamericanconservative.com/articles/will-israel-go-fascist

John Kerry Walks Up to the Truth
www.theamericanconservative.com/2014/04/30/john-kerry-walks-up-to-the-truth

The Presbyterian Victory
www.theamericanconservative.com/2014/06/25/the-presbyterian-victory

The Good Strategist
www.theamericanconservative.com/articles/the-good-strategist

Peace Candidate, '68 Vintage
www.theamericanconservative.com/articles/peace-candidate-68-vintage

Algeria, The Model
www.theamericanconservative.com/articles/algeria-the-model

Carter at Camp David: Triumph and Failure
www.mondoweiss.net/2011/03/the-history-of-the-camp-david-accords-reveals-that-the-president-is-incapable-of-standing-up-for-the-palestinians

Why I Owed Gore Vidal an Apology
www.theamericanconservative.com/2012/08/06/why-i-owed-gore-vidal-an-apology

NATO's Wrong Turn
www.theamericanconservative.com/articles/natos-wrong-turn

Washington Puzzled as Putin Doesn't Back Down
www.theamericanconservative.com/articles/washington-puzzled-as-putin-doesnt-back-down

Ferguson Is Not Palestine
www.theamericanconservative.com/articles/ferguson-is-not-palestine

Abandoned by the Left
www.theamericanconservative.com/articles/abandoned-by-the-left

The American Century Is Over
www.theamericanconservative.com/articles/the-american-century-is-over

Heather Mac Donald's Inconvenient Facts
www.theamericanconservative.com/articles/heather-mac-donalds-inconvenient-facts

Not So Huddled Masses: Multiculturalism and Foreign Policy
www.worldaffairsjournal.org/article/not-so-huddled-masses-multiculturalism-and-foreign-policy

Obama's Amnesty-Inequality Trap
www.theamericanconservative.com/articles/obamas-amnesty-inequality-trap

David Brooks's Dilemma (and Ours)
mondoweiss.net/2010/02/david-brookss-dilemma-and-ours

Ten Years in the Right
www.theamericanconservative.com/articles/ten-years-in-the-right

The Coming Love Affair with Iran
www.theamericanconservative.com/2013/09/30/the-coming-love-affair-with-iran

Israel and the Saudis, United in Jealousy
www.theamericanconservative.com/2013/10/25/israel-and-the-saudis-united-in-jealousy

The U.S.–Israel Politics Gap
www.theamericanconservative.com/articles/the-u-s-israel-politics-gap/

How Obama Can Stop Netanyahu's Iran War
www.theamericanconservative.com/articles/how-obama-can-stop-netanyahus-iran-war

How the Iran Deal Serves America
www.theamericanconservative.com/articles/why-israel-opposes-the-iran-deal

Netanyahu's Lobby vs. the World
www.theamericanconservative.com/articles/the-iran-deals-historic-politics

Christopher Caldwell's 'Reflections'
mondoweiss.net/2009/08/scott-mcconnell-on-christopher-caldwells-reflections

Not Your Father's National Front
www.theamericanconservative.com/articles/not-your-fathers-national-front

Z

Zionism, 12, 14, 16, 63, 64, 67, 68, 92, 94, 98, 107, 121-123, 125, 129
Zoabi, Hanin, 133, 134